The New Case for Bureaucracy

Dedicated to the memory of
Charles True Goodsell
1886–1941

The New Case for Bureaucracy

Charles T. Goodsell

*Virginia Polytechnic Institute
and State University*

Los Angeles | London | New Delhi
Singapore | Washington DC

Los Angeles | London | New Delhi
Singapore | Washington DC

FOR INFORMATION:

CQ Press

An Imprint of SAGE Publications, Inc.

2455 Teller Road

Thousand Oaks, California 91320

E-mail: order@sagepub.com

SAGE Publications Ltd.

1 Oliver's Yard

55 City Road

London EC1Y 1SP

United Kingdom

SAGE Publications India Pvt. Ltd.

B 1/I 1 Mohan Cooperative Industrial Area

Mathura Road, New Delhi 110 044

India

SAGE Publications Asia-Pacific Pte. Ltd.

3 Church Street

#10-04 Samsung Hub

Singapore 049483

Printed in the United States of America

Cataloging-in-publication data is available from the Library of Congress.

ISBN 978-1-4522-2630-9

This book is printed on acid-free paper.

Publisher: Charisse Kiino

Editorial Assistant: Davia Grant

Production Editor: Olivia Weber-Stenis

Copy Editor: Ellen Howard

Typesetter: C&M Digitals (P) Ltd.

Proofreader: Susan Irwin

Cover Designer: Michael Dubowe

Marketing Manager: Erica DeLuca

Certified Chain of Custody
SUSTAINABLE Promoting Sustainable Forestry
FORESTRY
INITIATIVE www.sfiprogram.org
SFI-01268

SFI label applies to text stock

14 15 16 17 18 10 9 8 7 6 5 4 3 2 1

CONTENTS

TABLES, BOXES, AND FIGURES

TABLES

BOXES

FIGURES

PREFACE

In our daily language the word "bureaucracy" is a term of vilification and ill will. Its popular meaning conveys disgust for nonfunctioning government that is slow to act, mired in technicalities, and probably bloated and controlling. No case at all could be made for such government, and I would be the last to try.

In this book I use the word very differently and without a negative emotional loading. It refers simply to the institutions that do the ongoing work of government, the agencies of public administration. These departments, bureaus, and local government administrations enable government to perform the exacting tasks expected of the public sector in a modern society. They are staffed by men and women who make it possible for a democracy to succeed over time.

I have written on the subject of bureaucracy in America for thirty years in successive editions of *The Case for Bureaucracy*. The volume you are holding is not, however, the latest version of that work. It is entirely different in two senses.

First, it is new in content, structure, and tone. Whereas the earlier "Case" was consciously written and labeled as a polemic, this volume is in the nature of an extended and rather personal essay. Instead of summarizing all scholarly research on the positive aspects of US public administration that make it defensible, the book identifies selected ideas and research findings for consideration, examines them in sufficient detail so readers can judge for themselves their importance, and allows me to express opinions based on a half century of study and reflection. In short, the former polemicist is now a more mellowed author who is still opinionated but wants his readers to think for themselves. Indeed, some sections of the book are not devoted to defending bureaucracy at all but to describing its scandals and shortfalls.

I seek to build this case for bureaucracy at all levels of American government, although the availability of research conclusions that can be generalized has been skewed by scholars in favor of the national government. Hence by necessity more attention is given in the book to federal administration than to government bureaucracies in the states and localities. This is unfortunate since it is at the state and local levels that most US public administration operates. I apologize for this imbalance to the millions of present and future state and local public employees who serve their citizens ably.

Mention of the book's federal emphasis brings us to the second sense in which this case for bureaucracy is "new." At this writing the federal government and the nation it serves face perilous times. The country's deep partisan divide, bitterly deadlocked Congress, and unresolved public financial status have created a crisis of governance. While centered in Washington, DC, the situation's adverse effects penetrate the entire federal system.

At the end of the book I offer my views on an appropriate role for federal agencies in this emergency. It is not passive, anxiety-ridden acquiescence, but rather being alert to opportunities for taking bold action. The stance I propose for bureaucracy includes a readiness to exercise political savvy in fighting for the funds needed to save vital missions and to take policy initiatives when necessary in the face of congressional inaction. In view of this perspective, I see the purpose of the new case for bureaucracy as more than correction of an overly pejorative view of bureaucracy. It is also to invoke a moral imperative for bureaucracy to stand tall in this difficult period of our nation's history.

Several events occurred in the closing months prior to finishing this book that pertain to this "new case" argument. A shutdown of the federal government revealed once again the importance of uninterrupted administration to public trust and it is discussed in Chapter 5. The bungled launch of the Affordable Care Act reminds us how important in-house bureau capacity is to complex governance and is commented on in an Afterword. Passage by Congress of a limited federal budget compromise effective through FY 2015 is a modest step beyond partisan stalemate, yet an enormous chasm of policy disagreement remains that will likely necessitate more proactive moves by agencies to protect their missions. As for revelations about the information-gathering activities of the National Security Agency, I ask you—upon reading this book—to work out your own opinions.

ACKNOWLEDGMENTS

My largest debt of gratitude is owed to Charisse Kiino, editor for social sciences at CQ Press. She encouraged the project from the beginning and has helped keep my morale up throughout. I could not ask for a better or more supportive editor and publisher.

Four persons kindly agreed to read the manuscript in advance of a Southeast Public Administration Conference at Charlotte, NC, on September 26, 2013, and then act as discussants at a panel dedicated to it. These individuals are Brian J. Cook of Virginia Tech; William M. Haraway III of the University of West Florida; Richard W. Jacobsen, retired public administrator at Mecklenburg County, NC; and Claire Mostel, retired public administrator at Miami-Dade County, FL. I greatly appreciate their comments, criticisms, and suggestions.

Others I would like to thank are Professor Maja Husar Holmes of West Virginia University for allowing me to try out early ideas on her classes; William C. Adams for sending me useful survey data; Michael B. Cooke for his explanation of tax code matters; Gautama Adi Kusuma for researching the social media and providing statistics help; Gregory B. Lewis for providing literature guidance; Ken Wylie for listening to my inner thoughts over coffee along the way; Ellen Howard, who performed as my able and dependable copy editor; and Olivia Weber-Stenis for her helpful assistance as production editor.

A personal expression of love and thanks goes to my wife, Mary Elizabeth MacKintosh Goodsell. As always, she was tolerant of my preoccupations with writing over these past two years and always ready to hear me vent on issues that arise. Liz is an unbelievably good speller and gladly helps out when I fall short in that area, which is often.

The dedication of this book to the memory of my father has special meaning. While writing the final chapters it came to my attention that his ashes had been unclaimed for over seventy years in a funeral home in Michigan. I was able to acquire them, and it was my pleasure to celebrate his life with family and friends present when I placed them in a columbarium niche in Blacksburg, Virginia, on May 11, 2013. He too was a teacher and author.

The New Case for Bureaucracy

WHAT, *DEFEND* BUREAUCRACY?

O ffhand, can you think of a more dumb idea than to defend bureaucracy? One of the great demons of our times?

Let me begin by assuring you I am not using the word in its common meaning of government offices so bound in red tape they can't help anyone. Or of arrogant bureaucrats who think they have the power to push people around as they see fit.

In this book we transcend such stereotypes and think concretely and broadly about the agencies of administration that do the work of government in this huge country. In it you will find that I contend the general quality and effectiveness of these departments and bureaus to be greater than most believe. Some are outstanding and stand as world exemplars in their field. This is why I make a substantive case for bureaucracy as it exists in this country.

It is entirely understandable if you are wary of my conclusion. Americans are known for their individualism and love of personal freedom and hence tend to be suspicious of big and powerful institutions. They benefit from the fruits of a market economy and frown on paying a good chunk of the fruits of their labor to a public treasury. Business executives and investors that make the economy productive dislike being constrained by government regulation. Hence this book is practically contrary to the American way! Actually, my pride of country is deep and made deeper for the relative competence and dedication I see in the civil servants who make our democracy work on a day-to-day basis.

I have a big job ahead of me as I present my case. I do not lecture at you as a know-it-all authority but as someone who wants to stimulate your own thinking. I hope you enjoy this intellectual journey we take together; contact me at goodsell@vt.edu if you wish to discuss a point.

SOME PRELIMINARIES

First we need to attend to some preliminaries. The term "bureaucracy" is derived from the Old French word *bureau*, initially referring to a heavy wool cloth that covered tables. Later on, *bureau* meant the table itself and then the desks at which people work in offices. Hence literally bureaucracy means "desk rule" or governance by those who work at desks.[1]

Max Weber's Model. The famous German sociologist Max Weber, writing in the context of early twentieth-century Prussia, theorized that bureaucracy is the form of organization that inevitably emerges when money-based societies take on complex tasks. The reason is that it is capable of unparalleled precision, speed, continuity, and technically optimal capabilities for advanced collective action. These assets are achieved, he said, because of the combined effects of several organizational features. Known today as the Weberian model of bureaucracy, these are: (1) fixed duties for officials that apply within a set jurisdiction, (2) a graded system of hierarchical authority from highest level to lowest; (3) the use of formal rules to guide the carrying out of duties; (4) the maintenance of written files over time; and (5) employees who are full-time, salaried, trained, tenured, and work at an office away from home. However, Weber warned, in addition to being technically superior, the tight efficiency of bureaucracy enables it to acquire political power. Hence a regime's top leadership is always in danger of becoming overwhelmed by the concentrated information, resources, and skills of its bureaucracy. Do you think this could be a danger in America?[2]

Since being translated into English in the 1940s, Weber's work has had a pervasive influence in public administration thought. At first scholars ambivalently admired his comprehensive compilation of administrative traits on the one hand, but took seriously his warnings about bureaucracy's threat to democracy on the other. By the 1960s academic critique of the model extended to the point of outright condemnation of the model's stress on hierarchy, rules, and expertise as inviting top-down dominance of the institution as well as organizational inflexibility. A few decades later this critique became the springboard for an antithesis theory of bureaucracy whereby nonhierarchical processes, multipoint collaboration, and minimization of the public-private distinction were championed. Still later a "governance without government" thesis emerged that repudiated the centrality of stand-alone bureaucracies in general as the heart of public administration in favor of a networked series of multiple, scattered, public and private actors acting jointly.[3]

These ideas that detract from Weber's model are attractive in many ways. They emphasize the importance of decentralization, partnerships, flexibility, decision influence upward as well as sideways, and participation by citizens in administration. Yet at the same time the classic attributes of precision, speed, and expertise are still needed in this era of electronic communication, nonstate wars, and global markets. Furthermore the cultural coherence and endurance of the stand-alone institution is still important as a basis of achieving pride, dedication, and self-identity in a workplace. From the standpoint of responsible and fiscally sound administration, a sharp focal point of official accountability is also indispensable. Perhaps you differ, but I believe the individual bureaucracy is here to stay as a keystone for a compatible bureaucracy-democracy fit; in a country like ours, governance must simultaneously involve desks, networks, and ballot boxes.

US Bureaucracy: An Overview. Bureaucracy has the reputation of being big and everywhere. Yes, from the financial standpoint, it looms large. The federal government's annual outlays are equivalent to a slice of the Gross National Product between 18 and 25 percent of the whole, depending on the state of the economy. State and local government expenditures augment federal outlays by approximately 40 percent, leading to total annual public sector spending in excess of $6 trillion at this writing. A gross expenditure figure overstates the cost of the bureaucracy itself, however; most public spending goes not to public payrolls and operating budgets but to entitlements to individuals, allotments to subsidized industries, payments to government contractors, and to a lesser degree grants and contracts with nonprofit service providers.[4]

A more direct measure of bureaucracy's magnitude is the number of bureaucrats employed. Table 1.1 provides total-employee numbers for each level of government in three years. The grand total for 2011 of roughly 22 million bureaucrats is about 12 percent of the economy's employed workforce. You can see big differences in magnitude among the three levels of government; clearly, most of American bureaucracy is not at the national level but in the states and localities, especially the latter. Variations over the three years are steady in overall scale, although it is notable that some 800,000 bureaucrats were added to the totals during the George Bush presidency and about 350,000 were lost to them in Obama's first term. Hence the overall amount of American bureaucracy is by no means determined alone by the ideology of the party that elects the president, as one might anticipate.

Another surprise, at least to me, is how when one disaggregates public employment figures into the number of workers per workplace, the image of bureaucracy as a mammoth phenomenon begins to dissipate. This is especially true for offices that deal directly with the public. A few years ago I calculated the average size of 40,671 postal and other federal offices around the country and found that 69 percent had staffs of ten or less and 53 percent had five or less. Similarly, 55 percent of Social Security field offices employed fewer than twenty people. For 53 percent of the nation's 1,872 local welfare departments, essentially the same situation obtained. Budget cuts during the recent recession and the federal sequester of 2012–2013 have driven these workplace numbers even lower.[5]

TABLE 1.1	Civilian Government Employment, 2005–2011 (includes part-time, in thousands)		
Level	2005	2009	2011
Federal	2,720	2,824	2,854
State	5,078	5,329	5,313
Local	13,926	14,480	14,099
Total	21,724	22,633	22,266

Source: Statistical Abstract of the United States, 2012, p. 300. Bureau of the Census website, "Government Employment & Payroll." Accessed July 19, 2013.

Disaggregating bureaucracy is necessary to understanding it from the standpoint of the type of organization as well. United States public administration is remarkably varied and pluralistic, just like the country itself. The classic bureau is common but by no means the only type. From the standpoint of continuous, empowered effort, however, it has many advantages, which is probably why it is pervasive (as Weber argued). These features include a legislative statute or local government charter that authorizes pursuance of identified goals; annual appropriations to enable the continuation of this work over time; a hierarchical organization that makes possible focused accountability and unified internal management; and staffing by a nonpartisan body of specialized civil servants.

The potential effectiveness of this workhorse of bureaucracy is implied by efforts of legislatures to create opposing but similar organizational forms as a counter to it. Placement of the bureau in an overhead structure like the Department of Homeland Security or National Oceanic and Atmospheric Administration augments political control by the elected chief executive. Establishment of nonexecutive bureaus like state legislative staff offices or a Government Accountability Office augments political control by elected representatives. Agencies like an Office of Director of National Intelligence provides operational coordination, while an Office of Management and Budget enables managerial supervision.

Other types of organizational entity do not augment control but affect capabilities in other ways. Government enterprises such as the US Postal Service make the activity dependent on its own earnings without the assurance of annual appropriations. Independent regulatory commissions replace unified top leadership with a bipartisan board whose members serve rotating terms. Public organizations financed by multiple governments, such as regional planning commissions, facilitate coordination across jurisdictions. Inspectors general and the Postal Inspection Service constitute insider watchdogs to look for wrongdoing. A paramilitary body of uniformed professionals like the US Public Health Service Commissioned Officer Corps transcends agency jurisdictions. So, my reader, variety is the spice of public administration as well as other aspects of life.

Downstairs or Upstairs? A major theme in the Masterpiece Theater television dramas "Upstairs, Downstairs" and "Downton Abbey" is how the servants on the lower level of the Edwardian English mansion have a distinctly inferior station in life from the aristocratic family upstairs. Nonetheless the butlers, valets, cooks, and maids working down there become inextricably involved in the lives of family members upstairs, albeit with the class distinction always preserved. Curiously enough, such spatial verticality was the same in the nation's early state capitols, where legislative chambers were on the second floor, the governor's office on the ground floor, and bureaucratic offices in the basement.[6]

Life in the Edwardian mansion has metaphoric possibilities for public administration. Those of us who teach and write in the field frequently refer to bureaucrats as "public *servants*." While our use of the term is based not on perceived inferiority but on a desire to grant respect, the upstairs-downstairs distinction can be compared to the field's classic distinction between politics and administration. Originally drawn to emphasize the need to keep administration nonpartisan, this "dichotomy" can, in a larger sense, embrace the basic point that in a democracy, elected officials *do* need to exercise *ultimate* authority over administrative agencies. A parallel dyad found in political science is between making public policy versus implementing it, and in organizational economics between the principals who give instructions and the agents who do or do not obey them.

These maxims reflect a profound truth, but not the whole truth. To return to our English mansion analogy, the *identities* of those involved—elected officials and political appointees upstairs and career bureaucrats downstairs—are undeniably distinct. However their *arenas of action* are shared. Both think over the same problems, assess their political implications, formulate possible proposals, listen to affected interests, consult with outside experts, consider implementation mechanisms, and evaluate eventual outcomes. In sum, while the big decisions are ultimately made upstairs, their nature is also shaped downstairs. Moreover, if a political crisis erupts on the second floor whereby ideological division paralyzes action there, it is not inconceivable that big short-term decisions would be made on the lower floor. At the end of the book I address this exact possibility.

BUREAUCRACY'S IMAGE

What does the bureaucracy look like to the public? Because in popular language the term bureaucracy is so pejorative, thoughts spawned by its image yield practically universal disgust. For example a vanity license plate issued in Virginia was lettered "GOVT SUX" (it is a conservative state). I have in my study a bumper sticker emblazoned "Bureaucrats Do It In Triplicate" (I'll let you interpret that). A television presidential-campaign spot aired a few years ago flashed "BUREAUCRATS" in upper case with the last four letters highlighted. Scores of books berating bureaucracy on the worst possible terms are in print, like *The Federal Rathole, Burning Money, Alice in Blunderland*, and *America by the Throat*.[7]

Some Concrete Images. But when the public is exposed to concrete details about government rather than mere stereotypes, the implanted images may still be negative–but more nuanced. Beverly Cigler and Heidi Neiswender examined how the subject of public administration is presented in eighteen introductory texts for college courses in American government. What is emphasized is the large size and permanence of bureaucracy, its alleged lack of efficiency compared to business, the use of unintelligible language, and the power of agencies to escape full control by the President.[8]

The depiction of governmental administration in television dramas can have significant effect on lay attitudes. Researchers at the Center for Media and Public Affairs at George Mason University in Virginia examined TV episodes aired between 1992–1998 and 1999–2001. They found that in the earlier period, three-fourths of the shows portrayed government as corrupt, cynical, and unrepresentative. In the second time period, however, three out of five episodes depicted an essentially effective public sector, although bureaucrats themselves were portrayed favorably only ten percent of the time.[9]

In a study of motion pictures, Michelle Pautz and Laura Roselle analyzed the ten top American films (in terms of gross receipts) released each year from 1992 to 2006. Among them were *Schindler's List, Clear and Present Danger, Pearl Harbor*, and *The Bourne Supremacy*. Coders assessed how government personnel were portrayed in them and noted characteristics written into their roles. Of the 105 pictures examined that included a significant governmental presence, 60 percent presented the bureaucrat as inefficient or incompetent and 40 percent as capable. In two-thirds of the negative portrayals, "the system" was construed as at fault rather than individuals. The five most common role characteristics of bureaucrats were, in descending order of frequency: (1) good looking or fit; (2) knowledgeable, wise, or smart; (3) dangerous, evil, or corrupt; (4) friendly or approachable; and (5) professional or rule-following.[10]

Beth Wielde and David Schultz assessed the portrayal of public professionals in 20 government-themed films issued between 1984 and 2003. Using content analysis, they uncovered five character types: (1) the Power Monger, exemplified by dismissive EPA official Walter Perk in *Ghostbusters*; (2) the Bureaucratic Criminal, illustrated by presidential aide Gloria Russell who covers up an act of murder by her boss in *Absolute Power*; (3) the Hyper Loyalist who sacrifices personal life to duty, the role of Deputy Mayor Kevin Calhoun in *City Hall*; (4) the Action Hero who rebels against by-the-book routines to save the day, as in Harry Dalton of the US Geological Survey in *Dante's Peak*; and (5) the Ethics Hero who reveals a presidential cover-up, as in the long-anonymous Deep Throat of *All the President's Men*.[11]

Bureaucracy on Facebook. Capturing the popular image of bureaucracy in the twenty-first century would be incomplete without noting what is said in the social media. However "bureaucracy" by itself is not a hot topic there. To get around that problem, the Facebook pages of leading newspaper and television outlets were sampled on days when aspects of administrative governance would likely come up. Selected were January 13, 2011, when President Obama presented an agency reorganization plan, and February 13, 2012, the day the FY 2013 federal budget was made public.

In order to solicit a range of opinion, the Facebook pages of the *New York Times*, *Washington Post*, and *Wall Street Journal* were examined for comments on the reorganization plan and the same was done for the budget on television news channels MSNBC, CNN, and Fox News. Entries touching on governance were picked out among the hundreds posted; and from that pool, 15 particularly revealing (and printable) comments were selected. Seven of these dealt with the reorganization plan (see Box 1.1) and eight the budget (see Box 1.2).

BOX 1.1   Facebook Comments on Obama's Reorganization Plan, January 13, 2012

New York Times

The problem is not the size or duplicative nature of the bureaucracy that is charged with all these functions. Rather, the problem is that there is a function at all. Congress and the President pass all these laws and mandates and obligations and some agency somewhere is charged with implementation. The fact that numbers must be hired to do this bidding, under one acronym or another, or several different acronyms, is not where the problem is. It is in the need for Federal intervention at all. Oh how lucky these congressmen and the President are to blame the Federal largess on the very machine that must carry out all these whims. It is the whims that are the problem. Do away with them and there is no need for the engine.

Conceptually, pulling the five agencies named by the president together under one umbrella will require building another layer of "management and supervision" that will serve only to slow down the larger process. Yes, they will be able to "consolidate some jobs" within the US government, and therefore save some small change, but they will inevitably make the function of those jobs much less efficient by adding the layers.

Every time I see someone slight the EPA, I have to wonder if they've ever googled "Cuyahoga River Fire." That's pre-EPA. While you're there, check out the reason for the FDA, another maligned agency.

Washington Post

The government is too big when people refuse to pay the taxes to support it. Sorry, but those who keep promising that someone else is going to come around and eliminate the deficit are kidding us and themselves. Even Obama is saying that the government should be streamlined. THAT is when you know government is too big and too inefficient.

When people start paying the taxes to support a bigger government, they can have one. Until then, asking for a bigger government with the expectation that someone else is going to come along and pay for it isn't the right way to go. Obama is cutting 1,000 jobs, through attrition, from a total of 2.1 million. Sounds like a very small step in the right direction.

(Continued)

(Continued)

Wall Street Journal

Isn't adding SBA as a cabinet post EXACERBATING bureaucracy? I have a hard time believing it belongs up there with departments of Defense, State, Treasury, and Justice without trivializing these latter important cabinet posts.

The initiative of cutting bureaucracy and/or costly dependences of the government looks good, but what is behind the new plan of the White House? Frequently, the politicians promise changes that after that nobody implements due to the difficulties or risks to make those changes. Do you remember the famous case of Guantanamo?

Source: Facebook pages of the media shown.

| BOX 1.2 | Facebook Comments on Obama's Budget for Fiscal 2013, February 13, 2012 |

MSNBC

I can't believe people are actually agreeing with this! 30%?!?!?! That's almost one third of their income. To support OTHER people.

I suppose we can close down all the schools, ambulance services, government offices, police forces, all because you do not think the rich should be taxed. In FDR's term they were paying 70 some percent in taxes and they were still doing just fine. It is NOT solely the middle class's job to support this country especially when the top 1% of this country, i.e. "the RICH AND FILTHY RICH" have all the money.

Fairness? How is it fair that the successful get punished and continually get raped by the government, while others are collecting food stamps, housing, welfare, unemployment, etc. Fair would be not having an entitlement system and have everyone pay the same % regardless. Taking from the rich is easy because of envy. Why should the responsible members of society foot the bill for the least responsible? Those programs weren't meant to be life long entitlements, which is what they have become.

Your idea of "fairness" seems to ignore all the systemic issues of unfairness already present in our economic and political system. Stop pretending that everyone in this country has the same access to opportunities and government that the rich do. From the very beginning the poor go to poor schools while the rich go to rich schools. Access to education is paramount in terms of an individual's ability to increase financial "success," but as a country we make sure that only the rich grow up in your utopia of opportunity. It is this lie of equal opportunity that has done and continues to do the most damage to our country.

CNN

Typical big government socialist. One year left of this jerk.

Socialist? What idiots you are to even say such a stupid thing! Do you think paying taxes for your police, firefighters, teachers, roads, bridges, and everything ELSE your dumb and sorry arse uses EVERY SINGLE day is a socialist thing?

FOX News

GOVT> is the problem.

We do have a spending problem ... and a lot of it is waste at the top of government ... we have people running key positions with no qualifications ... could any of us get jobs we don't qualify for ... I think not ... we spend for things on government contracts that we can buy cheaper at a hardware store ... it just makes no sense ... are there no common sense politicians ... sure doesn't look like it.

Source: Facebook pages of the media shown.

For background, Obama's reorganization plan called for consolidating all or parts of six agencies into a new but as yet unnamed cabinet-level department. These were the US Trade Representative, the US Trade and Development Agency, Export-Import Bank, Overseas Private Investment Corporation, Small Business Administration, and most of the Commerce Department other than the National Oceanic and Atmospheric Administration. The stated aim of the plan was to reduce duplication, focus more squarely on the needs of business, and eliminate 1,000–2,000 jobs by attrition.[12]

Four of the positions expressed on this plan were squarely on the cynical side: the functions of federal agencies are unneeded and are the product of politicians' whims (*New York Times*); if Obama admits the government should be streamlined, you know it is too big; cutting 1,000 jobs goes in the right direction but not nearly far enough (both *Washington Post*); and the plan looks good but will no doubt be fruitless (*Wall Street Journal*).

Two other plan comments are critical but more moderate in tone: a consolidation could help but will also create another layer of management (*New York Times*); and adding the SBA to a department trivializes that organizational unit (*Wall Street Journal*). Only one statement is clearly sympathetic to public administration: if you know about the Cuyahoga River fire, you know the EPA is important (*New York Times*).

Obama's 2013 budget proposed expenditures of $3.803 trillion against revenues of $2.902 trillion, generating an anticipated deficit of $901 billion. Although required by law and necessary for its wealth of detail on federal operations, Congress considered the document to be little more than a meaningless gesture; at that time the 2012 election campaign was underway, and no one knew what would happen to taxes and looming spending caps.

Of the eight comments on the budget, five were hostile to bureaucracy and three reasonably favorable. The most negative ones come right to the point: taxes are unbelievably high and only "support OTHER people" (MSNBC); Obama is a "big government socialist" jerk (CNN); clearly government "is the problem"; and waste is prolific (both Fox News).

Another commentator's reply to the "OTHER people" dismissal was that ordinary citizens benefit from government services but the "FILTHY RICH" don't pay their share of the cost (MSNBC). A retort to the "socialist" charge was that it is stupid to think we don't need things like fire fighters and roads (CNN).

In a longer interchange on the issue of fairness, one writer argues that successful citizens are "raped by the government" while irresponsible "others" benefit from free services. An entry answering this assertion states that it ignores the unfairness built into the system by having society's deck stacked against the poor from the start (both MSNBC).

You will have many reactions to these statements, and I wish I could hear them. To me, two points stick out. One is the predictable one that antibureaucracy feelings correlate with a conservative political posture. A less obvious observation is that those who express anger against government tend to speak in abstractions (politicians' whims, big-government socialist, raped by government) while progovernment commentators are more concrete in their references (firefighters, roads, the Cuyahoga River).

What About Trust? Public opinion polls offer the possibility of a more systematic—but not necessarily perfect—understanding of government's image. In its ongoing surveys the Gallup organization asks, "How much of the time do you think you can trust the government in Washington to do what is right?" In 2001, three weeks after 9/11, 60 percent of Americans said "just about always" or "most of the time." A year later the percentage dropped to 45 percent, and by 2005 it was 30 percent. In 2010 the figure was down to 19 percent.[13]

Yet Gallup has also found that the extent of governmental trust depends on what branch or level you pick. Table 1.2 offers five breakdowns from 1997 to 2012. As for the executive branch at the national level, it reached its zenith during the period in 2002 at 72 percent. This was the first such survey conducted immediately after 9/11. Over the following years it dropped quite steadily until a rise to 61 percent occurred in September of the year President Obama first took office, 2009. It then declined to 49 percent but rose once again to 56 in 2009, a month before his re-election. What this suggests is that the image of *who* is president as well as what happens to the country affects this poll number significantly.

By contrast, trust in Congress remained in or near the 60s until 2005 and then began a downward run to the 30s and was at 34 percent in 2012. The judicial branch has remained relatively stable in the 60s–70s range except for 80 percent in 1999. Both state and local governments hit their highest levels for the period in 1998, with the states typically in the 50s and 60s thereafter and the localities achieving the 60s and 70s. Like the other categories, they too showed upticks in 2012.[14]

One of the realities of polling is that the wording of the question often affects the responses given. A survey in 2011 conducted by Ipsos-Reuter asked, "On a scale of 1 to 10, where 1 means complete distrust and 10 means

TABLE 1.2	Percent of Public Expressing Trust in Government				
	Executive Branch	Legislative Branch	Judicial Branch	State Government	Local Government
1997	62	59	71	68	69
1998	63	61	78	80	77
1999	64	57	80	n/a	n/a
2000	65	68	75	n/a	n/a
2001	63	65	74	65	69
2002	72	67	75	n/a	n/a
2003	60	63	67	53	68
2004	58	60	65	67	68
2005	52	62	68	67	70
2006	46	56	69	n/a	n/a
2007	43	50	69	67	69
2008	42	47	69	67	72
2009	61	45	76	51	69
2010	49	36	66	52	70
2011	49	31	63	57	68
2012	56	34	67	65	74
Mean	56.6	53.8	70.8	63.3	70.3
Std. Dev.	9.077	11.128	5.057	8.848	2.625

Source: Trust in Government/Gallup Historical Trends. Accessed January 25, 2012 and July 24, 2013 at http://www .gallup.com/poll/5392/trust-government.aspx.

Note: For the national government, the question put is "Let me ask you how much trust and confidence you have at this time in the [branch named]." For subnational governments, it is "How much trust and confidence do you have in the [level of government] where you live when it comes to handling [level] problems? Percentages are the sum of the responses "a great deal" and "a fair amount."

complete trust, how much do you trust or distrust the following?" The outcome given for the federal government was pretty sour: 31 percent chose scores 1 to 3, 28 percent 4 to 5, 21 percent 6 to 7, and 18 percent 8 to 10. The interpretation given by the pollster was that 80 percent of the population harbored nonexistent, mild or lukewarm trust in Washington. When the same question was applied to local government, the outcome was slightly better at 76 percent. In another example, a Pew survey conducted in the same year asked how much respondents trust the information they receive from federal government agencies. The results were 6 percent a lot, 38 percent some, 32 not too much and 22 not at all, yielding a 92 percent other than fully satisfactory experience. Corresponding percentages at the state level of government were slightly better at 8, 43, 29, and 18.[15]

The best available data set for our purposes comes from the work of William Adams and Donna Lind Infeld at George Washington University. It is an annual nationwide poll called Battlefield that focuses on public attitudes toward the federal civilian workforce. To minimize partisan bias, Adams and Infeld asked leading pollsters associated with each of the two major political parties to help design and administer it. Battlefield's prime question is "Would you say that you have a great deal of confidence, a lot of confidence, some confidence, or very little confidence in federal civilian employees?" Table 1.3 presents the responses over four years, with percentages for the "great deal" and "a lot" options combined in the first column with the third column also incorporating the "some" option.

One could argue that these questions lean toward yielding progovernment answers just as the questions previously discussed lean toward the anti side. Yet I am prepared to conclude that they do show that the public appears to perceive the explicit referent of federal civilians as more trustworthy than such generalities as the "government in Washington" or "executive branch." Indeed, the mean percentage for at least some positive confidence is over 70 percent. As with the Facebook entries, we are encountering the phenomenon whereby particularized evaluations of bureaucracy are better than abstract ones.

Adams and Infeld looked for independent variables that have an appreciable effect on their results. A differential ranging from 14 to 24 points separates respondents who identify with the two major parties,

TABLE 1.3	Degree of Confidence in Federal Civilian Employees, 2009–2012 (in percent)				
	Great Deal or a Lot	**Some**	**At Least Some**	**Very Little**	**No Opinion**
2009	21	54	75	21	4
2010	19	47	66	27	7
2011	20	53	73	23	4
2012	22	46	68	28	4
Mean	20.5	50.0	70.5	24.8	4.8

Source: Articles in *PA Times* by William C. Adams and Donna Lind Infeld: "Surprising Majority of Americans Endorse Careers in Government," August 2009; "Trust in Federal Workers Continues to Erode," October 2010; "Federal Workers Gain in Public Trust," October 2011; "Americans Exhibit Increasingly Partisan Views of Federal Workers," October 2012.

with Democrats more confident in the bureaucrats and Republicans less so. A racial divide exists as well: in 2012, 20 percent of whites were in the great deal column as over against 27 percent of Hispanics and 35 of African Americans.[16]

In the annual Adams-Infeld data one thing caught my eye. Except for 2012's "great deal" response, over the four years an annual up-down-up-down movement occurred in the three confidence columns, with an inverse pattern in the "very little" response. Although probably not statistically significant, I cannot help but wonder whether this means public trust in bureaucracy tends to drop off in election years.

In addition Adams and Infeld offer comparative figures across institutions, as seen in Table 1.4. This is made possible by virtue of the fact that the Gallup organization asks similar questions for other parts of government. Keeping in mind that the table lists the institutions in order of high to low, the military and Congress stand by themselves as the top and bottom extremes respectively. In between are two clusters: the first is the police and Supreme Court and the second the criminal justice system, public schools and federal employees. The presidency follows in a category by itself. The fact that our national public servants rank alongside the schools and courts and above the presidency and Congress is definitely worth noting.

TABLE 1.4	Comparative Degree of Confidence by Institution, 2012 (in percent)				
	Great Deal or a Lot	Some	At Least Some	Very Little	No Opinion
The Military	75	18	93	1	6
The Police	56	28	84	16	0
Supreme Court	37	38	75	22	3
Criminal Justice System	29	40	69	29	2
Public Schools	29	40	69	30	1
Federal Civilian Employees	22	46	68	28	4
Presidency	36	27	63	36	1
Congress	13	34	47	52	1

Source: William C. Adams and Donna Lind Infeld, "Americans Exhibit Increasingly Partisan Views of Federal Workers," PA Times, October 2012.

Note: Question asked is the same as for Table 1.3, adapted to institution.

Workplace Violence. This seems like an odd topic to bring up in a discussion of bureaucracy's image. The reasons are twofold, both of which reflect my pro-bureaucracy slant. One, we should avoid being dismissive of low-paid government employees who perform bureaucracy's routine work; in this era of cutbacks they can face anxiety-producing workloads and layoffs. Two, we need to recognize that certain fringe elements of the society hate government so much they want to do violence to its employees.

The Department of Justice estimates that around a million cases of workplace violence occur each year in the American economy. Approximately 30 percent take place in government—double of what we would expect given the relative sizes of the private and public sectors.[17] In 2005, 4.8 percent of private employing establishments reported incidents, compared to 14.7 percent in local government and 32.2 in state government.[18]

On August 20, 1986, in a post office in Edmond, Oklahoma, postal worker Patrick Henry Sherrill suddenly pulled out a gun and killed two of his supervisors and 14 coworkers. Seven bystanders were injured. He then turned the gun on himself. Postal investigators found that Sherrill had been showing stress on the job, probably caused by a recent wage cut, fewer workers available in the office, and fear that he was about to lose his job. The incident was widely reported in the media and the term "going postal" entered the language.

After this incident came to light, it was discovered that similar occurrences had previously happened four times in the US Postal Service. In the following decade five more post office melees occurred, almost always involving firearms with the shooter committing suicide afterward. What the rampages had in common was antisupervisor rage, increased work pressure from cutbacks, and personal mental problems. Hoping to shed the stigma of the derisive "going postal" term, the USPS responded by placing "workplace environment analysts" in each of its 85 districts. Since that time no additional instances have been reported.[19]

An even darker face of the problem of workplace violence in government is attacks against government employees rather than by them. I refer here not to law enforcement officers who routinely face danger, but civilian bureaucrats who are unlucky enough to symbolize government authority to persons who are deranged or deeply resentful.

The first major domestic terrorist attack in the United States also occurred in the state of Oklahoma, nine years after the Sherrill shooting. On the morning of April 19, 1995, Timothy McVeigh parked a Ryder truck loaded with two tons of fertilizer explosive in front of the Alfred P. Murrah federal building in Oklahoma City. Just after hundreds of federal employees had arrived for work and deposited children in the building's daycare center, the truck's cargo exploded. The entire front of the eight-story building was ripped off, killing 168 people including 19 children. After he was captured and before he was executed, McVeigh made it abundantly clear that his motivation was bitter resentment against the national government of the United States.

In the years that followed, many additional antigovernment attacks occurred, especially against the Internal Revenue Service. In 2008 an Alabama taxpayer, after he and his wife had been arguing with an IRS agent on the phone, rammed his Jeep Cherokee SUV into the agency's offices in Birmingham, Alabama.[20] In 2009 a Florida man was sentenced to 30 years in prison for hiring an undercover FBI agent posing as a hit man to kill the IRS worker who was investigating his tax liability. In 2010 a disgruntled taxpayer piloted his private plane into the IRS office in Austin, killing one employee and himself. He had left a suicide note on his website saying, "Well, Mr. Big Brother IRS Man, let's try something different; take my pound of flesh and sleep well."[21] In 2011 a plot was uncovered in which four elderly Georgia men were conspiring to blow up offices of the IRS and Bureau of Alcohol, Tobacco, Firearms and Explosives, as well as scatter the deadly toxin ricin in cities by car or over them by plane. Inspired by Timothy McVeigh and an on-line novel titled "Absolved," the men had boasted of collecting a "bucket list" of government officials that needed to be "taken out."[22]

Another major target for antigovernment activity is agencies that manage federally owned public land, often in the far West but not exclusively there. Each year the Fish and Wildlife Service receives 10 to 12 threats or acts of violence against its personnel. The Bureau of Land Management experiences 20 to 30 such incidents, the National Park Service 100 or more, and the Forest Service 200 to 400. Examples of such activity are threatening to kill federal agents while they are enforcing grazing restrictions; running a truck over a Park Service ranger at Organ Pipe Cactus Monument; telephoning a BLS refuge manager to tell him his life is under a $15,000 contract; and placing a bomb in the front yard of a Forest Service district resource manager, destroying his car, and blowing out the front windows of his house.[23]

In recent years prosecutors and other prominent officials have been assassinated in Western states. In 2013 the executive director of the Colorado Department of Corrections was shot to death point blank when he answered a knock on the front door of his home. The suspected killer, who had the word "Hate" tattooed on his hand and a swastika on his stomach, was one of three notorious members of a white supremacist gang.[24]

According to the Southern Poverty Law Center, approximately 1,300 antigovernment, radical-right Patriot and Hutaree organizations and armed militiamen units exist in the United States, such as F.E.A.R., which stands for "Forever Enduring Always Ready." Some 100,000 individuals are also estimated to be active in the Sovereign Citizen movement, whose members reject the validity of US laws, deny the obligation to pay federal taxes, and refuse to get driver's licenses. The FBI categorizes the group as "domestic terrorist."[25]

WAYS THEORISTS CONDEMN IT

We now migrate in our discussion from how ordinary people perceive bureaucracy to how the experts do. Not surprisingly, they tend to be divided between those who regard it as a societal curse and those who see it as a societal asset. We begin by examining theorists who condemn bureaucracy and then turn to those that commend it. On each side, selected publications are discussed that raise issues about how well it works, its affects on people, and its relation to democracy.

It Does Not Work. Many academic critics argue that bureaucracy simply does not work, or at least not the way it should. A classic statement of this position is made in the 1944 book *Bureaucracy*, by Ludwig Von Mises. He was a pro–free market economist who came to the United States in 1940 as the German Nazi regime conquered Europe. In this country he taught at New York University where he influenced conservatives such as Milton Friedman and Ayn Rand. In his book, Von Mises contrasts two systems, Profit Management and Bureaucratic Management.

In the first, decisions are based on economic calculations designed to achieve profit maximization. In this explicit yet open-ended framework, managers are able to act freely and creatively in accord with market conditions. Personal freedom and political democracy flourish under this system. Bureaucratic Management, however, operates in the face of two powerful limits, the law and the budget. Such restraints do not free the manager to be creative, but to the contrary establish static norms and regulations that greatly limit decision freedom. Moreover, since bureaucracy's output has no cash value, no clear means of evaluating the activity exists. At the working level, meanwhile, a psychology develops whereby the combination of career tenure and seniority advancement attracts only mediocre talent, offers no incentive to accept change, and elevates to the top old men who have lost their vitality. With no opportunity or reason to excel, bureaucracy becomes institutionally dead and of prime use only to totalitarian regimes. Remarks Von Mises with contempt, "the main difference between a policeman and a kidnapper and between a tax collector and a robber is that the policeman and the tax collector obey and enforce the law, while the kidnapper and robber violate it.[26]

Another book which declares that bureaucracy is by its nature destined to work badly is by University of California professor emeritus Guy Benveniste. Published in 1983, it is also named simply *Bureaucracy* but written from a social-psychological rather than economics perspective. Moreover it considers bureaucracy in the private sector as well as in government. Benveniste's argument is elaborate but simple in its essence: "If we want to improve the efficiency and effectiveness of bureaucracies, we have to reduce the level of fear that exists within them."[27]

At the individual level, such fear stems from the harm that could be done to one's career if uncertain yet possible adverse events unfold over time. Examples are a decision that turns out to be unwise or an action that later damages the organization's image. Underlying the anxiety is a feeling that somewhere in the organization evaluators are assessing your work closely, and will delay your advancement or demean your status if something goes awry. This uneasiness operates at the edge of consciousness and causes the bureaucrat to be unduly cautious and conservative in his or her daily work. Byproducts are obsessive rule abidance, scrupulous documentation, distrust of others, and generally a joyless work life.

At the organizational level, Benveniste outlines a number of defensive "games" that are played to reduce uncertainty. In government these include inflating citizen demand for services, making clients wait to teach them a lesson, and engaging in trivial planning to legitimize decisions already made. Another strategy is "spreading" the organization by acting through intergovernmental bodies or stakeholder networks so as to deflect clear responsibility for failed outcomes. He regards the practice of organization development as a response to uncertainty rather than a way of defusing it, and sees citizen participation as possibly degenerating into a way to legitimize centralized control.

The most influential contemporary account of bureaucracy's purported ineffectiveness is *Reinventing Government,* by consultants David Osborne and Ted Gaebler. Since its publication in 1993, this book has stimulated reform efforts at all levels of government in the United States and in several foreign countries. Vice President Al Gore's National Performance Review during the Clinton presidency was built conceptually on the book, and it did much to inspire the New Public Management movement in academia.

Osborne and Gaebler believe that the agency-based concept of bureaucracy with its stable civil service workforce and centralized authority is a thing of the past. It originated in the industrial economy of the Progressive Era and New Deal, they say, and is now outdated with the onset of the information economy. They deplore traditional bureaucracies as staggeringly wasteful, a problem that cannot be rectified by budget cuts. This is because

> *waste in government does not come tied up in neat packages. It is marbled throughout our bureaucracies. It is embedded in the very way we do business. It is employees on idle, working at half speed—or barely working at all. It is people working hard at tasks that aren't worth doing, following regulations that should never have been written, filling out forms that should never have been printed.*[28]

How, then, should bureaucracies reinvent themselves? Although Osborne and Gaebler insist they know that government cannot be run like a business, their proposals have a strong private enterprise ring. Governments should focus on policy "steering" and devolve to others the "rowing" of direct service delivery. They should move from "government by program" to "market-oriented government" that catalyzes private suppliers, shares risk, and leverages investments. Administration by monopoly should be replaced by administration by competition, using such tools as vouchers, franchising, competitive procurement, load shedding, and internal profit centers. Also government itself should become enterprising, via fee-for-service mechanisms, joint investments, revolving funds, and profit centers. As for the bureaucrats, they should be hired with less red tape, subject to pay for performance, and evaluated for results, not just efforts.

It Is an Oppressive Force. A second category of writers denounce bureaucracy because it is seen as inherently oppressive of the human beings it serves as well as those it employs. A classic early article in this area is by Robert K. Merton, a prominent American sociologist who taught for many years at Columbia University. Titled "Bureaucratic Structure and Personality," it was published in *Social Forces* in 1940.

Merton points out that the authority of bureaucrats inheres in the offices they hold, not in the individuals who occupy them. Hence it is not surprising that their conduct is governed by the structure of this instrument of production, as Karl Marx would call it. The bureaucracy's purpose is to carry out the tasks assigned it in an efficient, precise, and predictable manner. To achieve this purpose, decisions must be made according to set rules, and clients must be treated depending on how they are categorized by those rules.

The problem of bureaucracy for Merton arises from what Thorsten Veblen termed "trained incapacity." This refers to how the carrying out of a narrow, single duty closes off one's horizons. A propensity for rigidity is reinforced by methodical and disciplined work habits, a culture that stresses devotion to the organization, and the desire to maintain a clean record so that regular promotions occur throughout the career. Collectively, these factors lead bureaucrats to overstep minimal needs for performance reliability and become so accustomed to ritualistic application of the rules that they value their content over the ends being sought, causing what sociologists call a displacement of goals.

The outcome of all of this, says Merton, is that when citizens arrive at a government office for assistance, they are greeted by a "public servant" whose bureaucratic personality makes a mockery of that phrase. They encounter instead an arrogant, impersonal, domineering, and inflexible official. All humanity is squeezed out of the pathos of a single citizen in need going to the sovereign state for help.[29]

A leading book on the actual practice of bureaucratic service to clients is Michael Lipsky's *Street-Level Bureaucracy*, first published in 1980. He defines "street-level bureaucrats" as public school teachers, policemen, welfare workers, and court employees. Although ideally these bureaucrats should treat every client equally and in accord with objective criteria, in practice they make discretionary decisions. More often than not, acute selectivity is forced by the compulsions of heavy caseloads and inadequate staff. The formal rules are not blatantly ignored, but they are applied in such a way as to make decisions quickly, in high volume, and in accord with the perceived demands of "the system."

Practices utilized to this end fall into three groups. One is to ration services. Access fees, long wait-time queues, selectively withheld information, triaging, and creaming are methods by which this is done. A second strategy is to take direct control of the client relationship. This is accomplished by means of physically intimidating offices, complex processing routines, isolating clients from each other, stigmatizing individuals by labels, and imposing strict rules on conduct. A third practice is to husband scarce resources by maintaining the existing backlog intact so as to discourage new work, using receptionists to screen out undesirables, and referring clients to other service providers. Lipsky's overall conclusion is that by means of these actions, street-level bureaucrats do not just implement public policy but make it. In the process they corrupt the ideals of their professions and perform as agents of social control over society's marginalized classes.[30]

If bureaucracy oppresses citizens, what does it do to its employees? In general, critical theorists and postmodernists believe it dehumanizes them. The most penetrating voice on this score is that of Ralph

Hummel, a long-time friend recently deceased. His book, *The Bureaucratic Experience*, presents his position; it first appeared in 1977, and its 5th and final edition was published in 2008.[31]

Hummel's ideas are sure to set you thinking. His starting point is that bureaucracy, which he defines as "rationalist administration driven by a single will," has become the dominant form of human organization in the world. People who spend eight or more hours a day immersed in its controlling, soulless grasp lose their identity, freedom, and individuality. Their relationships with others are no longer authentic and spontaneous but structured by the organization in terms of work assignment. Their cultural values are not inherited from a unique personal background but imposed by the organization, with prime emphasis on the virtues of efficiency, capitalism, and imperialism.

Turning to the process of dehumanization itself, the functions of gaining knowledge, obtaining mastery of one's work, and exercising moral judgment are taken over by the organization. Bureaucracy replaces the psyche; personal feelings and conscience are exiled, and capacities for imagination and sensibility disappear. The proactive, self-making, language-creating individual is lost from view. Bureaucracy confers a self-image derived from occupation of a particular office, which leads to alienation from the self and a de-centered psyche. People learn to think of themselves as means to bureaucratic purposes, not beings precious unto themselves.

It Is Antidemocratic. When at the beginning of this chapter I was discussing Weber's model of bureaucracy, I mentioned in passing that he warned of its political power. We need to cover this aspect of his thinking more fully.

Weber asserts that bureaucracy is, among all social structures, one of the hardest to destroy. Because of its discipline and technical competence, it is, in itself, a power instrument of the first order—to the one who controls it. Well, you might respond, in a democracy with regular elections, this instrument of power is blunted. Even so, more is involved. Since modern society would be impossible without bureaucracy, chaos would reign if it disappeared. Hence, in an ultimate sense, the bargaining chips are on its side (as in a government shutdown). Then too, regardless of whether a democracy or autocracy is in place, the degree of expertise and knowledge at the disposal of the bureaucracy cannot be matched by any other component of government. This imbalance gives it great heft in dealing with matters of state, and much more so if the bureaucracy decides to keep its operations secret (and it was the bureaucracy that invented the notion of "official secret," according to Weber). The overall consequence is that the very characteristics that make bureaucracy so effective also make it so powerful that it places the controlling capacity of even the regime's top officials in question. Two quotes translated from German:

> Bureaucratic administration means fundamentally the exercise of control on the basis of knowledge. This is the feature of it which makes it specifically rational. This consists on the one hand in technical knowledge which, by itself, is sufficient to ensure it a position of extraordinary power. But in addition to this, bureaucratic organizations, or the holders of power who make use of them, have the tendency to increase their power still further by the knowledge growing out of experience in the service. For they acquire through the conduct of office a special knowledge of facts and have available a store of documentary material peculiar to themselves.[32]

> Under normal conditions, the power position of a fully developed bureaucracy is always overtowering. The "political master" finds himself in the position of the "dilettante" who stands opposite the "expert," facing the trained official who stands within the management of administration.[33]

Another author translated from the German, Henry Jacoby, denounces what he calls "the bureaucratization of the world." In a book by that name, he insists man's existence in the modern world is controlled and directed by central agencies of government. The sole individual is unable to escape bureaucracy's regulation and manipulation, if for no other reason than it seems essential for a modern-day lifestyle. This myth of indispensability, as Jacoby calls it, prevents any return to spontaneous self-sufficiency.

Hence Jacoby concludes that the real problem with bureaucracy is not how well or badly it functions but its corroding impact on democracy. Speaking from his interpretation of European history, he says its impact is to undermine if not destroy the values of freedom of the individual, equal rights, the legality of government, and the division of governmental power. All of these attributes are suppressed by administration's own autocratic ways, he says. For one thing, the agencies are internally controlled by the use of hierarchy and rules. For another, bureaucracy's external relationships to other centers of power are manipulated by strategies of empty ritualism, procrastination in carrying out instructions, and quiet sabotage of policy initiatives. This is true despite the claim by bureaucrats that they are nonpartisan and politically neutral. "It is doubtful whether the virtue of 'neutrality' does in fact exist; mostly it exists only within certain limits. The continuity of the bureaucratic machine favors a predominantly conservative attitude."[34]

We end our tour of antibureaucracy writings with a contemporary law professor who believes the values of our legal system have been trampled upon by the discretionary powers conferred upon bureaucracy. Richard Epstein, in a book titled *Design for Liberty: Private Property, Public Administration, and the Rule of Law*, examines the intersection of the three elements in its subtitle. A proper balance between private rights and bureaucratic power has shifted so much from the former to the latter that protections of the law have been eviscerated. Epstein traces the origin of this megashift to the Progressive Movement but says it began in earnest with FDR's New Deal and has continued under Obama as exemplified by the Affordable Care Act and Dodd-Frank Wall Street reform law.

The leap in scale of the role of the federal government, although legitimized by a series of free elections, has endangered the very legal principles set down by the Constitution to protect us from runaway government, which Epstein sees as neutrality, generality, clarity, consistency, and prospective application. The author illustrates the degeneration of these values by recounting what has happened with respect to eminent domain takings, health and safety regulations, the permitting of building projects, and the allowing of popular protests in public places. The only proper policy domains that should be reserved for federal government action, Epstein believes, are law enforcement, infrastructure provision, and national defense.[35]

WAYS THEORISTS COMMEND IT

I now turn to theorists who do not condemn bureaucracy but commend it. With "bureaucracy" being tantamount to a hate word in the English language, one would expect them to be few. Actually that is not true. To illustrate, no less than two "cases for bureaucracy" were made using this title decades before your author took pen to the subject. In 1933 Charles and William Beard published such a piece to denounce the "frenzy" of attacks against New Deal agencies. Thirty years later Harlan Cleveland did the same to reject "canards" heaped upon the Department of State.[36]

It Can Be Made to Work. The first items we discuss on the "pro" side relate to whether bureaucracy works. My initial selection is a chapter by Christopher Leman found at the beginning of a volume titled *The Tools of Government*, edited by Lester Salamon. The book's overall theme is that in today's complex environment, public service delivery should be shifted more fully from public agencies to third parties. In the language of what is termed the New Governance, "direct" government gives way to "indirect" government via contracts, grants, loans, loan guarantees, government enterprises, vouchers, and tax expenditures. Leman's chapter gives bureaucracy one last chance to show its wares to the book's readers before delving into the chapters on alternative tools.[37]

One thing Leman does is to identify types of situations in which direct administration seems desirable. These are where (1) the exercise of legitimate force is involved, as in policing and incarceration; (2) adequate performance is so critical that it cannot be left to chance, as in controlling civil aircraft; (3) equity considerations are especially important, as in Head Start and Food Stamps; (4) no private providers are available to take over the activity; and (5) government reserve capacity is needed, for example stores of back-up emergency medical supplies.

In addition, Leman is willing to claim that in-house administration does have some inherent overall advantages. One is vertical integration. Possessing its own personnel, equipment, and other resources gives the agency full control over what it needs to carry out the mission. The complexity and uncertainty of relying on multiple parties with different goals are eliminated. Another advantage is that it avoids the extra transaction costs of coordinating and evaluating the activities of outside organizations. While private providers may produce repetitive concrete services more cheaply because of scale, coping with amorphous problems like child obesity or energy independence are better handled by government. Finally, undue delays or instances of corruption are harder to ferret out when spread among private organizations. Also disclosure of sensitive information or violation of employee due process may be less stoppable. Leman concludes by criticizing the federal government for its clumsy, outdated personnel system, but praises it for the many technological innovations it has spawned for society.

In another book named *On Thinking Institutionally*, Hugh Heclo of George Mason University lays the basis for thinking about bureaucracies in a way that transcends the mundane. Institutions are not simply instrumental "tools" at all but living organizational entities of inherent importance. Illustrated by everything from the institution of marriage to the local hospital, institutions are conveyances of values inherited from the past that have been adapted for the present. As a consequence institutions give purpose to collective social life and endow human efforts with shared meaning. While unquestioned belief in their rightness and wisdom should never be tolerated, so too should blanket, wholesale rejection of their authority. Heclo takes a midway position between these two extremes by advocating for a residue of skepticism and occasional dissent to be coupled with generalized acceptance and occasional devotion.

Heclo's institutions include those that comprise the operating arms of government. In fact he devotes several pages of his book to more particularized concepts of thinking institutionally that pertain especially to bureaucracy. He describes these as "tattered modern remnants" of past institutional practice that deserve "respect in depth" today. One is the concept of profession, a notion that gives seed to the possibility of engaging in a noble cause, such as serving the interests of one's community. A second is the notion of office, which envisions the carrying out of duties that call for responsible fulfillment of a public duty impartially and conscientiously. Third is stewardship, an idea that anticipates being faithfully attentive to the needs of others so that the trust of those others is deserved and won.[38]

As it happens, your author has developed an institution-based normative theory of bureaucracy—although when doing so, he had not yet encountered Heclo's work. It is described in a book named *Mission Mystique: Belief Systems in Public Agencies.* The project was the outcome of several years of field research on the qualities of six government agencies that were chosen because they are thought well of to a particularly high degree. My aim was to uncover the traits they might have in common. Four federal organizations were studied: the National Park Service, National Weather Service, Centers for Disease Control and Prevention, and the Peace Corps. One agency each was investigated at the state and local level: the Virginia State Police and the Department of Social Services of Mecklenburg County in Charlotte, North Carolina.

I was analyzing bureaucracy at its best because I wished to uncover in specified conceptual terms what "best" seems to mean in institutional terms for bureaucracy. Obviously these six organizations do not represent some kind of "median norm" in public administration. Their full set of attributes is probably rivaled by a small minority of the thousands administrative bodies in the US public sector. Yet the properties that came to my attention are generic in nature and adaptable to varied settings. Probably most extant bureaus already possess one or more of them in some degree. This realization led me to conclude that, at the very least, my framework could serve as a set of useful goals for improvement in public administration. In any case, I went away from the project with the firm conviction that American bureaucracy *can* work, indeed exceedingly well.

My normative framework is shown in Figure 1.1. It is called a template rather than a model since it constitutes only a recommended guide, not a precise recipe. The term "belief system" connotes value commitments that reinforce each other to create a whole. Their fulfillment yields an image or status I call "mission mystique." The first word in this term indicates the overriding importance of mission achievement as an institutional goal. The second word conveys my realization that what these attributes in combination seemed to do is create an aura of institutional charisma that radiates in two directions: inward to the workforce, where it fosters pride and devotion beyond what one would normally expect; and outward to external constituencies and the informed public, who regard the agency with unusual admiration and respect.

Figure 1.1 shows the full extent of relevant features I uncovered. The template's three columns and three rows form a matrix of nine numbered cells. A central mission purpose (cell 1), regarded by society as important (cell 2), and legitimized by a past record of achievement (cell 3), establishes an overall sense of institutional direction (the top row). This direction is pursued energetically (middle row) by virtue of the intrinsic motivation of personnel (cell 4), their common immersion in a mission-centered culture (cell 5), and knowledge of stories of the past that foster pride and identity (cell 6). The always-lurking danger of having an intense mission commitment become stale or perverted (bottom row) is forestalled by welcomed internal dissent (cell 7), opportunities for policy experimentation (cell 8) and organizational learning that enables agency self-renewal (cell 9).[39]

It Can Free and Enrich. Contrary to what we encountered above, commending theorists say that bureaucracy is not necessarily oppressive and, on the contrary, can produce freedom. Larry Preston, a political scientist at Northern Arizona University, states that freedom of choice is certainly limited when working in bureaucracy, but it is also enabled. For example, the existence of rules and standard operating procedures set boundaries for action but also confer independent exercise of choice within them.

FIGURE 1.1	The Mission Mystique Belief System: A Template

	Direction Column	Environment Column	Time Column
Purpose Row	1. Central Mission Purpose	2. Important Societal Need	3. Recorded Achievement
Energy Row	4. Intrinsic Motivation	5. Institutional Culture	6. Celebrated History
Vitality Row	7. Accepted Dissent	8. Qualified Autonomy	9. Ongoing Renewal

Source: Charles T. Goodsell, *Mission Mystique: Belief Systems in Public Agencies* (Washington, DC: CQ Press, 2011), p. 14.

The resources provided to bureaucrats for carrying out their duties permit professionals and technicians to practice their expertise freely. Bureaucracy even does something as fundamental as creating the stability and predictability necessary for engaging in the process of reasoned choice. Also the inevitable internal politics that take place in a bureaucracy offer the chance to make bargaining choices. Thus,

> *properly conceived, advancing bureaucratization need not mean a loss of freedom. Indeed, personal and social life centered around the rules and logic of bureaucracy can witness far greater freedom than was ever possible in our laissez faire or communal past.*[40]

In a book titled *In Praise of Bureaucracy*, British sociologist Paul du Gay contends in the same vein that bureaucracy does not crush the individual who works in it, as Hummel claims, but instead makes freedom compatible with sovereign authority. His position is developed from Max Weber's concept of ethos of office and runs parallel to Heclo's thoughts on the subject. The ideal "life order" conferred on bureaucrats who occupy an office is such that when on duty, they must not act in arbitrary or unpredictable ways, but otherwise are entitled to make prudent use of discretion. Existing between the separated boundaries of the rules' dos and don'ts is space for creative, independent action by the bureaucrat to seek goals in a spirit of fairness.[41]

In 1976 Canadian social psychologist Elliott Jaques presented ideas in his *A General Theory of Bureaucracy* that also take issue with the arguments of Hummel. Working in a hierarchical organization can be—but need not be—alienating, says Jaques. To the contrary, under the right circumstances it can become a setting conducive to a humane work life. The secret is to enable individuals to exercise their natural abilities to the full and to enrich their relationships with colleagues.

Jaques lays out three fundamental principles to achieve this result. The first is that the organization must be small enough to allow its members to know each other, at least by sight, making possible what he calls a "nodding" mutual recognition quality. This facilitates personal interaction, the building of social ties, authentic dialogue, and mutual respect.

Hence the defining workplace unit should not exceed 250 to 300 members; if that is impossible, subparts on that scale are separately identified.

A second principle is to locate the work activity in a single geographic place. This way, members can interact socially with each other on a private basis outside work. Third, Jaques advises that hierarchical levels be limited to three: head manager, section managers, and below that unsupervised work teams. Under this arrangement workers are free to employ their craft knowledge without continuous interference. Reporting is limited to a single immediate superior with appeal possible only one step away.[42]

Jacques' prescriptions for ease of contact, physical proximity, and a flattened hierarchy sound quaint today. Nonetheless it is very possible that they are feasible more than ever in an electronic age. The village-like qualities that he strives to create may now be possible for the first time in a mass society via e-mail, Linkedin, Facebook, and Twitter.

Democracy Counts on It. Early in this chapter I broached the metaphor whereby the bureaucrats generally work "downstairs" and elected officials hold sway "upstairs," even though the lower-level folk often ascend the stairs to advise the upper-level. Theories like those of Weber and Jacoby portray something of an invasion of the upper story by the lower, however. What would be a contrary view?

A classic early article on the question is "Fear of Bureaucracy: A Raging Pandemic" by Herbert Kaufman, author of many fine books in our field. This anxiety, he says, stems from the belief that bureaucracy is so powerful it is out of control. But, he asks, if this is true, who controls it? If we ask people who have been thwarted by bureaucracy, we find that everyone has a different answer. To use contemporary examples, Occupy on the extreme left sees bureaucracy as the tool of Wall Street, while the Tea Party on the far right blames big-spending Democrats. The coal-burning utilities tell us that global-warming activists are responsible for regulatory "overreach," but environmentalists believe that lobbyists for those who spew carbon into the atmosphere sabotaged the standard. Back in Washington, political appointees of the administration complain that committee chairs exercise too much influence in the agencies Downtown. Yet Republicans on the Hill are sure the White House is dictating agency actions. How, then, can anybody be behind bureaucratic power if everyone is? Kaufman's answer is that hyped rhetoric about the power of "bureaucracy" is an abstraction that says nothing cognitively meaningful and merely shows how political warriors need a devil to blame when they lose a fight. What better Lucifer than the bureaucracy?

The only way to comprehend the power of bureaus, Kaufman goes on, is to disaggregate the abstraction of "bureaucratic power" and assess the political influence individual agencies are able to bring to bear in concrete situations. It will be found that diverse factors determine how each organization is both empowered and constrained, in different degrees and ways, as it goes about its decision making. Particularizing the analysis this way does not give satisfying simple answers, but it does bring to light the absurdity of flat-out pronouncements that an identifiable, omnipresent, all-powerful, single vague force is always standing ready to sabotage democracy.[43]

If it is granted that bureaucratic influence is variable rather than inexorable, one can begin to think more imaginatively about a desirable role for the bureau in policy and power. It might even be possible, despite the specters raised by bureaucracy's critics, for it to *contribute* to democracy. This is the thesis of a book named *Bureaucratic Representation* by Canadian professor H. T. Wilson. He urges us to look to the administrative implementation process for ways for government to act affirmatively and actively in behalf of necessary public and social interests. A major reason that such action is needed is the failure of traditional electoral representation to transcend its proestablishment, conservative biases, Wilson says. Hence ostensibly neutral civil servants should practice bureaucratic representation.

What Wilson means by this phrase is a form of interaction between bureaucrats as they deal with practical problems and policy makers as they make policy. It involves the exercise of "constructive discretion" by bureaucrats, which consists of conveying insights gained during the process of implementation to policy makers as a source for appropriately adjusted policy content. This allows a "closing the loop" in the policy process whereby past outputs of legislatures are turned into fresh policy-making inputs, made possible by learning from direct encounters with public needs. The prime opportunity for that to happen is the rule-making process, where the problems that lead to regulatory intervention are systematically heard. Informal discretionary experiences with agency clients can also be drawn upon for improvement ideas. Wilson readily admits his idea is sure to set off a howl of protest from the legislative and legal communities. Yet somehow we must convince representative bodies to shift away from the pattern of giving agencies wide discretion and then slapping them later for what they come up with.[44]

The final item of literature to review is *Pragmatist Democracy*, by Christopher Ansell at the University of California, Berkeley. Like Wilson, Ansell proposes an expanded role for bureaucracy in policy making, but his vision for it is considerably more sweeping. He calls upon the administrative agency to become the linchpin for a newly conceived form of democracy. It entails a public deliberative process comprised of several intertwined elements: open consideration of new ideas; a holistic comprehension of issues; deliberate pooling of information; a problem-solving mentality; and a readiness to think reflexively, engage in joint discussion, and permit consensus to evolve.

Last but not least, pragmatist democracy requires a willingness to get the hands dirty in real-world policy experimentation. This is not laboratory experiments to attain objective knowledge in the positivist vein, but actual trial runs of promising intervention approaches followed by subjective assessment of outcomes. It is often valuable to carry out a series of reiterative experiments to capture the full yield of pragmatist thinking.

The bureaucratic agency does not monopolize this activity yet acts as its prime sponsor. To make a bureau capable of this role, it is necessary to modify the principle of hierarchy so that authoritative influences move upward as well as downward. Decentralization as well as centralization are imparted to give localized grassroots groups sufficient space to formulate ideas and launch initiatives. Authority is thought of in relational rather than legal terms in order to nurture authenticity and social bonding. Then, on a practical level, top officials and street-level bureaucrats join forces to fashion workable implementation schemes. The end product is that public administration performs not only at the tail end of the policy process but at its front end as well, concludes Ansell.[45]

SO WHAT'S OUR STARTING POINT?

I bring this first chapter to a close by tying together tightly the points we have covered to give you the best starting point possible for working out your own thoughts on bureaucracy.

In this book I do not use the term "bureaucracy" as a synonym for failed government. It refers, rather, to American public administration and, in particular, its agencies.

Defined this way, bureaucracy is massive in scope with respect to both dollars and personnel numbers. But its organizations and people are spread out among all three levels of our federal system—with most at the local level—and operate in every corner of the country, often in small offices.

Its image is poor among Americans when viewed as an aggregate phenomenon. However, when considered concretely as particular agencies and programs, it receives warmer reviews—including being awarded more trust than Congress.

Published academic thought on bureaucracy ranges across a wide spectrum. For many years the preponderance of scholarly writing was critical. In recent years a substantial amount of countering literature on the other side has appeared.

One point in contention is bureaucracy's effectiveness. Condemning theorists say its monopolistic form causes agencies to be static and mediocre, whereas private firms are more dynamic because they face competition. Accordingly, a movement exists to devolve their activities to the private sector, particularly through contracts. The pro side responds by saying the bureaucracy's career service gives it unparalleled expertise and knowledge. Also many of its activities are life-and-death in nature and should be kept in-house. When the agency culture stresses the importance of its mission to employees, an impressive degree of dedicated service can be generated.

Another split in the literature concerns the attitudes and motivations of the bureaucrats. On one side, critics charge that the hierarchical and specialized structure of bureaucracy, along with its need to use rules, cause its personnel to be narrow, rigid, and rule obsessed. Other ills are a fear of failure and the possibility of arbitrary actions toward clients. Ralph Hummel, bureaucracy's most penetrating critic, contends that people who work in bureaucracy become dehumanized.

In contrast, favorable writers argue that the stability and predictability of bureaucracy provide an opportunity for reasoned judgment, autonomous choice, and personal fulfillment. It is also possible to impart more humanity to bureaucracy if aspects of organization size and communication are rethought. Ascribing evils to bureaucratic behavior using abstract deductive reasoning leads us to ignore the fact that individual agencies are living institutions. They embody core values of the society and put professionalism, a sense of duty, and possibilities for earning trust to work in behalf of the public.

A final point of contention is bureaucratic power. On one side, its huge aggregate size and the fact that bureaucrats are not elected lead critics to charge that bureaucracy circumvents and crushes democratic values and principles by invading private rights and sidestepping legislative power. It possesses a near monopoly of information that gives it the ability to dominate elected officials.

The counter argument is that a mythic concept of overall bureaucratic power is a product of blame laid on government by individuals for its failure to obey their will. The political influence actually exercised within bureaucracy must be assessed at the level of the individual bureau; and, in that light, its amount, use, and impact vary greatly. Bold theorists on the pro side who propose radical new policy roles for administration go beyond implementation of policy and say it could achieve more democracy than we now derive from elected legislatures.

ENDNOTES

1. Erick Partridge, *Origins: A Short Etymological Dictionary of Modern English* (New York: Greenwich House, 1989), 64–65.
2. H.H. Gerth and C. Wright Mills, eds., *From Max Weber: Essays in Sociology* (New York: Oxford University Press, 1946), ch. 8.
3. R.A.W. Rhodes, "The New Governance: Governing Without Government," *Political Studies* 44 (1996): 652–657.
4. *Statistical Abstract of the United States: 2012* (Washington, DC: US Bureau of the Census, 2011), 268, 310.
5. Charles T. Goodsell, *The Case for Bureaucracy: A Public Administration Polemic*, 3rd ed. (Chatham, NJ: Chatham House, 1994), 136, and 4th ed. (Washington, DC: CQ Press, 2004), 113.

6. Goodsell, *The American Statehouse: Interpreting Democracy's Temples* (Lawrence: University Press of Kansas, 2001), 113–115.

7. Donald Lambro, *The Federal Rathole* (New Rochelle, NY: Arlington House, 1975). J. Peter Grace, *Burning Money: The Waste of Your Tax Dollars* (New York: Macmillan, 1984). Jack Anderson and John Kidner, *Alice in Blunderland* (Washington, DC: Acropolis Books, 1983). George Roche, *America by the Throat: The Stranglehold of Federal Bureaucracy* (Old Greenwich, CT: Devin-Adair, 1983).

8. Beverly A. Cigler and Heidi L. Neiswender, "'Bureaucracy' in the Introductory American Government Textbook," *Public Administration Review* 51, no. 5 (September–October 1991): 442–450.

9. Center for Media and Public Affairs, "Changing Images of Government in TV Entertainment," *Public Voices* 6, nos. 2–3 (n.d.): 70–72.

10. Michelle C. Pautz and Laura Roselle, "Are They Ready for Their Close-Up? Civil Servants and Their Portrayal in Contemporary American Cinema," *Public Voices* 11, no. 1 (n.d.): 8–32.

11. Beth A. Wielde and David Schultz, "Wonks and Warriors: Depictions of Government Professionals in Popular Film," *Public Voices* 9, no. 2 (n.d.): 61–82.

12. David Nakamura and Ed O'Keefe, "Obama Seeks Power to Streamline Government," *Washington Post*, January 14, 2012.

13. Trust in Government/Gallup Historical Trends. Accessed July 24, 2013 at http://www.gallup.com/poll/5392/trust-government.aspx.

14. Ibid.

15. Data obtained from the iPOLL database maintained by the Pew Research Center for the People & the Press, Storrs, CT.

16. William C. Adams and Donna Lund Infeld, "Americans Exhibit Increasingly Partisan Views of Federal Workers," *PA Times*, October 2012.

17. Lloyd G. Nigro and William L. Waugh, Jr., "Violence in the American Workplace: Challenges to the Pubic Enterprise," *Public Administration Review* 56, no. 4 (July–August 1996): 326.

18. *Statistical Abstract of the United States*, 2012, p. 428.

19. Charles Montaldo, "It's Official: 'Going Postal' is Epidemic" and Wikipedia article "Going Postal." Accessed January 27, 2012.

20. Ed O'Keefe, "IRS Investigates Flurry of Threats Against Its Workers and Facilities," *Washington Post*, March 12, 2010.

21. William Branigan and Spencer S. Hsu, "Pilot Slams into IRS Offices in Texas," *Washington Post*, February 19, 2010.

22. "Novel Believed to Have Inspired Terror Plot," *Roanoke Times*, November 3, 2011.

23. Public Employees for Environmental Responsibility, "Violence vs. Employees—Home." Accessed January 27, 2011.

24. Associated Press, "Colorado Prisons Chief Killed at His House," *Washington Post*, March 21, 2013; "Prison Chief's Slaying Suspect Had Troubled Life," *Roanoke Times*, March 29, 2013; "Gang Member Arrested in Death of Prisons Chief," *Roanoke Times*, April 6, 2013.

25. Southern Poverty Law Center, *SPLC Report* 42, no. 1 (Spring 2012), "Radical-Right Movement Explodes," 1, 3.

26. Ludwig Von Mises, *Bureaucracy* (New Haven: Yale University Press, 1944), with quote at p. 76.

27. Guy Benveniste, *Bureaucracy*, 2nd ed. (San Francisco: Boyd & Fraser, 1983), with quote at p. xvii.

28. David Osborne and Ted Gaebler, *Reinventing Government: How the Entrepreneurial Spirit Is Transforming the Public Sector* (New York: Plume, 1993), quote at pp. 22–23.

29. Robert K. Merton, "Bureaucratic Structure and Personality," *Social Forces* 17 (1940): 560–568. Reprinted in *Reader in Bureaucracy*, ed. Robert K. Merton, Ailsa P. Gray, Barbara Hockey, and Hanan C. Selvin (New York: Free Press, 1952), 361–371.

30. Michael Lipsky, *Street-Level Bureaucracy: Dilemmas of the Individual in Public Services* (New York: Russell Sage Foundation, 1980).

31. Ralph P. Hummel, *The Bureaucratic Experience: The Post-Modern Challenge*, 5th ed. (Armonk, NY: M.E. Sharpe, 2008).

32. Talcott Parsons, *Max Weber: The Theory of Social and Economic Organization* (New York: The Free Press, 1947), 339.

33. Gerth and Mills, *From Max Weber*, 228–235.

34. Henry Jacoby, *The Bureaucratization of the World* (Berkeley: University of California Press, 1973), with quote at pp. 162–163.

35. Richard A. Epstein, *Design for Liberty: Private Property, Public Administration, and the Rule of Law* (Cambridge: Harvard University Press, 2011).

36. Charles and William Beard, "The Case for Bureaucracy," *Scribner's Magazine* 93 (April 1933): 209–214 [reprinted in *Public Administration Review* 46, no. 2 (March–April 1986): 107–112]. Harlan Cleveland, "The Case for Bureaucracy," *New York Times Magazine*, October 27, 1963, 19, 113–114.

37. Christopher K. Leman, "Direct Government," ch. 2 in *The Tools of Government: A Guide to the New Governance*, ed. Lester M. Salamon (New York: Oxford University Press, 2002), 48–79.

38. Hugh Heclo, *On Thinking Institutionally* (Boulder, CO: Paradigm, 2008). See 130–149 for the last point.

39. Charles T. Goodsell, *Mission Mystique: Belief Systems in Public Agencies* (Washington, DC: CQ Press, 2011).

40. Larry M. Preston, *Freedom and the Organizational Republic* (Berlin: Walter de Gruyter, 1992), ch. 4 with quote at p. 140.

41. Paul du Gay, *In Praise of Bureaucracy: Weber, Organization, Ethics* (London: Sage, 2000). See also his chapter "Bureaucracy and Liberty: State, Authority, and Freedom" in *The Values of Bureaucracy*, ed. Du Gay (Oxford: Oxford University Press, 2005), 1–13.

42. Elliott Jaques, *A General Theory of Bureaucracy* (London: Heinemann, 1976).

43. Herbert Kaufman, "Fear of Bureaucracy: A Raging Pandemic," *Public Administration Review* 41, no. 1 (January–February 1981): 1–9, with quote at p. 3. Readers may wish to consult a revisiting of this topic twenty years later by Kaufman in "Major Players: Bureaucracies in American Government," *Public Administration Review* 61, no. 1 (January–February 2001): 18–42.

44. H.T. Wilson, *Bureaucratic Representation: Civil Servants and the Future of Capitalist Democracies* (Leiden, the Netherlands: Brill, 2001).

45. Christopher K. Ansell, *Pragmatist Democracy: Evolutionary Learning as Public Philosophy* (Oxford: Oxford University Press, 2011).

BUREAUCRACY UNDER THE MICROSCOPE

S cientists use microscopes so they can look at objects more closely than is possible with the naked eye. The data they obtain help them understand their subject better. Although this is a work of social inquiry and not social science, this chapter has the same ends.

CLIENTS' IMPRESSIONS

I start with one of my earliest ventures in researching bureaucracy. When I presented its results to a faculty audience interviewing for a job, I was told I simply could not have it right. I got so angry that I determined to write what became the first edition of the forerunner to this book.

Parking Lot Interviews. Merton and Lipsky tell us to expect that bureaucrats treat their clients with arrogance, dominate and control them, and are preoccupied with obeying the rules. To find out if this is true, I once stood in the parking lots of welfare offices around the country and asked clients departing from the social services building several questions about their just-completed experience. This was done in two medium-sized cities and two big cities. In each place three types of bureaucracy were evaluated: Social Security offices, departments of public welfare, and unemployment compensation offices. Table 2.1 provides the findings from this "exit polling," as it would be called today.

I was impressed that rather than hearing a barrage of reports of disappointment, hurt, or anger, the encounters were usually successful from the client's point of view and in most instances far from unpleasant. Most

TABLE 2.1	Client Evaluation of Three Welfare Programs (in percent)		
Clients Who:	Social Security	Public Welfare	Unemployment Compensation
Achieved what they came for	85.0	70.0	68.8
Argued with office personnel	2.5	6.3	11.3
Felt the worker really listened	79.5	65.8	60.8
Felt the worker really tried to help	74.3	67.1	60.3
Felt personnel were very courteous	74.7	61.3	61.3
Felt personnel were very efficient	67.1	51.3	39.7
Felt personnel were very sympathetic	47.8	33.3	31.6
Were "very satisfied" with how the office handled their problem overall	68.4	46.8	35.0
Expect to remember something "really nice" about the encounter	70.7	49.1	40.0
Expect to remember something "really unpleasant" about the encounter	29.3	50.9	60.0

Source: Charles T. Goodsell, "Client Evaluation of Three Welfare Programs," *Administration & Society* 12, no. 2 (August 1980): 123–136.

Note: In the two "achieved" and "argued" questions, the percentage shown is the number saying yes in a yes-no option. In the five "felt" questions, it includes those volunteering a strong affirmative answer such as very, really, or lots (with no choices offered). In the one "problem overall" question, four options were given: very satisfied, fairly satisfied, somewhat dissatisfied, and very dissatisfied; the percentage shown is the first option only. For the two "expect to remember" items, the percentage means yes if the respondent expected to remember anything, which occurred 51.3 percent of the time for Social Security, 66.3 percent for Public Welfare, and 50.0 percent for Unemployment Compensation. All interprogram differences were statistically significant ($p < .05$) except for the argued, tried to help, very courteous, and very sympathetic items.

of the respondents said they got what they wanted inside the office and dealt with a worker whom they perceived as courteous, a good listener, and trying to help. Only a few reported arguing with the individual. Client gender and city size did not affect outcomes, but elderly applicants tended to be more pleased than young people and whites more satisfied than minorities.[1]

Yet the three programs produced quite different results with respect to perceptions of worker efficiency and sympathy, overall satisfaction, and anticipated recollections. In all of these areas Social Security offices produced the most favorable responses with positive scores in the high 60s or low 70s, except for perceived sympathy. Public welfare was regularly in second place on these variables and unemployment compensation at the bottom, with scores in the 40s or 30s.

The fact that significant contrasts showed up even within the single general category of social assistance demonstrates vividly that any notion that all bureaucracies are more or less the same is faulty. It is perfectly understandable that client impressions of these three programs would differ. Most (but not all) of Social Security benefits are earned by payroll deduction. Public assistance is a straight gift and means-tested, and one cannot receive unemployment compensation without falling into the humiliating status of being jobless.

The ACSI. The American Consumer Satisfaction Index (ACSI) queries some 70,000 consumers annually in order to measure the degree of satisfaction they experience from what they buy. Its methodology is to reach randomly selected US residents by phone or e-mail and ask what products or services they have recently purchased or received. If the item originates from one of 225 private companies or 200 government programs currently being evaluated, respondents are asked standardized questions on (1) prior expectations of quality, (2) degree of satisfaction with the quality encountered, and (3) any complaints that they have lodged. For commercial transactions only, respondents are also queried on feelings about price paid and future plans to buy.

When in this process a target of 250 or more respondents has been reached on a given item, numerical values assigned to responses are fed into a computer program to yield an index score of consumer satisfaction between 0 and 100. ACSI then makes available selected results at various levels of aggregation, periodically over time. For the private sector—the original target for ACSI evaluations—these levels are industry, firm, and product. In recent years the public sector has been tested by government (federal or local), agency and program. A summation score for the over-all national economy includes both private and public sectors.[2]

Table 2.2 shows, for the years from 1999 to 2011, scores for the federal and local governments in comparison to the national economy. Note they are all quite closely grouped within the 62–76 point range. This sug-gests a relatively satisfied consuming public overall. Differences from the national economy are all negative, indicating a persistent gap in degree of favorable impression between the private and public sectors. Nonetheless the size of that gap is more marginal than harsh skeptics of government would likely expect. Some of it might be due to the fact that the ACSI was designed for commercial, not bureaucratic clients; the purpose of public goods and services is not to please customers but create a desirable soci-ety for all.

While most ACSI questions are about specific organization-product experiences, in recent years the Ann Arbor–based company has gone

TABLE 2.2	American Consumer Satisfaction Index Scores, 1999–2011				
Year	National Economy	Federal Government	Difference from Economy	Local Government	Difference from Economy
1999	72.3	68.6	−3.7	68.7	−3.6
2000	72.7	68.6	−4.1	65.7	−7.0
2001	72.2	71.3	−0.9	67.9	−4.3
2002	73.0	70.2	−2.8	66.3	−6.7
2003	73.9	70.9	−3.0	66.5	−7.4
2004	74.2	72.1	−2.1	62.7	−11.5
2005	73.2	71.3	−1.9	65.9	−7.3
2006	74.5	72.3	−2.2	67.7	−6.8
2007	75.2	67.8	−7.4	68.0	−7.2
2008	75.3	68.9	−6.4	72.9	−2.4
2009	76.0	68.7	−7.3	68.3	−7.7
2010	75.7	65.4	−10.3	68.3	−7.4
2011	75.7	66.9	−8.8	67.1	−8.6
Mean	74.2	69.5	−4.7	67.4	−6.8
Std. Dev.	1.37	2.09		2.30	

Source: American Consumer Satisfaction Index, "National Quarterly Scores" and "Public Administration/ Government Sector Scores," ACSI website. Accessed April 19, 2012.

Note: These scores are on a low-high scale of 0–100. National Economy scores, which include both private and public sectors, are calculated as means of the four quarters for that year.

beyond its original focus and also asked questions on generalized trust in government. In 2010 it reported that 41 percent of respondents expressed overall trust in the federal government, a proportion that declined to 36 in 2011. When the question is directed only to persons who recently had actual transactions with national agencies, scores of 68 for 2010 and 69 for 2011 were yielded. This abstract-concrete differential echoes a theme we have already encountered. ACSI commented,

> *Once someone has experienced services from a particular agency, that person tends to look at the agency more favorably and have far greater trust in it. Contrary to popular belief, it seems that the more people come into contact with and receive services from federal agencies and departments, the more they like them.*[3]

We can pursue this point further by examining ACSI scores for particular public institutions. Table 2.3 gives them for twelve federal departments or agencies and two local government functions, with seven private industries and sectors thrown in for comparison purposes. Looking down the list ordered high to low, we note that private sector organizations essentially occupy its upper half; their mean score is 75.4 and that of the fourteen public organizations is 69.3. Hence the somewhat lower evaluation of government just mentioned is still evident. Yet we also notice that two government scores are among the top five, both slightly above the global score of 75.7 for the national economy. Remarkably, these are metropolitan trash collectors and the Defense Department, not producers one would normally put in the same league with hotels, hospitals, and insurance companies for customer satisfaction.

In the middle of the list, above the federal government global score, is a cluster of cabinet departments: Agriculture, State, Commerce, Veterans Affairs, Health and Human Services, and Transportation. Going one step deeper in level of analysis, ACSI calculated scores on individual programs in each of these departments. In Agriculture's Rural Development division, beneficiaries of a community facilities loan-grant program rated it at 77. State's Bureau of Consular Affairs issues over 13 million passports to US citizens every year, and in so doing earned an 83 from

TABLE 2.3	ACSI Scores for Industries and Agencies, 2011
Score	
79	Hospitality and food industry
78	Health care industry
77	Metropolitan solid waste management
76	Finance and insurance industry
76	US Department of Defense
[75.7]	[National Economy as a whole]
75	Retail trade
75	Utilities (not publicly owned)
74	US Department of the Interior
74	US Postal Service
73	Transportation industry
72	Information industry
72	US Department of Agriculture
72	US Department of State
71	US Department of Commerce
70	US Department of Veterans Affairs
69	Social Security Administration
[67.1]	[Local Government as a whole]
67	US Department of Health and Human Services
67	US Department of Transportation
[66.9]	[Federal Government as a whole]
65	Metropolitan police departments
59	US Department of Homeland Security
57	US Department of the Treasury

Source: "ACSI Commentary January 2012," "Citizen Satisfaction by Federal Department," "Public Administration/ Government Sector Scores," and "Scores by Industry," ACSI website. Accessed April 19, 2012.

applicants. Householders rated Commerce's National Weather Service at 84 for its weather forecasts. Users of the VA's Information and Technology office were satisfied at the level of 73 with its skills and responsiveness. The Bureau of Clinician Recruitment and Service in HHS provides medical school scholarships to future doctors who promise to practice in underserved communities, and participants scored the program at 78. Airline managers and heads of aircraft repair centers rated the Federal Aviation Administration's flight safety oversight at 68. Once again, the closer one gets to bureaucratic institutional life, the better it looks.[4]

Local Government Surveys. The nation's municipal and county governments conduct hundreds of their own citizen satisfaction surveys every year. Utilizing a statistical concept known as Percent to Maximum (PTM), Thomas Miller and Michelle Miller have done a meta-analysis of 261 separate municipal surveys administered over ten years that involved 215,000 respondents. Theoretically these represent the opinions of 40 million people living in 40 states. PTM solves the integration problem caused by differing rating scales among these surveys by calculating how far, percentagewise, each act of assessment went in the direction of achieving the highest possible score.

The mean adjusted PTM for all services conducted in all jurisdictions was 67.2. In other words, the "glass" of how Americans feel about their local government services is two-thirds full. The water level for individual services varied from just over half to more than three-fourths. Cultural and arts programs scored 76.7, public safety 75.1, parks and recreation 71.5, public utilities 69.5, administrative support services 67.8, public works and transportation 62.8, health and human services 62.6, and planning and growth management 55.4.[5]

A recent survey by Michael Herian and Alan Tomkins of citizen opinion in Lincoln, Nebraska, penetrates the survey-research imagery of municipal bureaucracy unusually well. Their methodology consisted of both placing random telephone calls and encouraging citizens to participate online. The survey was publicized in advance by the mayor and local newspaper and resulted in 607 telephone and 1,024 online responses. The authors divided their probes into two categories, satisfaction with city services and "derived-importance outcomes." I recategorized them for our purposes by separating the first category into perceptions of (1) city government as a whole and (2) the quality of city services, with their second category then becoming (3) the effects of city services. Although descriptors in their 5-point scale differed, in all instances the two most favorable ratings were reported, as shown in Table 2.4.[6]

TABLE 2.4	Citizen Perceptions Of Government In Lincoln, Nebraska	
City Government as a Whole	**Telephone Responses**	**Online Responses**
I receive good value for my tax dollars	3.16	2.94
I have great confidence in the city government	3.17	2.63
It can usually be trusted to make decisions right for all	3.14	2.66
Its officials treat residents with respect	3.59	3.12
Its officials base decisions on facts, not personal interests	2.92	2.48
All neighborhoods and areas are treated fairly and equally	2.79	2.27
Overall, how would rate its performance?	2.64	2.51
Mean rating	3.06	2.66
Approval of City Services	**Telephone Responses**	**Online Responses**
Building safety permits and inspections	3.42	3.06
Recycling and sustainability efforts	3.72	3.31
Fire and ambulance	4.09	3.81
Health department	3.72	3.39
Management of sewage and storm water	3.87	3.68
Snowplowing of streets	3.42	3.00
Street maintenance	3.17	2.51
Zoning and growth management	3.25	2.76
Mean rating	3.58	3.19
Effects of City Services	**Telephone Responses**	**Online Responses**
Availability of affordable quality housing	3.68	3.37
Ease of bicycle travel	3.95	3.53
Ease of bus travel	3.18	2.72

Effects of City Services	Telephone Responses	Online Responses
Ease of car travel	3.49	2.94
Employment opportunities	3.25	2.81
Job creation and economic development	3.02	2.68
Overall quality of libraries	4.35	4.09
Overall quality of life	4.25	3.81
Overall quality of parks	4.10	3.72
Recreational opportunities	3.89	3.52
Cleanliness of city	4.15	3.69
Number of unsightly or blighted properties	3.15	2.72
Overall appearance of city	4.10	3.57
Safety and security of city	4.07	3.82
Mean rating	3.76	3.36

Source: Michael N. Herian and Alan J. Tomkins, "Citizen Satisfaction Survey Data: A Mode Comparison of the Derived Importance-Performance Approach, *American Review of Public Administration* 42, no. 1 (January 2012): 67–86, 74–75.

Note: Specific performance aspects are rated on a 1–5 scale of Strongly Disagree, Disagree, Neutral, Agree, and Strongly Agree. Overall performance is rated on a 1–5 scale of Poor, Fair, Neutral, Good, and Excellent. Services and results are rated on a 1–5 scale of Very Dissatisfied, Dissatisfied, Neutral, Satisfied, and Very Satisfied. Omitted items are Community spirit of citizens, Overall natural environment, and a general Trust and confidence scale.

In examining the table, one notes that these three ways of looking at municipal government in Lincoln yield quite different degrees of perceived quality. Whereas none of the scores for city government as a whole are above 3.66 (the level at which two-thirds approval is registered), four items on city services surpass that standard in phone responses and two in online responses. As to the *effects* of these services, nine surpass 3.66 in phone interviews and five in online entries. As can be seen, the mean ratings for the three perspectives are 3.06, 3.58, and 3.76 for phone respondents and 2.66, 3.19, and 3.36 for online contacts.

This three-step depth in citizen evaluation of Lincoln's government is not unlike what we saw in the ACSI data. There, perceptions of governmental level, individual agencies, and selected programs exhibited progressively more favorable impressions as one got closer to actual operations. In the Lincoln study, this ascendancy covers (1) global assessments of city government as a whole, such as what is going on inside city hall; (2) chance evaluation of specific city services based on observations of their being carried out; and (3) direct personal appraisal of extant living conditions, the deepest connection to citizen experience of all.

The difference between telephone and online ratings, I speculate, is probably due to the nature of the sampling process coupled with the social situation involved. In phone interviews, a random sample of respondents is participating in a survey that has been implicitly endorsed by the mayor and the media as legitimate and authoritative. This method provides a more accurate cross-section of opinion but creates social pressure to offer reasoned replies that will be seen as those of responsible citizens. Online participation, by contrast, is self-initiated and involves respondents who are either eager to volunteer positive feelings or desirous of telling about unpleasant experiences in the safe environment of anonymity. It would appear that the enthusiasists are outnumbered by the complainers.

Drawing together common strands in these client impressions, we repeatedly encountered a phenomenon whereby bureaucracy looks better the more intimately it is encountered. In my parking lot interviews, I was talking to men and women who had just had their personal lives affected by the actions of bureaucrats—and the responses were surprisingly positive. In the ACSI satisfaction scores, the polling organization itself found it worth commenting that respondents look more favorably on federal departments than the federal government as a whole—and furthermore this tendency extends to some evaluated individual programs. Then, in the municipal PTM scores, citizens evaluated more highly some individual city programs than they did the city administration itself. In the Lincoln study it was found that questions on the city services were higher than those for city government as a whole, with impressions of the actual consequences of programs drawing an even higher level of appreciation.

OUTPUT AND OUTCOME DATA

Evaluating bureaucracy by means of the opinions of clients is valuable, but we need also to assess its outputs directly. Whenever this is possible on a quantitative basis all the better, even though that requirement leaves out much of what government can accomplish.

The Federal Productivity Index. From 1967 to 1994, the US Bureau of Labor Statistics (BLS) compiled what was known as the Federal Productivity Index. This was undertaken in response to a request from Congress to see if government's labor productivity is anything like that of the private economy. The BLS already tracked the productivity of the private economy and was assigned the task. For technical reasons the agency determined that outputs should be measured on a gross rather than net basis. Beginning with a base number of 100, the index was continued for 27 years until 1994, the year when Republicans seized control of the House for the first time in thirty years. Over time, the index incorporated more and more program outputs until it covered 60 agencies, 225 organizations, and the work of two-thirds of the civilian executive branch workforce.[7] (See Figure 2.1.)

The overall upward thrust of the graph indicates that yes, it is possible for the productivity of the federal government to grow, and over time substantially. By 1994 the index reached 134.3. The average rate of growth over the twenty-seven-year period is 1.1 percent; between 1967 and 1982 it was 1.5—approximating a typical private economy rate—but fell to .6 in 1982–1994. Reasons ascribed to the improvement are the introduction of computers, increased automation, better facilities, and added efficiencies in management and operating systems. Handling above-normal workloads imposed by wars, recessions, emergencies, bad weather, and natural disasters is another factor. It is unfortunate that the index is not still being calculated so we could assess the efficiencies being produced by present-day technologies.

Social Security Productivity. We have already encountered the Social Security Administration (SSA) in my parking lot interviews and the ACSI satisfaction ratings. One of the most famous bureaucracies in America, SSA is headquartered in Woodlawn, Maryland, near Baltimore. By means of its 1,300 field offices and 70,000 employees located around the country, it administers two prime programs. The oldest is Old-Age, Survivors, and Disability Insurance (OASDI), which provides pensions and disability assistance earned by a lifetime of payroll deductions by working Americans. The second major program is Supplemental Security Income (SSI), created in 1974. It is a means-tested welfare program

FIGURE 2.1   Federal Productivity Index, 1967–1994

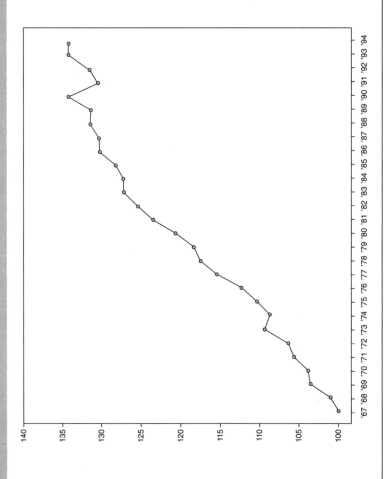

Source: Donald Fisk and Darlene Forte, "The Federal Productivity Measurement Program: Final Results," *Monthly Labor Review* 120, no. 5 (Spring 1997): 22.

that provides survival income for over five million elderly, children, and the blind and disabled, financed from general revenues.

Performance outputs and outcomes available for our consideration include the productivity and timeliness of Social Security hearings, of which more than a half-million are conducted each year. These relate mainly to settling disputed claims of OASDI eligibility, of which three-quarters have to do with disability payments. The mammoth litigation task this amounts to is undertaken by one of the largest administrative law systems in the world, a unit within the agency known as the Office of Disability Adjudication and Review (ODAR). It has 169 local offices around the country, operates by its own code of procedure, and employs some 1,300 administrative law judges. These civil servants function in a manner comparable to a criminal or civil judge although with somewhat less formality. Supported by a staff of 7,000, the judges receive hearing requests, study and hear evidence, and conduct recorded sessions in hearing rooms before claimants and their representatives. Decisions are handed down in writing and have the force of law. If the claimant wishes to appeal, an SSA Appeals Council is the first court and the closest US District Court the second.[8]

Figure 2.2 contains three bar graphs that pertain to these hearings, taken from the 2011 Performance and Accountability Report issued by SSA.[9] Each of the graphs presents actual performance data along with targeted performance figures over a period of six fiscal years. The figure's upper graph shows the number of hearings completed per employee work year. That number has risen each year, with the exception of 2010 when it remained steady at 105. Targets were not reached in four of these years, although in 2008 and 2011 they were exceeded. The high of 109 in 2011 is in part the consequence of improvements made in what is called FIT, or Findings Integrated Templates. FIT is Microsoft Word software that allows claimants or their representatives to prepare disability requests in exactly the same format that ODAR staff processes them. This way, the submitted document may become the draft of a potentially favorable decision, saving much time for everyone.

The middle graph in Figure 2.2 indicates the average processing time between receipt of the hearing request by ODAR and its final disposition. The fact that this period exceeded 365 days for many years caused SSA administrators much concern. A couple of steps were taken to address the problem. A predictive model was perfected that assesses what factors indicate a positive eligibility decision is likely, allowing many cases to be

FIGURE 2.2	SSA Hearing Productivity, Processing Time, and Backlog, 2006–2011

SSA hearings case production per workyear

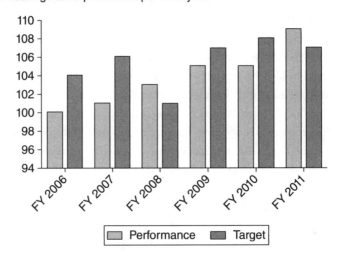

Average processing time for hearing requests (in days)

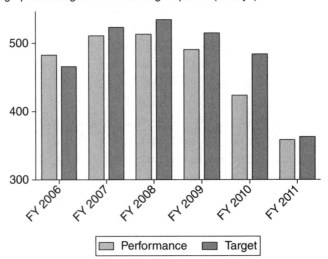

Number of hearing requests pending

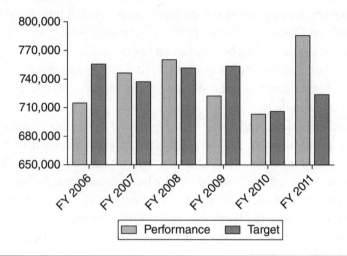

Source: Social Security Administration, "FY 2011 Performance and Accountability Report," pp. 51–56, SSA website. Accessed on May 28, 2012.

fast-tracked. Along with this, a compassionate allowance list of medical conditions that would almost certainly trigger that eligibility was lengthened from 88 to 100. As a result, mean processing time dropped from an average of 514 days in 2008 to 360 in 2011, an improvement of 30 percent.

The number of hearing requests pending at the end of the fiscal year is shown in the bottom graph of Table 2.2. Despite the overall productivity growth shown in the top graph and gains in processing time shown in the middle one, by 2011 the backlog had spiked to 787,190, or 8 percent above target. The principal reason was that for three years in a row, the number of incoming new requests had reached record levels. Additionally, greater attrition than normal was being experienced in the number of administrative law judges. In light of the situation, every effort was made to eliminate at least the oldest cases, defined as 775 days and above. By the end of 2011, only 103 were left—.09 percent of the 111,792 then pending. Eventually efforts to reduce the backlog apparently worked, for by 2013 Republican Darrell Issa, chair of the House Committee on Oversight and Reform, was complaining that administrative law judges were being too lax in their decisions and driving up program costs.[10]

Another performance area of concern is payment accuracy rates in the SSI program. Income payments are based on the client's individual funding needs and thus are affected by the discretionary judgment of social workers. Many facts must be checked and periodically rechecked, such as level of income, amount of assets, and marital status. As a result, SSI error rates are higher and more variable that those for OASDI, which are calculated by formula.

Added SSA data are provided in Figure 2.3. The upper two graphs indicate percentages of SSI payments free of error for each year. Two kinds of payment error occur. One is overpayment: that is, providing an amount in excess of that justified. As the top graph shows, the percentage of payment free of such overage ranged between the high 80s and low 90s, well below targeted levels except for 2010. The second kind of error is underpayment: that is, instances when a transfer is insufficient. Information on this is given in the middle graph, where we see a comparatively high and steady error-free percentage, around 98.

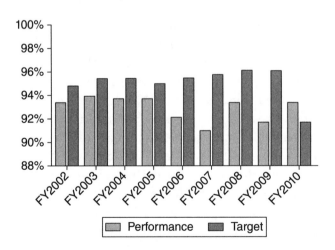

FIGURE 2.3   **SSI Payment Accuracy Rates and Access to SSA 800 Number, 2002–2011**

Percent of Supplemental Security Income payments free of overpayment error

Percent of Supplemental Security Income payments free of underpayment error

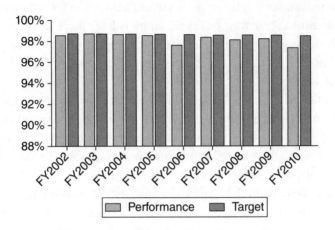

Speed in answering National 800 Number calls (in seconds)

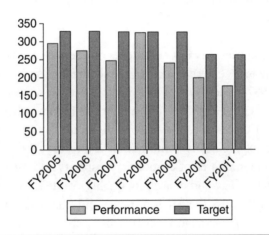

Source: Social Security Administration, "FY 2011 Performance and Accountability Report," pp. 68, 75–77, SSA website. Accessed May 28, 2012.

Two features of these data are striking. One is that all but one of the average annual error-free calculations in the two graphs are above 90 percent. This overall finding seems remarkable in light of the SSI's complex, individualized, decentralized, and vast programs. The second notable point is the sizable difference between overpayment accuracy and underpayment accuracy. This phenomenon appears not just in Social Security but in food stamps and unemployment benefits as well. A main reason for it is that clients are not anxious to report new income when it comes their way, but the change is later discovered from bank records or wage inquiries. Despite the complex and time-consuming nature of this process, the percentage of payments free of overage increased from 89.7 in 2008 to 93.3 in 2010.

The third performance dimension for which we have SSA data is how long incoming callers to SSA must wait for an operator to answer. The agency takes pride in keeping this wait time short; in 1995 Dalbar, a Boston financial services company, reported that SSA's telephone performance was superior to that of Southwest Airlines, Nordstrom, L.L. Bean, Xerox, and the Disney Companies.[11] According to the bottom graph in Table 2.3, the time a caller waits in a queue before making voice contact shrank from 296 seconds in 2005 to 250 in 2007, then spiked to 325 seconds in 2008; but by 2011, it had dropped to 180 seconds, that is, three minutes.

Societal Outcomes. My last comments on measured government performance relate to its external societal consequences. As part of a book published in 1997 titled *Why People Don't Trust Government*, Derek Bok, former president of Harvard, took an unusually comprehensive look at US government outcomes as they affect the entire country. He developed a list of over sixty objectives the nation is presumably seeking to attain. These include measures of economic prosperity and income; the state of research, technology and education; quality-of-life issues regarding housing, neighborhoods, the environment, and the arts; matters of equal opportunity, health care, job security, and public safety; and lastly, values of personal freedom, personal responsibility, and minimizing poverty.

Bok then set about evaluating where the country is and where it is going on these dimensions. He first compared conditions in the 1990s with those in the early 1960s. His conclusion is that "the United States has made definite progress over the past few decades in the vast majority of cases." Second, in an attempt to evaluate the rate of progress, he contrasted the amount made in 1960–1975 versus 1975–1990. Here the record is mixed, he says; on one hand, the pace had slowed for economic growth, improvement in racial integration, and access to health care; but on the other hand, it had quickened for environmental protection, crime fighting, and student test scores. On balance, he concludes, the positives outweigh the negatives.

Yet in a third way of assessing the government's outcomes, Bok's rosy appraisal darkens. He contends that in all too many areas, the United States lags behind the attainments of other industrialized democracies, particularly Britain, France, Germany, Japan, and Sweden. In roughly two-thirds of the sixty measures we are falling behind them, he says. He gives America a "below average" grade in 11 measures and "at or near the bottom" in 34. Especially troublesome are per capital growth, the rate of capital investment, student achievement, workforce training, job safety, preschool education, racial segregation, fear of crime, air pollution, recycling of waste, teen pregnancy, infant mortality, child vaccination, life expectancy, trade union influence, violent crime, teenage pregnancy, and severity of poverty.

In light of the themes of this book, it is particularly interesting that although Bok's work is published in a volume on why people don't trust government, he is himself circumspect in attacking it. In many areas of decline, he concludes, the ability of the government to affect the situation is limited since progress depends on citizens taking responsibility. Moreover there is little evidence the barrier is government inefficiency; that which exists is mostly not because of inept administration, he says, but poorly designed programs. While efforts to improve bureaucratic efficiency are certainly worth making, "if one is after truly major savings, the place to begin is almost certainly Congress much more than the executive branch."[12]

Personally I agree with this aspect of Bok's conclusions. However I would like to make one added observation. After reading his analysis about the "below average" and "at or close to the bottom" measures of comparative achievement, I was moved to look in my statistical abstract for time-series data on those indicators. After eliminating statistics that had little or nothing to do with the programmatic outputs of concrete government agencies, I was left with the eleven measures contained in Table 2.5. Notice as you go through them that all save one show improvement over time, albeit at different rates. This suggests that the steady

TABLE 2.5	Statistics Related to Bureaucracy's Impact on Society, 1980–2009				
	1980	1990	2000	2008	2009
Life expectancy (years)	73.8	75.4	76.8	78.0	78.3[1]
Infant mortality rate (per 1,000 births)	12.2	8.95	6.97	6.64[2]	n/a
Incidence of tetanus (in thousands)	95	64	35	19	18
Nursery school enrollment (in millions)[3]	0.06	1.2	2.2	2.6	2.7
Percent of births to teenage mothers	n/a	12.8	11.8	10.4	n/a
Number of criminal offenses (in millions)	13.4	14.5	11.6	11.2	10.6
Worker deaths (per 1,000 employees)[4]	8	5	3	2	2
CO_2 emissions (in millions of tons)	185.4	154.2	114.5	77.7	n/a
Percent municipal solid waste recycled	9.6	16.2	29.7	33.4	33.8
Education and training payments ($ billions)[5]	4.1	12.3	21.9	45.6	56.7
Percent persons below poverty level	13.0	13.5	11.3	13.2	14.3

Source: Statistical Abstract of the United States for 2012 unless other year is indicated. Life expectancy, p. 77. Infant mortality, 2002, p. 78; 2012, p. 85. Tetanus incidence, p. 125. Nursery enrollment, p. 149. Teenage births, p. 69. Criminal offenses, p. 196. Worker deaths, p. 426. CO_2 emissions, p. 229. Waste recycled, p. 231. Education payments, 2002, p. 340; 2012, p. 351. Below poverty level, p. 464.

Notes: 1. Projection for 2010. 2. Figure for 2005. 3. Public only. 4. Manufacturing only. 5. Federal only.

work of bureaucracy, operating day by day for the most part out of the headlines, is quietly helping our nation move ahead. The one exception is poverty, a pernicious problem that we simply cannot seem to lick.

BUREAUCRACY COMPARED TO BUSINESS

We continue our microscopic look at bureaucracy by examining data that shed light on the contention that business is inevitably more efficient than government, a position that Ludwig Von Mises would surely have endorsed.

Is Business More Efficient? "The 'Government Should Be Run Like a Business' Mantra" is the title of an article by Julia Beckett. In a resentful tone she points out that the assumption that government is plagued with bad features while business is filled with good ones can be traced back to the beginning of the field, when municipal research bureaus were created to depoliticize City Hall and install Main Street efficiencies. This thinking has silently underlain many of the field's reform movements, from Reinventing Government to the New Public Management and now the New Governance. Without distinguishing mom-and-pop stores from giant corporations, Beckett says, the proposition that business is inherently superior is based not on evidence but on a mythology rooted in capitalism.[13]

One place to look for actual evidence on the question is the literature on privatization. Graeme Hodge has done the field a service by conducting a detailed worldwide study of the literature's verdict on the performance outcome of privatization, in particular with respect to the contracting out of services. In a survey of 38 scholarly studies on the subject that analyzed the consequences of contracting out by over 6,000 organizational units, he comes to this conclusion: "There is little doubt the weight of evidence appears to support the notion that on average the unit costs of services are reduced through competitive tendering of public services." Although some contrary evidence is available, Hodge finds on a net basis mean savings of around 6 to 12 percent, assuming a few percent to pay the cost of the contracting process.[14]

Nonetheless Hodge encountered wide divergences within the contracting out record. The amount of savings depends heavily on what is outsourced. In cleaning services, building maintenance, and refuse collection, governments save money but not in more complex areas like engineering services and the training of personnel. The where, when, how, and who of the empirical studies of the subject seem to affect results. United States comparisons show less monetary gain than those carried out in Britain and Australia. Work done on the subject before the year 1990 is more glowing in its findings than that done in later years.

Studies that utilize sophisticated statistical methods yield lower savings than those that do not. Even the discipline of the researcher makes a difference: investigators from finance, accounting, and business report more positive effects than those from economics, politics, and law.

Hodge examined also the noneconomic consequences of service outsourcing. He found no tendency for the quality of the outsourced activities to be either better or worse than that provided in-house. Although management accountability can be improved via contracting, external transparency is not. An adverse social consequence he noticed is that when in-house employees are displaced, it is disproportionately female part-timers and members of minorities that lose out. As to political impacts, one phenomenon he noticed was that when government contracts out, it exposes itself to added risks with respect to undesirable political influence and the occurrence of corruption.[15]

Another student of the subject, Barbara Stevens, compared the productive efficiency of contractual versus internal provision of local government services in the Los Angeles area. Eight services were examined: street sweeping, refuse collection, janitorial cleaning, traffic light maintenance, asphalt street resurfacing, tree care along streets, grass mowing, and payroll preparation. For each comparison, at least ten cities using each mode of operation were included in the study.

Using direct observation, ratings by professionals, and documentary evidence, Stevens found that the overall quality of the work done was found to be essentially at the same level. Also no meaningful differences were uncovered with respect to numbers of assigned crews, means of communication, or the kind of equipment used. Although wage and benefit levels were a few dollars higher for contract personnel, the difference was not statistically significant even though pay was incentive-based.

With respect to overall costs, for nearly all of the eight services studied by Stevens, in-house provision was more expensive than contracted work. The single exception was payroll preparation, where only personnel inside the organization knew enough to do the job well. Private sector savings occurred in both funded monetary costs and number of work hours expended. Percentagewise, total average cost differentials were 37 for tree maintenance, 40 for grass mowing, 42 for refuse collection, 43 for street sweeping, 56 for traffic light maintenance, 73 for janitorial work, and 96 for asphalt laying. Thus, from a purely economics stand-point, privatization in these areas was the smart move.

Yet Stevens goes on to point out that dollar savings from contracting out can incur nonfinancial costs. Contract workers tend to be part-time, a few years younger, and more short-term with respect to tenure. They are hired to perform one task alone and possess few additional skills and almost no experience that make them of value to the city beyond this narrow capability. In addition, socially they are outsiders; contract personnel do not attend staff meetings, are left out of agency social events, and generally do not know "what was going on" in the organization. In short, these people are of city hall but not in it.

In contrast, city employees occupy a bigger work world. They are routinely trained not only to operate the equipment they use but to maintain it as well. As long-term staff they are expected, over time, to rotate among several tasks conducted by the department and grow in their responsibilities. Unlike contract workers, their first-line supervisor alone does not have the authority to hire, discipline, or even fire them. Instead, personnel matters are handled by established and documented processes of due process and fair play. Hence workers are not mercenaries hired to do one thing on the cheap, but members of a social institution in which bonded relationships and mutual obligations develop.[16]

The Case of Public Transit. Insights into differences between public and private provision can also be gained from comparing areas of business enterprise that employ both. Urban mass transit is a case in point, where five kinds of organizational arrangement exist in the United States: (1) private, for-profit ownership and management; (2) public ownership and operation by cities or counties; (3) ownership by such governments but operational management contracted out to a private company; (4) ownership and operation in the hands of a special-purpose, public transit authority; and (5) ownership by such an authority but management and operations outsourced. Substantial empirical study has been conducted over the years in this field, especially for bus transportation. Examining this research allows us to reflect more deeply on our subject.

The work of James Perry is central in this area. In 1984 he prepared a report for the Urban Mass Transportation Administration (UTMA; now

Federal Transit Administration) that summarized the results of twenty studies on the comparative efficiency of private and public transit systems. Of these, seven concluded that privately owned systems are more efficient, six found in favor of public ownership, and seven came up with mixed results or a finding of no significant difference.[17]

In 1986 Perry and Timlynn Babitsky published the results of a study they had personally conducted, drawing from quantitative data that had been submitted by common carrier bus companies to UMTA for the years 1980–1981. They report that factor analysis of 25 variables related to the operation of nearly 250 transit systems identifies eight performance indicators by which to compare in detail the various organizational arrangements. Their most important finding is that transit systems that are private in both ownership and management are positively and significantly related to the output per dollar indicator and hence superior in productive efficiency. An expectation that systems owned and operated by municipal governments would be more efficient than those run by transit authorities was not supported.[18]

This research was replicated in 2009 by Susanne Leland and Olga Smirnova, using comparable data from 2004–2005. During the intervening twenty-plus years, a shift had occurred in the industry from private to public ownership. Many for-profit providers had gone bankrupt, and government bodies were taking them over and operating them on a subsidized basis to preserve a continuity of service. More often than not, they did not run the systems but contracted out their management. In this changed environment, the authors conclude, privately owned and managed transit systems are no longer first with respect to efficiency and effectiveness. In a society where private automobiles almost totally dominate the transportation picture and monopolistic bus systems do not face competition, the vaunted superiority of private enterprise had evaporated. Now, Leland and Smirnova conclude, the data tell us that municipal and county governments operate more efficient systems than transit authorities. The reason is that public administrators are more capable than business managers in dealing with conflicting pressures from multiple stakeholders such as riders, bond holders, unions, and suburban interests.[19]

Hence, in assessing the competence of public bureaucracy vis-à-vis private business, we need to go beyond easy slogans. Contracting out certain kinds of government functions to the private sector frequently saves money but can have unexpected consequences, such as less quality, reduced transparency, attachment of "stranger" mercenaries to the agency culture, and handing a politically charged governmental function over to apolitical private sector managers.

THE MAGNITUDE OF BUREAUCRACY

We turn next to claims that government, even in a society innately suspicious of it, has an innate tendency to grow in size, which by definition means that the numbers of bureaucrats must increase. This assumption is implicitly or explicitly advanced by economists who suspect administrative leaders of building empires for self-advancement, by political scientists who expect bureaucracies to mobilize power in order to enlarge turf, and by antigovernment ideologues who are convinced that bureaucracy is no more than a tool of the political left to subvert the free market and undermine personal liberty.

Is Growth Inevitable? Do these theories of self-promotion, manipulation, and conspiracy mean bureaucratic growth is inevitable? Let us see. If we look at changes in the overall size of the federal civilian workforce year by year over a period of time, we encounter not just steady expansion but other movement as well. When I examined yearly annual changes in the total federal workforce size during the forty years between 1970 and 2010, increases in government employment occurred in twenty instances and declines took place in twenty. During the first twenty years of this forty-year period, upward change occurred thirteen times and downward seven. Strangely enough, during the second twenty years, the reverse occurred, down seven and up thirteen.[20]

At the individual organizational level, the same kind of mixed pattern also obtained. When employment size is examined in the civilian federal cabinet departments for the five decades between 1960 and 2010, none consistently showed a net gain at the conclusion of each decade. State and Commerce experienced growth in four decades and decline in one; Treasury, Defense, Interior, Labor, and Veterans Affairs saw expansion in three decades and loss in two; Agriculture, Health and Human Services and Housing and Urban Development show increases in two decades but decreases in three. In a replicating analysis of independent agencies, NASA, the Small Business Administration, and the Tennessee Valley Authority experienced growth in two of the five ten-year intervals while the General Services Administration gained more employees in only one. Calculating an overall score for the joint record of all fourteen organizations, net decade expansion occurred in thirty instances and contraction in forty. In short, "inevitable" growth occurred only 43 percent of the time.[21]

The picture is quite different in state and local government, however. The history here is less mixed and more stable. Statistically we would expect this, for the categories are aggregated data, meaning individual variances are swallowed up in a single measure. Nevertheless, long-term trends can be detected. In fact, for both levels of government the summed number of employees in place over six mostly five-year intervals in 1982–2009 showed increases at the end of every interval. Over the twenty-seven years as a whole, the state figure increased by 40 percent and the local number by 57.[22]

As for differences among states, during the single interval of 2000–2009, public workforces grew in size in forty-two states, decreased in four (Louisiana, Maryland, Missouri, and South Carolina) and showed no significant change in four others (Connecticut, Idaho, Maine, and Rhode Island). With respect to cities, of the ten largest metro areas in terms of population, employment size enlarged between 2000 and 2009 in seven (New York, Los Angeles, Houston, Phoenix, Philadelphia, Dallas, and San Jose) and declined in three (Chicago, San Antonio, and San Diego).[23]

The Employment-Population Ratio. If the task of public servants is to serve the public, as the "public" grows one would think the bureaucracy in employment terms should grow too, discounting for any productivity gains as noted earlier in this chapter. Otherwise the capacity to attend to the needs of each citizen declines. To pursue this matter I worked out the ratio of numbers of government employees per 1,000 population over time. Table 2.6 displays the outcome over a seventy-year period spaced by intervals of five years. I was quite surprised with what emerged.

TABLE 2.6	Number of Government Employees Per 1,000 Population				
	Federal Executive Civilian Employees		State and Local Employees		All Employees
Year	Number	% of All	Number	% of All	Number
1940	8	24	25	76	33
1945	25	52	23	48	48
1950	14	33	28	67	42
1955	14	31	31	69	45
1960	13	27	35	73	48
1965	13	24	41	76	54
1970	14	22	50	78	64
1975	13	19	56	81	69
1980	13	18	58	82	71
1985	13	19	57	81	70
1990	13	18	61	82	74
1995	11	15	63	85	74
2000	9	12	64	88	73
2005	9	12	64	88	73
2010	9	12	64	87	73

Sources: Federal data: For 1940–1965, "Civilian Employment by Federal Government" table in *Statistical Abstracts of the United States* for 1970 and 1975; and thereafter in "Federal Civilian Employment and Annual Payroll by Branch," *Statistical Abstracts* for 2001 and 2012. State, Local, and All Governments data: For 1940–1945, "Public Employment by Type of Government" table in *Historical Statistics of the United States, Colonial Times to 1957*; thereafter from the "Government Employment and Payrolls" table in *Statistical Abstracts* for 1970, 1980, 2002, and 2012. Population data: "Population and Area," "Population," and "Resident Population Projections" tables, *Statistical Abstract* for 2012.

Note: Legislative and judicial branch employees of the federal government not included. The final state and local figure is for 2009.

The "all employees" column gives the results for total civilian public employment over these seventy years. The ratio doubled from 33 to 69 between 1940 and 1975 and then leveled off to a relatively stable plateau in the low 70s. While one is tempted to say the period of expansion was set off by the New Deal of Roosevelt and continued by the Fair Deal of Johnson, it also included the presidencies of Eisenhower, Nixon, and Ford. Hence ideology seems not to be a factor in proportionate government hiring, probably because the ratio is rarely calculated and hence ignored.

Comparing ratios between the federal sector with state and local government yields provocative results. After the war year of 1945, the federal number has gone into slow decline, dropping to the teens and then sliding to the single-digit realm of 9, at nearly the 1940 level. Probably the main factor here is an explosion of private outsourcing plus devolution of programs elsewhere within the federal system. For its part, the state-local column registers a substantial and steady expansion of bureaucratic adequacy, hinted at by the steady rise of employment numbers in that sector described above. It, too, is currently stuck at one data point, 64. Remarkably, this is seven times the federal ratio.

This massive shift of in-house human resources from the national level to the subnational level is the most startling conclusion to be drawn from employment-population ratio analysis. While the feds collect the most taxes, wield the most power and receive the most antigovernment attack, they are a relatively small crowd compared to their less de-bureaucratized state and local brethren.

At what kind of level *should* an employment-population ratio be to provide adequate governing? At the program level, it depends on how labor intensive it is. Sending welfare checks requires fewer bureaucrats per capita than responding to family violence. In thinking about this question more broadly, about all we can do is note how our country compares to others. Insight on this score is offered in Table 2.7, which presents 2006–2008 ratio figures for thirty selected countries plus the United States.

America's ratio of 21.8 does not jibe with what was shown in Table 2.6, which can be explained by the likelihood that those who reported our figures to the International Labour Office included uniformed personnel and perhaps workforce elements across the federal system. Assuming all countries reported similarly (which could easily not be the case), the United States is definitely on the low side. Most industrialized democracies are substantially higher, including all English-speaking countries and most European nations. Does this mean American bureaucracy is really a quite slender creature and not bloated at all?

CHANGE IN BUREAUCRACY

I conclude this chapter with some discussion of change in bureaucracy, a subject that draws our attention if for no other reason than several writers assume it to be static and conservative.

TABLE 2.7	Number of "Public Administration, Defence and Compulsory Social Security" Employees Per 1,000 Population in Selected Nations of the World, 2006–2008		
Country	Number of Employees	Country	Number of Employees
Peru	5.6	Canada	27.4
China	9.7	Spain	27.5
Philippines	10.7	Sweden	28.8
Turkey	16.3	Australia	30.0
South Korea	16.4	New Zealand	31.2
Japan	17.6	Netherlands	31.5
Israel	17.7	Portugal	31.8
Mexico	18.1	Denmark	32.2
Argentina	18.6	United Kingdom	33.6
United States	**21.8**	Germany	34.5
Brazil	22.3	Norway	34.6
Poland	24.4	Greece	35.5
Egypt	24.5	Russia	38.8
Italy	24.7	France	40.4
Finland	26.5	Belgium	41.9
		Saudi Arabia	58.4

Source: *Yearbook of Labour Statistics: Country Profiles* (Geneva: International Labour Office, 2009). Calculated from "total employment" figures given under tabulation category L, "Public Administration and Defence: Compulsory Social Security."

Do Agencies Age? The answer to this question is yes, according to two classic life cycle theories spelled out in the literature. The earlier one, published in 1955, originated with Marver Bernstein, an authority on independent regulatory commissions. Bernstein's cycle consists of four periods. The first is *Gestation*, at which time sentiment emerges that a public problem exists and requires regulatory intervention. A political battle ensues in which reformers demand that a statute be passed in order to create an agency with strong powers to act. Meanwhile established interests favoring the status quo engage them in strenuous political struggle. If a compromise is reached, a "treaty" is negotiated on appropriate statutory language, whose mandate is often left vague for political reasons.

The second period is *Youth*. Following enactment of an organic statute, the organization is filled with a sense of optimism and crusading spirit. Commissioners and staff take a broad view of their powers and envision an expansive role in the regulated domain. Soon, however, public and media interest begins to fade as supporters assume the problem is now solved. Meanwhile antagonistic special interests—usually associated with the regulated industry—mobilize to fight the agency on all vulnerable fronts and restrict its powers.

Maturity comes next. The agency becomes adjusted to an environment in which accommodation to the regulated industry is reached. Attention is turned from achieving change to preserving established precedents and policies. Vitality is lost while complacency and lethargy set in. Leaders and staff grow older and consider the possibility of retiring to a job in the affected industry, and replacements often come from that source. The agency's work becomes essentially judicial in nature and lawyers dominate policy discussions.

The fourth and final period is *Old Age*. Established procedures become set in stone, and traditional thinking guides the commission in all respects. Funding is curtailed as legislative subcommittees sense what is happening, resulting in the accumulation of case backlogs. Apathy, poor management, and doubt over true objectives grow. The agency lives on indefinitely in quiescent stasis, unless a scandal or calamity breaks out, which is when an investigation is launched. This may lead to the organization's termination, but that is not likely.[24]

In 1978 Kenneth Meier and John Plumlee tested Bernstein's model empirically. They measured quantitatively external support of agencies, cross-recruitment of personnel between the regulators and regulated, and manifestations of organizational rigidity. Time-series data on these variables were gathered from the year of origin for eight federal regulatory agencies. On political support, the authors found that appropriations, personnel, and budget growth tended to be high early in the history of the agencies, but primarily because they were starting from scratch. Later, the rates did not consistently decline, but instead fluctuated. On cross-recruitment, appointments from industry usually decreased over time rather than increased. In like manner, movement by agency people to the regulated industry became less frequent. "None of the data unambiguously support the contention that regulators and the industry form a more symbiotic relationship as time passes," Meier and Plumlee conclude. "In most cases the data directly refute the hypothesis."

As for the contention that aging produces an emphasis on procedures and rigidity, the researchers did find that the proportion of agency leaders with legal training tended to increase with time. The median age of top executives rose, but slowly. No important correlations were discovered between organizational age and leader turnover, percentage of top appointees without prior substantive expertise, end-of-year case backlogs, or number of cases handled per employee. The authors conclude, "the future does not look right for an aging theory of regulatory agency decay."[25]

Another well-known theory of bureaucratic decline is that of Anthony Downs. He addresses the topic more broadly and theorizes about government bureaus in general rather than regulatory commissions. The model is organized not by stages but tendencies; yet, like Bernstein, he paints an overall picture of evolution from vital organizational interest in policy change to a conservative, proestablishment stance.

The bureau is initially led by advocates and zealots, but eventually they are replaced by (or converted into) climbers and conservators. Over time personnel get older, the rate of turnover lessens, and promotion opportunities dry up. The proportion of administrators confined to offices increases and the presence of hands-on expertise declines. Formal rules become more elaborate, adherence to procedures becomes more important than program achievement, and paperwork generated by internal controls expands. The rapid path of growth experienced at the beginning of the bureau's life eventually decelerates and attention is increasingly shifted from institutional success to institutional survival.

At the same time, however, Downs concedes that major changes during the life of the bureau can occur. Innovations are more likely to stem from external opportunities that come along rather than deliberate, preplanned renewal efforts. The likelihood of this happening depends on the degree of diversity that exists among program activities and between points of view within the organization. Also important are the extent to which vacancies are filled by outsiders rather than insiders and the degree to which the bureau engages in interaction with other organizations in its daily work.[26]

Howard McCurdy has reflected on the extent to which the life history of the National Aeronautic and Space Administration matches Downs' predictions. In an article published in 1991, he examined what happened to NASA from the time it was founded in 1958 up through the Apollo moon landing in 1969. This was followed by a troublesome twenty-year period in which the Challenger exploded, the Hubble Space Telescope malfunctioned, construction of the space station faltered, and appropriations to NASA lessened.

McCurdy's conclusion is that in the post-Apollo period, the Downs model was on target with respect to workforce aging, declining promotion opportunities, and an increase in paperwork and procedures. Also the proportion of Washington-based versus operating center employees grew, as did the ratio of desk-bound support personnel to scientists, engineers, and technicians. Yet not all of this change was due to internal bureaucratic deterioration. The space program was maturing from a small set of research laboratories to a large, multifaceted program that had to be managed. Congressional oversight increased after three astronauts were killed in a test capsule in 1967. White House policy review became more intense, and political leaders were insisting on more and more contracting out. Yet from a survey of NASA personnel, McCurdy found that faith in the underlying cultural norms of test and exploration remained alive and well; determination persisted to develop new technologies, push new programs, and accept the inevitable risks of failure.[27]

In a follow-up book in 2001, McCurdy confirmed Downs' observation that even an elderly agency can, with a prod from circumstances, renew itself. Beginning in 1992, NASA embarked on a spurt of small-size, technically advanced projects that opened a new chapter in the agency's life. Instead of mounting massive programs that took years to develop, a number of unmanned spacecraft with specified missions were quite quickly conceived, developed, and launched. Mostly but not always succeeding, they included fly-bys and landings on Mars and asteroids, a search for water on the moon, the collection of comet material, and study of interstellar clouds. The vehicles used were equipped with less elaborate instrumentation, designed with minimal redundancy, and kept light by microtechnology control systems. McCurdy likens this burst of innovation by a fifty-year-old government bureau to the revolution against traditional Himalayan mountain climbing that occurred in 1975. The 26,470-foot Gasherbrum I was quickly ascended, not by using armies of porters and numerous base camps and supply caches, but by individual climbers carrying their own light-weight, high-tech equipment and ascending alone from a minimal camp below and a single supply depot on the way up.[28]

Innovation and Renewal. Is such innovation and renewal rare or more common? There is no shortage of conflicting literature on this point. Gerald Caiden joins Guy Benveniste in saying that dedication to the status quo, fear of change, inability to learn, and a lack of imagination (among other traits) mean bureaucracy invariably preserves routines, perpetuates shortcomings, and repeats mistakes.[29] On the other side of the argument, Louis Bragaw, in a book on the US Coast Guard, says that the history of this agency reveals that a "hidden stimulus" for innovation exists in bureaucracy, comparable to the competitive market for businesses. This is the need of the organization to combat threats that arise from time to time; for the Coast Guard they were absorption attempts by the Navy, fiscal starvation following wars, and moves to liquidate their programs.[30]

For many years the Kennedy School at Harvard has administered an Innovations in American Government award program, financed by the Ford Foundation. Sanford Borins wrote a book on innovation in state and local government based on documents submitted by award winners. Among his conclusions the point was made that the bureaucrats, not elected officials or department heads, initiated most of the changes.[31] In a later book on the same kind of program but aimed at the federal establishment, John Donahue likewise concluded: "Not one of the innovations celebrated in this volume would have been possible without the purposeful engagement of bureaucrats in the trenches."[32]

Let us pursue this point about the key role of bureaucrats in innovation by examining the emergence of probably the most revolutionary innovation of our time, creation of the Internet. Over the final forty years of the last century the World Wide Web and all of its manifestations came into being because of the activities of many categories of innovators, acting in various complex and intertwined ways. These were isolated geniuses, huge corporations, government contractors, academic researchers, public and private laboratories, and agencies of the federal government.

In an extensive article on this subject, Juan Rogers and Gordon Kingsley state that the contribution made by government to this immense contribution to our modern world has been systematically denied by historians and others. The authors contend that four myths surrounding this history have distorted our understanding of how the Internet came into being.

The first myth is that single scientists working essentially alone deserve the credit. Journalists recounting the Internet's development emphasize, for example, that J.C.R. Licklider and David Englebart first spawned the idea of a computer information network. Paul Baran and Donald Davies originated packet switching, Len Kleinrock first applied the mathematics of queuing theory to the idea, and Robert Kahn and Vinton Cerf invented the transport control protocol that was eventually adopted. About the only bureaucrat mentioned in these stories is Robert Taylor, who as an office director in the Pentagon's Defense Advanced Research Projects Agency (DARPA) oversaw implementation of the pioneer ARPA Network that initially linked university computer systems.

A second myth that has been perpetrated is that in debates over world-wide standards for the Internet and what networks should be developed beyond ARPANET, the engineers and programmers working on the project had to fight off staid, hierarchical bureaucracies in government and corporations in order to bring to the fore such radical notions such as blurring public-private sector boundaries and decentralizing the information system's management. The impression is conveyed that only members of the professional Internet community had the technical sophistication and vision to think of these possibilities.

The third obscuring myth given life is that government was a follower in this whole process rather than a leader. This view is advanced despite the fact that the Department of Defense and DARPA, the National Security Agency, NASA, and the National Science Foundation (NSF) were the primary funders during the four decades of originating work through countless grants, contracts, and arrangements for collaboration. While this point is not itself denied by historians, they imply that these bureaucracies helped only to build constituencies within the technology sector and make alliances with corporate America generally. A sidebar to the myth is that President Bill Clinton and Vice President Al Gore were brought into the loop to win their political support.

The final myth fostered plays to romantic adulation of the egalitarian or even anarchist aspects of the Internet. Its perpetrators suggest that the World Wide Web's creation set in motion a new narrative on how the new technology affects contemporary innovation. The concept of hierarchical bureaucratic government is now obsolete. Outdated notions of lawful order, governing authority, and state control are a thing of the past. Liberated cyberspace has replaced the conventional "public square" of biased and corrupt elected officials and sclerotic government agendas. The bureaucracy's obsession with secrecy has been foiled by the prying eyes of computer hackers. Oligopolistic giant corporations are left in the dust as small apps entrepreneurs and dot-com companies spring up. Most important, the Internet became society's central protector of free enterprise, free speech, and grassroots influence.

Rogers and Kingley state that these accounts grossly minimize and even ridicule the contributions of government and bureaucracy to the creation of the Internet. Deliberately selective stories are told about who was responsible. Individual heroes are highlighted, but key institutions such as DARPA and NSF are discounted. Technological development is decontextualized from early formative developments made possible by small contracts, seed grants, and first-time practical uses of the technology by bureaucracy, such as tabulating the census. Many of the involved scientists and engineers worked for the government on a career or temporary basis. Early attempts by contractors and grantees to privatize the Internet by placing it on a for-fee basis were emphatically rejected by NSF and other agencies.

Thus while government did not administer the Internet's invention as a state project as was the case with the Manhattan Project in World War II, it was its facilitator, cheerleader, and funder. Despite a strong presence of the private sector all along, today's Internet is

> *the congealed product of a government dynamic that took place over a period of about a decade. It is not the result of a top-down government program implemented by its officers. However, it*

grew out of a process squarely situated within the regular opera-
tion of government and a clear embodiment of public value as
understood by its officers.[33]

THE MICROSCOPIC VIEW SUMMED UP

What did we learn from this microscopic view of American bureaucracy?
What new insights came into focus?

One is that citizen opinion of bureaucracy improves when public
administration is seen up close rather than considered abstractly. Clients
interviewed just after they exited welfare offices report they were usually
treated courteously and given the help they need. Managers of the American Consumer Satisfaction Index are impressed with how survey
responses are more favorable to individual agencies and programs than
to government as a whole. Municipal satisfaction surveys indicate that
residents of America's cities and towns express general approval of their
governments, but responses are even more positive when they are asked
about specific city programs and their effect on community life.

With respect to organizational effectiveness, plenty of evidence exists
that bureaucracy can do well. An index compiled by the Bureau of Labor
Statistics showed that between 1967 and 1994 the federal government
experienced a 34 percent increase in labor productivity. Attempts to
make Social Security's half-million client hearings a year more productive and timely achieved significant positive results, although the case
backlog has recently grown because of increased applications. Derek Bok
examined the performance of the federal government over several
decades in meeting 60 national goals, and concluded that in 50 of them
major improvement was attained.

Comparing the bureaucracies of government and corporations reveals
a mixed bag, but the public sector's showing is not bad. Private contractors can be more efficient in routine, repetitive services. Yet the quality of
the work is not necessarily better, and many problems can be introduced
by outsourcing. These are less accountability, not as much transparency,
a less broadly trained workforce, and added opportunities for corruption.
Performance comparisons between private and public urban mass transit
systems have shifted over time from favoring the first to leaning toward
the second.

Contrary to common opinion, bureaucratic employment does not inevitably grow. At the federal level, civilian employment falls as much as it rises; at the state and local level, it has grown slowly over time but has currently dipped because of the recession. A measure of the bureaucracy's human-resource adequacy, the number of bureaucrats per 1,000 population, increased significantly between 1950 and 1980 but has remained stable since then at about seventy-three. Yet it seems quite remarkable that the federal ratio fell drastically from twenty-five to nine between 1945 and 2010. Compared to other industrial democracies, the US figure is definitely on the low side.

Academic predictions that bureaucracies inevitably age and wither have many counterexamples, one of which is NASA's shift to exciting far-space probes following the end of the manned space program. Theories of inherent bureaucratic conservatism are belied by the widespread incidence of agency innovations, many of which are initiated by career bureaucrats. The history of the Internet's development reveals that despite myths about the contributions of brilliant engineers and the importance of networked laboratories, a number of federal bureaucracies played an indispensable sponsorship and facilitation role in bringing into existence this revolutionary aspect of our existence.

ENDNOTES

1. Charles T. Goodsell, "Client Evaluation of Three Welfare Programs: A Comparison of Three Welfare Programs," *Administration & Society* 12, no. 2 (August 1980): 123–136.
2. "ACSI Methodology," from ACSI web page. Accessed April 19, 2012.
3. "ACSI Commentary January 2012," from ACSI web page.
4. "ACSI Scores for U.S. Federal Government 2011," from ACSI web page.
5. Thomas I. Miller and Michelle A. Miller, "Standards of Excellence: U.S. Residents' Evaluations of Local Government Services," *Public Administration Review* 51, no. 6 (November–December 1991): 503–514.
6. Michael N. Herian and Alan J. Tomkins, "Citizen Satisfaction Survey Data: A Mode Comparison of the Derived Importance-Performance Approach," *American Review of Public Administration* 42, no. 1 (January 2012): 67–86.
7. Donald Fisk and Darlene Forte, "The Federal Productivity Measurement Program: Final Results," *Monthly Labor Review* 120, no. 5 (Spring 1997): 19–28.

8. Social Security Administration, "Hearings and Appeals," from the SSA website. Accessed on May 28, 2012.

9. Social Security Administration, "FY 2011 Performance and Accountability Report," pp. 51, 52, 54, from SSA website. Accessed May 28, 2012. This document is also the source for the remaining SSA discussion, at pp. 53, 56, 56, 68, 75–77.

10. Stephen Ohlemacher, "Lawmakers Question Disability Claims," AP article appearing in the *Roanoke Times*, June 25, 2013.

11. A copy of the unpublished Dalbar report, titled "World-Class Benchmarks" and dated April 1995, was furnished to me by the then Commissioner of Region IV of the Social Security Administration, Gordon M. Sherman.

12. Derek Bok, "Measuring the Performance of Government," in *Why People Don't Trust Government*, Joseph S. Nye, Jr., Philip D. Zelikow, and David C. King, eds. (Cambridge, MA: Harvard University Press, 1997), pp. 55–76.

13. Julia Beckett, "The 'Government Should Run Like a Business' Mantra," *American Review of Public Administration* 30, no. 2 (June 2000): 185–204.

14. Graeme A. Hodge, *Privatization: An International Review of Performance* (Boulder, CO: Westview Press, 2000), ch. 7, p. 107.

15. Ibid., pp. 117–156.

16. Barbara J. Stevens, "Comparing Public- and Private-Sector Productive Efficiency: An Analysis of Eight Activities," *National Productivity Review* 3, no. 4 (Autumn 1984): 395–406.

17. James L. Perry, *Organizational Form and Transit Performance: A Research Review and Empirical Analysis*, UMTA Report No. CA 11–0027-2 (Washington, DC: Urban Mass Transportation Administration, 1984).

18. James L. Perry and Timlynn T. Babitsky, "Comparing Performance in Urban Bus Transit: Assessing Privatization Strategies," *Public Administration Review* 46, no. 1 (January–February 1986): 57–66.

19. Suzanne Leland and Olga Smirnova, "Reassessing Privatization Strategies 25 Years Later: Revisiting Perry and Babitsky's Comparative Performance Study of Urban Bus Transit Services," *Public Administration Review* 69, no. 5 (September–October 2009): 855–867.

20. Data obtain from various editions of the *Statistical Abstract of the United States*: 2002, p. 320; 2008, p. 322; 2010, p. 320; 2012, p. 326.

21. Ibid.: 1976, pp. 249–250; 1992, p. 330; 2012, p. 327.

22. Ibid.: 2012, p. 300. Because of vagaries in available statistics, one interval was three years long and one four.

23. Ibid., 2012, pp. 304, 305.

24. Marver H. Bernstein, *Regulating Business by Independent Commission* (Princeton, NJ: Princeton University Press, 1955), pp. 74–95.
25. Kenneth J. Meier and John P. Plumlee, "Regulatory Administration and Organizational Rigidity," *Western Political Quarterly* 31, no. 1 (March 1978): 80–95, with quotes at 91 and 95.
26. Anthony Downs, *Inside Bureaucracy* (Boston: Little, Brown, 1967), chs. 2, 12, 16.
27. Howard E. McCurdy, "Organizational Decline: NASA and the Life Cycle of Bureaus," *Public Administration Review* 51, no. 4 (July–August 1991): 308–315.
28. Howard E. McCurdy, *Faster, Better, Cheaper: Low-Cost Innovation in the U.S. Space Program* (Baltimore: John Hopkins University Press, 2001).
29. Gerald E. Caiden, "What Really is Public Administration?" *Public Administration Review* 51, no. 6 (November–December 1991): 486–493.
30. Louis K. Bragaw, *Managing a Federal Agency: The Hidden Stimulus* (Baltimore: Johns Hopkins University Press, 1980).
31. Sandford Borins, *Innovating With Integrity: How Local Heroes Are Transforming American Government* (Washington, DC: Georgetown University Press, 1998), pp. 37–39.
32. John D. Donahue, ed., *Making Washington Work: Tales of Innovation in the Federal Sector* (Washington, DC: Brookings Institution, 1999), p. 14.
33. Juan D. Rogers and Gordon Kingsley, "Denying Public Value: The Role of the Public Sector in Accounts of the Development of the Internet," *Journal of Public Administration and Theory* 14, no. 3 (July 2004): 371–393, with quote at 386.

THE BUREAUCRATS FRONT AND CENTER

I n the military, the command "front and center," spoken on the parade ground while facing a formation of troops as observers look on, calls forward a designated complement of soldiers for special scrutiny. In this chapter, we call forward from the country's 310 million citizens its 23 million public servants for special study.

SOME INITIAL FACTOIDS

Our task is to find out more about our bureaucrats, how they compare with fellow citizens, and the degree to which they deserve the brickbats and bouquets they get. While stereotypes of bureaucrats abound, underneath it all they are flesh-and-blood human beings and as such are intriguing to look at more closely. To begin, I offer several factoids about them that convey small but telling nuggets of information.

- Thirteen percent are employed by the federal government, 24 percent by the 50 state governments, and 63 percent by the nation's 90,000 cities, counties, townships, school districts, and special districts.

- Almost half of federal civilian employees work to defend the country or to serve those who have done so. Over half of state employees and also over half of local personnel are engaged in public education one way or another.

- The average age of federal bureaucrats is 46.8 and their average time in government service 15.5 years, although the first figure has been tending upward and the second downward.

- In 2010 the US population was 35 percent minority and the federal workforce 34 percent minority. Two decades earlier these percentages were 16 and 27 percent, respectively.

- The ratio of men to women in the federal workforce is 56–44 and in state and local government 54–46. A generation ago, a ratio of 60–40 would not have been unusual.

- The public sector is the employer of choice for returning veterans. Twenty-two percent of federal employees exercised veterans' preference when hired. Seven percent of federal workers are individuals with disabilities.

- Thirty-six percent of public employees in the country are union members. Seven percent of private sector workers are unionized. In terms of membership numbers, however, the two sectors are approximately equal at 7 million.

- The percentage of US taxpayers who in 2001 failed to file an income tax return or owed back taxes was 5.2 percent. Only 2.8 percent of federal workers were delinquent in this way, a differential that has continued for years.[1]

THEIR STATUS: INCOME AND EDUCATION

Civil service pay levels at the federal level have been a topic of lively political controversy for some time. Antigovernment conservatives insist bureaucrats are paid better than in private industry and hence cost far more than they are worth. In his 2012 campaign for the presidency, Mitt Romney contended that federal workers are overpaid by 30 to 40 percent. Right-wing think tanks back him up: the American Enterprise Institute puts the federal pay advantage at 14 percent, while the Heritage Foundation sets it at 22 percent. The Cato Institute claims 58 percent, with the differential said to have increased 25 percent over Obama's first term.[2]

The most valid studies refine the analysis to the point of identifying dimensions of public-private comparability in order to make contrasts valid. Some of these analyses assess the nature of the duties performed. Although a step forward, this method has the shortcoming that under certain circumstances, publicly paid professionals doing the same general work need to be especially skilled and dependable. Examples would be meteorologists and epidemiologists. To overcome this difference, another approach is to attain comparability on the basis of the needed qualities and qualifications of the persons who perform the job. A determination is made of the number of years of education or experience possessed by individuals doing the same type of work, with mean pay and benefits calculated by statistical decomposition and multiple regression and then aggregated by sector.

In 2012 the Congressional Budget Office (CBO) published a report produced in this manner. It concluded that, overall, federal pay is higher than compensation to private counterparts by 2 percent. When educational level is considered, the differential varies significantly however. In an analysis covering the years 2005–2010 that expresses all monetary remuneration in terms of hourly amount, the CBO found that civilian federal workers with a high school education or less earned $23.50 compared to $19.40 for private sector counterparts. For employees with some college education, the amounts are $27.10 public versus $23.60 private. For those holding a bachelor's degree the difference almost disappears, at $35.30 compared to $34.80. Persons with postgraduate degrees tip the scale in the other direction: $41.20 government versus $43.40 private sector for a master's degree and $48.50 versus $60.20 for a professional degree or doctorate.[3]

State and local government employees are not paid as well as those of the federal government. An analysis and replication of existing studies by the Center for Retirement Research at Boston College concludes that in the 2006–2010 period, on a global basis state and local workers earned 9.5 percent *less* than their private counterparts. Yet the differential still depends on level in the organization, measured in this instance by thirds in wage distribution: the lowest third was paid 2 percent more, the middle about the same, and in the top third 21 percent less.[4] A second recent study, by analysts at the Center for State & Local Government Excellence and National Institute on Retirement Security, found that in 2008 average monetary income received by state workers was 11.0 percent less than that obtained by comparable private employees and 11.6 percent below the private level for local government personnel.

Moreover this differential has grown over the years and increases with level of education.[5]

Supplementary noncash benefits have also been compared. Here the critics are right: government workers do better. The CBO found that, for federal workers, the value of the overall benefit package in hourly terms is worth six to seven dollars more at all educational levels except for the most highly trained, for whom the benefits are largely the same. State and local government benefits are also more generous. While conservatives are dismayed by such a difference, it indicates an advantage for young people considering a career in government—especially since the trend in private sector is to drop defined benefit compensation plans.

A byproduct of the CBO and Center for Excellence pay studies is some interesting comparative sector data on level of education, as seen in Table 3.1. The general pattern to prevail is that proportionately there are many more less-educated workers in the private sector than in the public. Conversely, a greater proportion of highly educated individuals is employed in government, especially at the postgraduate level.

In short, federal bureaucrats are comparatively well paid, especially at the lower levels. This is not as true for personnel in state and local government, however. In all of government, generous benefit packages are more common than in industry. At the upper levels of responsibility in government a greater number of advanced degrees are found than in the private sector, but their holders are paid less than business counterparts.

THEIR RACE: AN ENDURING ISSUE

Public administration researchers have studied closely the racial and ethnic composition of bureaucracy. The subject is a crucial aspect of knowing who the bureaucrats are and to what degree diversity policies have led to satisfactory amounts of inclusiveness. Wide consensus exists that fairness requires that those who do the people's business should mirror the people as much as possible.

Just How Inclusive? I approach this sensitive subject using census data not predigested by others. Accepting current census racial categories

TABLE 3.1	Relative Proportion of Educational Attainment in the Public and Private Sectors (in percent)	
Federal Level, 2005–2010	**Public**	**Private**
High school diploma or less	20	41
Some college	29	29
College degree	31	22
Master's degree	14	7
Professional degree or doctorate	7	3
State Level, 1983–2008	**Public**	**Private**
High school diploma or less	27	50
Some college	25	27
College degree	23	16
Post college	25	7
Local Level, 1983–2008	**Public**	**Private**
High school diploma or less	29	50
Some college	23	27
College degree	23	16
Postcollege	25	7

Sources: Congressional Budget Office, "Comparing the Compensation of Federal and Private Sector Employees," January 2012, p. 4. Center for State & Local Government Excellence and National Institute on Retirement Security, "Out of Balance? Comparing Public and Private Sector Compensation Over 20 Years," April 2010, p. 7.

Note: In both reports, data were obtained from the annual Outgoing Rotation Group results of the US Census Bureau's monthly Current Population Survey, in which data are gathered from 50,000–60,000 households for each time period. Federal data are for civilian employees.

(now being changed), the American population is roughly 65 percent white (Caucasian, non-Hispanic), 12 percent black (African American), 16 percent Hispanic, and 7 percent Asian (a category that includes American Indians; natives of Alaska, Hawaii, or other Pacific islands; and mixed).

When holding the distribution of 65–12–16–7 against the demographic composition of bureaucracy, we find the following. The federal government at the civilian, nonwage, and OPM-databank level is 68–18–7–8. At the state and local level the allocation is 67–19–10–4. Hence equivalency between the American population and its bureaucracy is approached but not attained. On a purely numerical basis, whites are somewhat overrepresented, blacks considerably overrepresented, and

Hispanics much underrepresented. As for Asians and others, the match is close at the federal level but low in the states and localities.[6]

The high proportion of black employment in government is the consequence of several factors. Following World War II, many African Americans moved from the South to Washington and northern cities for jobs. In 1948 President Truman desegregated the Armed Forces, stimulating a rethinking of racial attitudes within the civilian government. In 1954, the landmark Supreme Court decision *Brown v. Board of Education of Topeka, Kansas* desegregated the public schools. The Civil Rights Movement of the 1960s, led by Martin Luther King and many others, laid the basis for one of the country's major cultural revolutions. The 1964 Civil Right Act outlawed segregation of public accommodations, banned it in the workplace, and prohibited discriminatory voting practices. Later, equal opportunity offices were established in public institutions to press for affirmative action hiring practices. By 1973 the proportion of black employment in the federal government had reached 16 percent and in state and local governments 14 percent.[7]

Obviously, a complete assessment of the racial inclusiveness of bureaucracy cannot end by noting the relative proportions of overall employee numbers. Bureaucracies are of course hierarchical organizations with ranks of varying importance; and to assess matched equivalency, we must consider as well job level and type.

Table 3.2 provides data in this regard for civilian employees of the federal government, excluding the postal system and agencies not included in the OPM database. Pay levels in the federal civil service system are used as a proxy for hierarchical rank. The table provides percentage figures for five pay levels, listed in descending order, for each of four years. Hence each percentage states the proportion of employees at that level for that year within one of four racial categories, with all four percentages at that rank in that year adding to 100, allowing for rounding.

The main observation that springs from the table is that for the most part, during the time period covered, the proportion of white persons in all five ranks declined while a minority presence rose in each. Only a few exceptions to the pattern exist: an uptick in whites occupying the GS 9–12 and GS 1–4 levels in 2008; downturns in Executive blacks in 1990 and 2008; no change in blacks at GS 5–8 in 2008; and reductions by them

TABLE 3.2	Federal Executive Branch Employment by Race, National Origin, and Pay Level, 1980–2008 (in percent)			
	1980	1990	2000	2008
White, non-Hispanic				
Executive/senior	92.9	92.3	86.5	79.8
GS grade 13–15	91.5	87.3	86.5	79.8
GS grade 9–12	85.1	78.7	72.6	79.8
GS grade 5–8	73.8	66.7	60.3	58.8
GS grade 1–4	67.1	57.9	55.2	58.6
Black				
Executive/senior	4.8	4.7	7.1	5.7
GS grade13–15	4.9	6.4	9.7	12.5
GS grade 9–12	9.1	11.6	14.9	16.7
GS grade 5–8	19.8	22.7	25.2	25.2
GS grade 1–4	24.0	28.5	26.9	24.2
Hispanic				
Executive/senior	xx	1.5	3.0	4.1
GS grade13–15	1.7	2.6	4.0	4.7
GS grade 9–12	3.2	4.9	6.6	8.3
GS grade 5–8	4.1	5.7	8.0	8.7
GS grade 1–4	4.9	6.9	8.5	7.2
Asian and Other				
Executive/senior	xx	1.5	3.0	10.4
GS grade 13–15	1.9	3.6	5.5	7.3
GS grade 9–12	2.6	4.8	5.9	6.8
GS grade 5–8	2.4	4.9	6.5	7.3
GS grade 1–4	4.0	6.7	9.4	10.1

Source: *Statistical Abstract of the United States*, 1982–1983, p. 269; 2012, p. 328.

Note: The designation "xx" means less than 50 individuals; in 1980 Hispanics and Asians together constituted 2.4 percent of the executive/senior level. The "other" race category refers to American Indians, Alaskan Natives, and Pacific Islanders.

at GS 1–4 in 2000 and 2008. Clearly the Bush II years were not a good time for diversity. Yet the broad picture is that a revolution in bureaucracy's racial composition has occurred—overwhelming dominance by the white majority has given way to a significant expansion of minority presence.

As can be seen by the table, at the very top executive/senior level, white occupancy of these jobs declined 13.1 percentage points over the

1980–2008 period. African Americans rose from 4.8 percent in 1980 to 7.1 percent in 2000, but then fell to 5.7 under Bush. Hispanics and Asians advanced from practically zero to 4.1 and 10.4 percent by 2008, respectively. Comparing the 2008 executive breakdown to the current racial composition of the population, whites remain overrepresented by about 15 points; African Americans and Hispanics are still underrepresented by 6.3 and 11.9 points, respectively; and Asians advanced to an overrepresented margin of 3.4 points. A power shift at the top among the minorities had taken place; while some progress was made up the ladder by blacks and Hispanics, it was primarily the Asians who surged forward.

At the lower levels of the federal civil service similar shifts occurred, but with African Americans doing better. At the middle-management/ professional level of GS 13–15, whites lost 11.7 percentage points. Among the minorities, blacks gained 7.6, Hispanics 3, and Asians 5.4. Thus by 2008 the black percentage of 12.5 placed that group on a par with their presence in the population, a significant achievement at this relatively senior rank. Meanwhile in the GS 12 rank and below, whites generally lost ground and minorities gained ground, with some backsliding by blacks in 2000 and 2008.

Table 3.3 presents corresponding data for state and local government, albeit with different years and occupation categories as indicators of rank. Looking at the data set as a whole, the proportion of whites consistently diminished over the four years in all occupations. Minority gains were made for all four racial categories in all six occupations with the exception of losses by African Americans for protective service in 2009, paraprofessionals in 1999 and 2009, and service/maintenance in 1999.

The results of these shifts for mirroring the population are that by 2009, Caucasians are overrepresented in the state-local officials/ administrators category by 15 points, almost the same amount found at the federal level in 2008 for executive/senior positions. By 2009 state and local governments were led at the top level by a much higher proportion of blacks, 11.8 or almost precisely their proportion in the population— far higher than the 5.7 percent in the federal category of executive/senior. Hispanics and Asians clearly continue to be much underrepresented at the top of state and local governments; this is different from the federal government, where Asians but not Hispanics obtained access to the

TABLE 3.3	State and Local Government Employment By Race, National Origin, and Occupation, 1976–2009 (in percent)			
	1976	1989	1999	2009
White				
Officials/administrators	92.0	85.6	82.4	79.3
Professionals	86.9	79.4	74.3	69.6
Technicians	85.0	76.9	73.1	68.2
Protective service	87.8	78.0	71.5	69.3
Paraprofessionals	66.5	62.3	59.4	56.2
Administrative support	80.9	71.0	66.6	62.5
Skilled craft	84.0	77.6	74.1	70.9
Service/maintenance	64.0	57.8	54.8	51.9
Black				
Officials/administrators	5.4	9.9	11.1	11.8
Professionals	8.5	12.7	14.9	16.4
Technicians	11.0	14.9	15.4	16.0
Protective service	9.0	15.3	18.2	17.5
Paraprofessionals	28.4	30.6	30.2	29.6
Administrative support	13.7	19.4	20.3	20.4
Skilled craft	10.8	14.0	15.3	15.8
Service/maintenance	29.0	31.8	31.2	31.3
Hispanic				
Officials/administrators	1.8	3.1	4.2	5.8
Professionals	2.3	4.0	5.8	7.3
Technicians	2.9	5.6	7.5	10.1
Protective service	2.7	5.7	8.4	10.8
Paraprofessionals	4.2	5.5	7.8	10.8
Administrative support	4.1	7.1	9.7	12.9
Skilled craft	4.4	6.3	8.0	10.0
Service/maintenance	6.3	8.9	11.2	13.7
Asian and Other				
Officials/administrators	0.8	1.4	2.3	3.1
Professionals	2.3	3.9	5.1	6.7
Technicians	1.1	2.6	4.0	5.7
Protective service	0.5	1.1	1.9	2.3
Paraprofessionals	0,9	1.6	2.7	3.3
Administrative support	1.3	2.5	3.4	4.2
Skilled craft	0.8	2.0	2.5	3.3
Service maintenance	0.7	1.5	2.8	3.1

Source: Statistical Abstract of the United States, 1978, p. 320; 1991, p. 306; 2002, p. 297; 2012, p. 301.

Note: Percentages for each occupation level sum to 100 among the four race categories for that year. Whether "White" excludes all Hispanics is not stated. "Other" presumably includes Asians but is not specifically said. Even though data for the Paraprofessional category were not given for 2009, they could be deduced from residuals not accounted for by other categories.

corridors of power. With respect to the lower paid state-local occupational categories, by 2009 African Americans were overrepresented in all of them, especially paraprofessionals and service/maintenance. Meanwhile the other minorities have made gains but were not yet at parity with their population proportion.

Although we have treated inclusiveness in terms of gross numerical presence and hierarchical placement separately, it is possible to combine the two kinds of measure. Vernon Greene and Sally Selden have developed what they call a Rho statistic that incorporates both by weighting rank. Applying this methodology to 1955 Equal Employment Opportunity data for state and local governments, they found that the Rho score is lower than the proportion-alone score for African Americans and Native Americans, meaning they have lots of jobs but not at high levels. The opposite is true for Asians, especially men. As for whites and Hispanics, the men score high on Rho but the women do not.[8]

Since the data contained in these tables was collected, the racial breakdowns just discussed have not changed much. Overall, by 2010 white representation in the federal bureaucracy was reduced from 68 to 66 percent, mainly due to marginal gains by Hispanics. The position of blacks is essentially unchanged. Although Hispanics are still the most underrepresented minority, their presence in top federal positions has doubled.[9]

Representative Bureaucracy. A large body of academic research in this area falls under the heading of "representative bureaucracy." The term was coined by J. Donald Kingsley in a book he published in 1944. As an American who studied public administration in Britain, Kingsley was impressed by how the UK civil service was stratified by educational background, with top positions held almost exclusively by the products of prestige public schools and universities. Contending this created a climate of snobbish, narrow elitism, he concluded,

> *The democratic State cannot afford to exclude any considerable body of its citizens from full participation in its affairs. It requires at every point that superior insight and wisdom which is the peculiar product of the pooling of diverse streams of experience. In this lies the strength of representative government.[10]*

In 1952 my late colleague Norton Long stated a similar position on the subject from a US perspective. Noting that the American civil service is relatively open compared to more exclusionary hiring practices in many countries, he wrote in a much-quoted article that the nation's bureaucracy is actually more representative than its supposedly most representative public institution, Congress:

> If one rejects the view that election is the sine qua non of representation, the bureaucracy now has a very real claim to be considered much more representative of the American people in its composition than the Congress. This is not merely the case with respect to the class structure of the country but, equally significantly, with respect to the learned groups, skills, economic interests, races, nationalities, and religions. The rich diversity that makes up the United States is better represented in its civil service than anywhere else.[11]

Many writers on representative bureaucracy take a conceptual step beyond the expressive, mirroring concept of bureaucratic representation found in these classic statements. They seek not merely a "re-presentation" of the population's varied group traits, but an agential or advocatory role whereby members of designated subgroups within the public service use their official positions to advance that constituency's interests. In the literature this is heralded as active representation as over against passive representation. The constituencies usually examined for this behavior are African Americans and women. The following is how two lead scholars of active representation, Jessica Sowa and Sally Selden, articulate this perspective.

> Active representation takes the assertion that certain attributes such as race, ethnicity, and gender—which lead to early socialization experiences and, in turn, shape the values and attitudes of administrators—a step further than passive representation. These values and attitudes then can be conceived of as directly influencing the behavior of administrators, directing them toward using their discretion to foster improved equity for those who have been underrepresented in the implementation of public programs.[12]

Seldon's research on this matter includes a book on the Farmers Home Administration (now Rural Housing Service) in which she discovered that field offices staffed mainly by minority employees granted proportionately more loans to minority applicants than primarily white offices. Also African American county supervisors tended to be more supportive of minority interests than their white colleagues.[13]

Other scholars have found some evidence of such favoritism but not without complications. Sylvester Murray and associates surveyed members of the Conference of Minority Public Administration and found that they endorsed advancing minority goals in their jobs but at the same time expressed support for established organizational policies, no matter what their racial implications.[14]

Kenneth Meier and Kevin Smith studied minority influence in Florida school districts and uncovered not intentional active representation but what appeared to be reciprocal influences regarding appointments. Over time, increases in black school board membership seemed to lead to hiring additional black administrators, who in turn brought in more black teachers. Then more black teachers led to more black administrators, followed by expanded African American membership on boards.[15]

In a study of racial profiling in the San Diego Police Department, Vicky Wilkins and Brian Williams discovered that it is possible for African American hires to create adverse outcomes for minorities with respect to police conduct. From both interviews and stop records, they concluded that informal organizational pressures to be "a 100% cop" caused black San Diego officers to outdo their white colleagues in racial profiling in order to prove themselves.[16]

While I can certainly understand the desire of public administration scholars to conduct research framed around the need to compensate for the historical inequities visited upon minorities, I personally favor the goal of an outcome whereby *all* citizens are treated fairly and equitably on a color-blind basis. The important point is that bureaucracies mirror the presence of all demographic groups to the point that each one's perspective on what *is* fair and equitable is embedded in their workforces.

THEIR GENDER: THE EQUALITY IDEAL IN PRACTICE

Inclusiveness in the realm of gender is an issue that cuts across all racial groups and adds to the social challenges faced by bureaucracy. It too is difficult to attain, so efforts must be ongoing.

How Much Parity? An initial point to make is that while women constitute 50.6 percent of the US population, they are 47.3 percent of the civilian workforce.[17] Hence, whereas 50–50 is a laudable goal in employment terms, a doable standard is more like 53–47. I call this parity, or practical equivalence.

As for simply job-holding presence, according to the most recent census data female employees of the federal government constitute 44.1 percent of total federal workers. In state and local governments the figure is 45.8 percent. Hence attainment of parity is not quite there.[18]

But even this level was a long time in coming. At the end of World War II in 1945, women's employment was 34 percent of the federal workforce nationwide and 56 percent in the Washington, D.C. area, due to the absence of so many men at war. The levels fell sharply after 1945 however, and did not rise again for many years. Throughout the 1950s and 1960s the federal figure was in the twenties and did not rise above 30 percent until 1974. By 1988 it exceeded 40 percent, and from 1993 on the percentage has hovered between 44 and 45. At the state and local level, interestingly enough, 30 and 40 percent levels arrived several years earlier, although a 44–45 percent plateau also began in 1993.[19]

Making comparisons to other sectors of the economy, the percentage of female employment in manufacturing is 28, transportation 23, public utilities 22 and construction 9. Sectors thought of as "feminine" (much to the disgust of feminists) are retail trade at 49 percent, hotel and food service 53, finance and insurance 57, education 69, and hospitals 77. The reason, unfortunately, is that these figures reflect many women placed in low-status roles, such as store clerks, waitresses, cleaning staff, nurses' aides and office assistants.[20]

International comparisons on this subject are enabled by Table 3.4, whose data are drawn from the same source used for Table 2.7 in chapter 2 on employment-population ratios. The percent given in the table for the United States, 45.2, coincides with the figures just given. This level is five points above the mean for the 31 countries named, contrasting to the low side of the scale the United States occupied in Table 2.7. Nonetheless, all English-speaking nations rank higher, with some boasting 50+ percentages.

The key aim for women with respect to parity is to get their share of positions of importance and power. The federal Senior Executive Service (SES), a corps of 7,500 top-ranking civil servants (and some political appointees), had less than 10 percent of its positions filled by women for several years after its establishment in 1978. Between 1990 and 2000 the percentage nearly doubled, reaching 23 percent. By 2009 it stood at 30 percent, still far short of parity.[21]

A similar conclusion arises from an examination of the US General Schedule as a whole. In 2009 the average GS grade for men stood at

TABLE 3.4	Female Employment in "Public Administration, Defence and Compulsory Social Security," Selected Governments of the World, 2006–2008 (in percent)		
Government	Female Employment	Government	Female Employment
Saudi Arabia	2.2	Argentina	42.2
Turkey	13.9	**United States**	**45.2**
Egypt	23.3	Israel	45.6
Peru	24.0	Germany	45.8
China	27.6	Belgium	46.4
South Korea	31.9	Australia	47.6
Italy	34.0	Finland	47.6
Mexico	34.6	Norway	48.1
Portugal	35.4	United Kingdom	48.9
Greece	36.9	Poland	50.1
Netherlands	37.1	Denmark	50.2
Brazil	38.3	Canada	50.9
Philippines	39.0	France	52.0
Russia	39.5	New Zealand	52.1
Spain	40.8	Sweden	54.8
Mean = 40.1		Japan	55.2

Source: *Yearbook of Labour Statistics: Country Profiles* (Geneva: International Labour Office, 2009).

Note: Percentages are for tabulation category L, titled "Public Administration and Defence: Compulsory Social Security."

10.4, compared to 9.3 for women. Yet continued forward movement seems underway. At the senior pay levels of GS 13, 14, and 15—considered the "feeder" pools for the SES—the percentage of women grew from 11 percent in 1990 to 24 in 2000. Moreover each new grade cohort rising up contains more females than the last—as of 2009, GS 15 was 33 percent female; GS 14, 39 percent; and GS 13, 40 percent.[22]

Table 3.5 shows that in state and local government, the position ranking of women has improved greatly in recent decades also, but still falls short. The proportion of female officials/administrators rose from 19.5 in 1976 to nearly 38.8 in 2007. Perhaps most encouraging, the proportion of those holding professional positions is now well over half. A downside is present even in these trends, however; in 2009 female administrators in the federal government earned a median salary of $2,000 less per year than male, and women professionals received $9,000 less than their men counterparts.[23]

Another observation that can be taken from the table is that although traditional female areas of paraprofessional and administrative support (i.e., secretaries) are remaining relatively stable over time, women have made significant inroads on the traditionally masculine jobs of technician, protective service (security guards), and service/maintenance. Still, their pay lagged behind men by $10,000 for technicians and guards and $8,000 for janitors.

TABLE 3.5	Female State and Local Government Employees by Occupational Group, 1976–2007 (in percent)		
	1976	1989	1999	2007
Officials/administrators	19.5	30.8	34.5	38.8
Professionals	40.8	49.3	54.0	56.6
Technicians	33.3	40.0	42.0	41.9
Protective service	6.3	12.2	17.4	19.7
Paraprofessionals	67.5	71.9	73.5	73.0
Administrative support	84.7	87.5	86.5	86.3
Skilled craft	4.9	3.8	5.3	5.1
Service/maintenance	17.7	20.2	22.8	24.3

Source: Statistical Abstract of the United States, 1978, p. 320; 1991, p. 306; 2002, p. 297; 2011, p. 301.

Data are available on the ascension of women to the position of agency head in state administrative agencies. Research conducted over the years by the late Deil Wright and his associates shows that the proportion of such posts occupied by women rose from the 5–6 percent range in the 1970s to 14 percent in the 1980s, 22 percent in the 1990s, and 26 percent in 2004. The types of agencies most commonly headed by women are social services (39 percent), public health (33 percent), and public education (31 percent). Although critics will dismiss these as "feminine" fields, a substantial female presence was also found in regulatory and economic development bureaucracies (21 percent for both) and in agencies where heads are elected (22 percent). One of Wright's more interesting findings is that as new departments were created, the mean level of female leadership in the newest group doubled, from 16 percent in the 1960s to 34 in the 1990s.[24]

In a recent study Amy Smith and Karen Monaghan made a count of women serving at senior positions in federal regulatory bodies. They found that 39 percent of first-rank positions in 118 organizations were occupied by women. These include regulatory commissioners, who are nominated by the President and confirmed by the Senate. The authors point out that these organizations are more gender inclusive than congressional committees and corporate boards. Women were at the top in 29 percent of the agencies whose mission is masculine oriented, 45 percent where it is feminine oriented, and 49 percent of those that are neither. Smith and Monaghan also noted a tendency for women to be placed in charge of agencies facing a high risk of failure, but only those that are less visible politically.[25]

Bureau Women in Action. As the presence of women in bureaucracy grows and they move up the ladder of authority, to what extent can they operate on an equal basis with men? Some feminists question whether this is possible, as they see hierarchical bureaucracy as an inherently masculine domain that privileges male values such as exercising power for its own sake and reducing all thought to "objective" rational analysis. These tendencies suppress traits like personal warmth, intuitive thinking, and a readiness to compromise. As a consequence, unless women are willing to take on male attributes, they are inherently disadvantaged as they seek promotion and influence.[26]

Is, then, bureaucracy such a male bastion that women cannot prosper in it without losing their identity? Or can female bureaucrats turn the bureaucratic structure to their own advantage? Leisha DeHart-Davis explored the question by interviewing female employees of four Midwestern cities. One interviewee was a female emergency dispatcher operator who was bombarded by filling out different reporting forms for each of the 14 police, fire, and EMS departments she served. To overcome each unit's insistence on having its own form, she got them to accept a single common form by pointing out it would be more efficient, a solid male value they could not ignore.[27]

In another publication to emanate from the four-city Midwestern study, DeHart-Davis and coauthor Shannon Portillo investigated how male and female employees compare in their attitudes toward compliance to organizational authority. They asked survey respondents to rate themselves on a five-point scale separating four paired reactions: going-along versus arguing, accepting the system versus questioning it, accepting authority as opposed to resisting it, and in general conforming or rebelling. Sure enough, the women scored more toward the conforming side than the men. Yet, interestingly, female rule-conformity was higher at more elevated points in the hierarchy than lower down. The investigators expected the reverse, on grounds that lower level, younger women would be less confident and thus more intimidated. DeHart-Davis and Portillo speculate the reason is that New Public Management-style entrepreneurial norms required male administrators at the top to be bent on independent action and risk taking; and to do battle with them successfully, female managers had to have the rules on their side.[28]

Portillo undertook another study in which she asked male and female police officers and city managers to tell stories about occasions on which their authority was questioned. Two contrasting narratives emerged. High-status, older white men conceded that existence of a written rule gave an extra edge to the authority they saw themselves as already possessing, but they also lamented that it could box them in when they wanted to act autonomously. Female, nonwhite and younger respondents tended to see the rules as the essential foundation of the authority they found themselves exercising, yet this unfortunately opened them to being picky—and "bitchy" in the case of the female cops.[29]

In yet another investigation, Julie Dolan asked women and men SES careerists to indicate how much influence they feel they can exercise in various aspects of policymaking. Table 3.6 gives the opportunities for influence she named and the outcome scores. Remarkably, on every item the women scored themselves higher than the men. One way to look at this result is that despite all the obstacles of lingering sexism and masculine dominance, these female executives picture themselves as

TABLE 3.6	Perceived Influence Over Policy by Members of the Senior Executive Service, by Gender, 1996	
	Mean Score on Degree of Influence Scale	
Activity	Women	Men
Give advice to supervisor or those above me	3.66	3.54
Keep abreast of issues and new developments	3.56	3.42
Persuade others to follow my recommendations	3.56	3.42*
Gather information	3.50	3.32*
Set priorities for organization	3.45	3.30
Recommend changes to polices or programs	3.40	3.13**
Interpret and apply laws and regulations	3.40	3.00***
Initiate policy ideas	3.38	3.32
Choose among alternatives for achieving goals	3.29	3.13
Make budgetary decisions	2.89	2.73
Cultivate public support for policies	2.73	2.30**
Recruit employees	2.60	2.44
Draft rules and regulations	2.19	2.10

Source: Julie Dolan, "Gender Equity: Illusion or Reality for Women in the Federal Executive Service?" *Public Administration Review* 64, no. 3 (May–June 2004), p. 304.

Note: Scale ranges from 1–4, indicating extent to which respondent perceives she or he is able to influence policymaking in the organization: 1 = to no extent; 2 = to a limited extent; 3 = to some extent; 4 = to a great extent. *$p < .05$. **$p < .01$. ***$p < .001$.

equivalent to if not surpassing their male colleagues in clout. Another way to interpret the findings is that when filling out the survey, the women overstated their power as a defensive gesture.

Do women who gain power in bureaucracy use their position to advance women's causes, in accord with the active representation doctrine mentioned earlier? Judith Saidel and Karyn Loscocco surveyed 215 state agency heads and found that 50 percent of female respondents— compared to 35 percent of the men—place a priority on woman's issues such as pay equity and action against domestic abuse.[30] In another research project on priorities, Vicky Wilkins examined field supervisor conduct in the Missouri Division of Child Support Enforcement. Under state law, when the division is successful in obtaining delinquent child support payments from absent fathers, the funds are remitted to one of two destinations: the mothers or, if they are currently receiving Temporary Assistance for Needy Families (TANF), to the state treasury as a way of recouping monies spent on the grant. In her study, Wilkins surveyed program supervisors to determine how much priority they gave to allotting scarce caseworker time to TANF versus non-TANF cases. She found that female supervisors were significantly more favorable to the latter kind of case than were male supervisors, a pattern she interprets as consistent with active representation in behalf of women.[31]

Kenneth Meier (whose work on minority bureaucratic representation was described above) and Jill Nicholson-Crotty examined US Department of Justice data on metropolitan police departments and found that squads with a larger percentage of female officers report more incidents of sexual assault. Meier and Nicholson-Crotty note, however, that this outcome could result not from conscious profemale performance of duty but simply from the presence of officers who by their gender are naturally more attuned to the experiences of women. They suggest this explanation is more in keeping with passive representation, not active.[32]

ARE BUREAUCRATS REALLY THAT BAD?

In large part, this book has been written because many Americans— including public administration scholars—assume that government employees are as a class guilty of multiple sins. Among them are being too liberal, too inflexible, too controlling, and too irresponsible. A heavy indictment!

Leftist Leanings. The first count against them is that they lean to the left politically, and this fact becomes one reason why we have such big government. The argument is that because of their personal politics, strong turnout at elections, and consistent voting for liberal candidates, election outcomes are tilted leftward from where they would otherwise be. This is called the "bureau voting model" of government growth.

An influential early study comparing the political opinions of bureaucrats with those of other citizens is by James Garand and coauthors. They examined survey data from the National Election Studies during the Reagan presidency for 1982, 1984, and 1986. In all three elections the voting turnout by bureaucrats was indeed better than that of the general public, by an 8–10 percentile difference. To test for partisanship, the researchers adopted a 7-point scale of from 0 = Strong Democrat to 6 = Strong Republican, making 3 the midpoint between the two. In 1982 the score difference was 2.20 for bureaucrats to 2.50 for the public, with 2.26 to 2.85 in 1984, and 2.34 to 2.68 in 1986—that is, somewhat on the Democratic side. To measure personal ideology, a similar scale was used whereby 0 = Strong Liberal and 6 = Strong Conservative. The outcome this time was 4.12 bureaucrats to 4.37 general public in 1982, 4.45 to 4.57 in 1984, and 4.14 to 4.62 in 1986—also a tendency left of the public. Yet what is odd about these figures is that whereas the party percentages are on the left of the midpoint of 3, the ideology percentages are on the right of 3; hence bureaucrats vote Democratic more often than Republican but see themselves as moderate conservatives, not liberals.

Garand and associates also calculated comparative support for funding government programs in several areas. These survey responses were even more confusing; the bureaucrats were more enthusiastic than the public for space, health, and education in 1982; crime, science, and defense in 1984; and the environment, student aid, and civil rights in 1986. The researchers conclude that although the evidence "is not as clean and unambiguous as one might like, these results provide at least moderate support for the bureau voting theory of government growth."[33]

Other scholars have questioned the bureau voting model. Gregory Lewis inquired more systematically into opinion differences in several policy areas and encountered a substantial tendency for public servants to echo the public's views quite closely. The only major differences were stronger bureaucrat support for expenditures on national defense and space exploration, less concern about pornography and homosexuality, and less approval of wiretapping and more tolerance for free speech. On the social issues of abortion, marijuana use, gun control, capital punishment, fundamentalist religion, and aspects of female and minority rights, no significant differences surfaced.[34]

In a study of views on environmental protection, David Konisky analyzed the degree of opinion congruence or lack thereof between state environmental regulators and the general public. Respondents were asked to indicate their position on a 1–7 point scale whereby 1 = "current regulations to protect the environment are already too much of a burden on business" to 7 = "need tougher regulations on business in order to protect the environment." The mean replies were 4.74 for the officials and 4.14 for the citizens, a difference of only 0.6. As for political views, Konisky found that compared to citizens, managers tended to identify themselves as independent, nonpartisan voters, and philosophical liberals rather than either moderates or conservatives.[35]

Jason Jensen and associates tested the bureau-voting model cross-nationally. This was done by using public opinion survey data collected within two weeks of national elections held from 1996 to 2000 in eighteen countries, including the United States. Being a government employee along with other variables were correlated with (1) possession of a left-leaning political ideology, (2) turning out to vote, and (3) voting for a left-leaning party. The authors found that in ten of the eighteen countries, a significant and positive relationship existed between being a bureaucrat and harboring left-leaning views. However, significant correlations to voting turnout appeared in only seven countries and to voting leftist in only two, Australia and Slovenia. For the United States, the prediction regarding turnout was well supported, but for ideology only marginally so, and for voting not at all.[36]

A Bureaucratic Personality. We recall from chapter 1 Merton's classic theory of the bureaucratic personality. It portrays bureaucrats as narrow minded and inflexible rule enforcers. Much contemporary research in this area centers on the concept of red tape. This favorite epithet to hurl at bureaucracy pictures it as causing inordinate delays, producing endless paperwork, and demanding obedience to pointless rules. Barry Bozeman, the lead scholar on this subject, defines red tape more precisely, making it possible to conduct empirical research on the subject. To him, red tape consists of rules that once may have been useful but are still retained despite being a burden and not achieving their intended purpose.

Upon reviewing evidence on the extent and proliferation of red tape defined this way, Bozeman believes that it is more common in the public sector than the private sector, at least to some degree. His reasoning is that government agencies more than corporations are subject to extensive supervision within their immediate institutional orbit, along with stiff oversight from outside it. To survive and prosper under this heavy scrutiny, agencies subject their personnel to a proliferation of rules to forestall wayward actions for which they will be held responsible.[37]

In an extensive review of the literature on red tape, my former colleague John Foster examined a number of empirical studies that tested for rule inflexibility among bureaucrats. The purview of his search included scholarship on practices of rule abidance, the erection of procedural barriers, government worker attitudes, and observational studies of rule behavior. He concluded from this inquiry that virtually no evidence exists to support a generalized, widespread presence in government of the kind of rule behavior Merton anticipated. Indeed, he concludes that actually its existence "may be reasonably rare."[38]

I had a research experience several years ago in which I unexpectedly ran into a practice in bureaucracy of taking initiatives in behalf of clients not contemplated by the rules. From in-depth interviews with some 25 workers and clients, I learned that eligibility workers in a county public welfare department sometimes keep an eye out for help wanted notices and educational opportunities they happen to see on grocery store bulletin boards and similar places. They then bring these tidbits of information to the attention of favored clients whom the workers like personally and feel have life improvement potential. I called this departure from standard procedures whereby decisions are made according to formal categories "positive discrimination."[39]

In a more recent study, Zachary Oberfield examined agency socialization efforts of newly recruited police officers and social workers with respect to rule behavior. He was particularly interested in how initial training on the importance of following the organization's operating rules stuck with the recruits after going on the job. Approximately 130 new recruits of each type were surveyed upon their arrival and a subsample interviewed. The surveys and interviews were then repeated after one year of being on duty and a third time at the end of two years. Oberfield discerned three kinds of rule orientation among them: strict rule followers, discretion exercisers, and those in between. After the second year on the job, the strict followers fell from 85 to 60 percent for the police officers and from 60 to 39 percent for the social workers. In large part the shift away from rule abidance was toward case discretion for the police and to either discretion or a mixed posture for the social workers. The author concludes that rule-oriented individuals had been most influenced by training instructors and the discretion-oriented personnel by workplace peers or veteran personnel.[40]

Leisha DeHart-Davis has also written on red tape, and in her bold manner calls for a reframing of scholarly discourse on the subject. We should think about red tape not negatively in terms of bad rules that impair effectiveness, she contends, but positively in terms of good rules that promote it. This approach invites us to consider what "green tape" might be like. Her prescribed model of that, developed from the same study of four city governments mentioned earlier, is that rules should have five characteristics: (1) be in writing, allowing the bureaucrat to point to a printed version if necessary; (2) be recognizable as actually helpful in reaching the desired objective; (3) be tailored in degree of forcefulness, that is, neither overcontrolling nor undercontrolling for the particular situation; (4) is applied consistently so as to convey equal fairness to all; and (5) is presented so that its ultimate purpose is clearly obvious. DeHart-Davis tested her theory by surveying the employees of her four cities to see whether respondents who see themselves as effective users of rules tend to subscribe to these characteristics. By and large this was the case although in their eyes attributes (3) and (5) were seen as more important than (1) and (2), while (4) was deemed unimportant.[41]

The Dehumanized Bureaucrat. In addition to criticizing bureaucrats for dehumanizing clients, Hummel says that the bureaucrats themselves are dehumanized by working in a bureaucracy. To sum-marize his position, it shreds the individual's psyche by imposing on it a fragmented structure of specialization; subverts independent think-ing by immersing it in a hierarchical atmosphere; undermines the ego and super ego by oppressive managerial control; and displaces imagi-nation with rationalistic reasoning.[42]

An early piece of empirical research that at least touches on the issues raised by Hummel is that of sociologist Melvin Kohn. By means of a large survey he attempted to assess the personality traits of 3,101 men employed as civilians in bureaucratic organizations, both public and pri-vate. The existence of a bureaucratized milieu was defined in terms of large size and numerous supervisory levels. Kohn's survey questions assessed: how respondents value conformity to authority; the degree to which they demonstrate authoritative, legalistic, and noninnovative ori-entations; their scores on perception and problem-solving intelligence tests; and their use of leisure time.

Kohn's main finding was relatively simple: bureaucratized features of the milieu did not seem to be turning out authority-oriented, noncreative and rule-driven individuals, but instead people who tend to be individu-ally thoughtful and self-directed and even intelligent users of their leisure time. Kohn believes that one reason for this is that bureaucrats typically have more education than most workers. Another possibility is that the very nature of bureaucratic jobs actually attracts independent and cre-ative people. While added layers of hierarchy may tighten supervision, large size and extension specialization actually create enclaves of auton-omy, he speculates.[43]

Other studies of this kind could be described, but I prefer to conclude this discussion of Hummel's work in a different way. As mentioned ear-lier, Ralph and I were friends, and I recall conversations with him in which he stressed how scholars in our field should pay more attention to the concrete feelings experienced by bureaucrats in their day-to-day work. As it happens, one such bureaucrat wrote a review of his book and described it by drawing on just such feelings. This is Claire Mostel, then coordinator of the Office of Neighborhood Compliance in Miami-Dade County government. In her review she called for more active dialogue between public administration academics and practitioners, a motion

I am sure Ralph would second. In all sincerity I do not think he would have minded if I share some of her comments.

Mostel concedes from the start that many bureaucrats "do not exercise independent thinking, do not appear to be good listeners, and seem to have lost their individuality and forgotten the human aspect." She then goes on:

> My current work experience is the antithesis of the bureaucracy depicted by Hummel. I have been fortunate to work in a progressive environment in local government for the past 13 years. Although the department is a bit schizophrenic, with code enforcement and outreach divisions, staff are encouraged to be creative and to treat our citizens with respect and care. While we do have to operate within the boundaries of ordinances and regulations, our enforcement emphasizes compliance, not punitive action. Our outreach staff have the luxury of being able to work with our residents to ensure service delivery and to address quality-of-life issues. I recognize that my experience is not the norm in public service; however, I believe that there are many agencies and departments throughout the public administration world that are moving in this direction.

She concludes with this personal reflection:

> At the end of my grueling journey through The Bureaucratic Experience, I was left cold, uncaring, programmed, uninspired, powerless, and unable to relate to the human beings portrayed in the text. The good news is that tomorrow morning, I get to go back to work and do what I came to public service to do: provide assistance to those in need in a caring and personal manner, using common sense and flexibility whenever possible.[44]

The Subordinate Agent. A final alleged bad trait of bureaucrats to be considered is suspicion as to whether they can be trusted to live up to the instructions of their superiors. In organizational economics and management theory, this issue is seen as the principal-agent "problem." This refers to the assumed difficulty on the part of principals—seen as those in charge—to depend on the reliability of agents, who are their subordinates, to carry out instructions. An example in the private sector would be corporate shareholders depending on hired management, and in the public sector elected officials relying on the bureaucracy.

The "problem" lies in differentials in the diverging interests of the two parties along with different amounts of information possessed by each side. Although the agent's duty is to advance the principal's interests in all aspects, the subordinate who is immersed in the work being carried out knows far more about what is happening in practice and what can be accomplished. This informational asymmetry allows the agent to take various forms of liberty with respect to the agent's interests, such as depart from the principal's instructions; take unwarranted risks with the principal's assets; or misinform the principal of outcomes. The common remedy offered by principal-agent theorists is to manipulate the agent's financial rewards so as to create monetary incentives so that the agent will be motivated to achieve the desired results. Typically this is done by commissions on sales, performance pay, profit-sharing schemes, bonuses, or tips. This way rational self-interest takes over without having to develop mutual personal trust or foster motives beyond personal self-gain—qualities we hope are not always strangers to the public sector.

Carole Chaney and Grace Saltzstein examined police behavior in California using the principal-agent idea as a conceptual framework. Conformity by the police (agents) to laws enacted by city council members and state legislators (principals) is the matter at stake. At issue is whether the police will obey a legal requirement to arrest automatically the aggressors in violent domestic disputes. The law was passed out of suspicion that male officers cannot be relied upon to take into custody other men found to be attacking women and children. Instead, it was felt, they are inclined to take milder steps such as give warnings, order the husband to leave, or urge counseling.

To determine whether the automatic arrest law actually worked, Chaney and Saltzstein surveyed the directors of police department research and planning units and analyzed documented case files. Their finding was that yes, officers in departments covered by the law did become, after its passage, more forceful in their actions. Arrest and apprehension of the perpetrator occurred 99 percent of the time if police arrived at the scene as the abuse was taking place. If it had occurred prior to their arrival, the arrest rate was 81 percent. Even when threats only had been made but no actual violence took place, a 40 percent arrest rate occurred. The authors conclude, "[P]olitical principals apparently can influence the behavior of bureaucratic agents through issuance of direct orders, even in a difficult-to-control setting dependent upon the actions of street-level bureaucrats."[45]

The results of studying principal-agent theory in the field of social work are described in the book *Working, Shirking and Sabotage,* by John Brehm and Scott Gates. Their title refers to three possible modes of conduct on the part of these street-level bureaucrats: actively and reliably pursuing the tasks assigned them ("working"), not doing so because they are lazy or dislike the tasks ("shirking"), and actively undermining the work assigned ("sabotage"). The last two courses of action are predicted by principal-agent theory. To test this possibility the authors examined federal employee surveys, other empirical studies, computer simulations and their own survey of social workers in Durham County, North Carolina. The outcome was that Brehm and Gates encountered little evidence to support shirking or sabotage. Social workers in Durham County take paperwork home at night, hardly a case of avoiding work. They do not commit sabotage by fudging reports or bending rules. Indeed they demonstrate commitment to the job, mindfulness of the rules governing their work, and dedication to their clients' welfare.

Brehm and Gates then go on to discuss why the congenital suspicion of subordinates at the heart of principal-agent theory is not necessary to governance. Pure self-interest faces two countermotivators. One is recognition of the larger objective importance of the work the bureaucrats are doing. The other is loyalty to a common work ethic shared with work colleagues. The authors thereby propose we should "turn the phraseology, if not the meaning, of principal-agent theories around: bureaucracy works in the United States because of 'principled agents.'"[46]

The profound significance of this small linguistic switch inspires me to make the observation that when one thinks about it, principal-agent theory and public administration are antithetical worldviews. The first orientation is based on the assumption that only self-interest drives human action; the second one recognizes that people are moved also by other-directed dedication to shared common purposes. To put it another way, the principal-agent perspective is dominated by suspicion of wrongdoing while the public administration perspective assumes a healthy amount of trust is essential.

Moreover, in taking on social tasks the two worldviews contemplate opposing forms of interaction. At its core, principal-agent theory is built on the elegant but simplistic notion of rational game playing between two unitary sides. Public administration, by contrast, recognizes that both principals and agents are made up of multiple actors in and of themselves, for example various legislative factions on one side and differing agency subunits on the other. This means that interaction between the two organizational realms involves bargaining and negotiation within each side and between the two sides, all at the same time. The consequence is far from elegant, but more compatible with the realities of democratic governance in a pluralistic society.

ARE BUREAUCRATS ACTUALLY PRINCIPLED?

We conclude this chapter on American bureaucrats by looking for evidence to see whether public servants actually *are* "principled."

Asking Them About Their Work. We start with a direct look at federal bureaucrats' own perceptions. The source is the same government-wide survey consulted by Brehm and Gates. Conducted by the US Office of Personnel Management, it was once called the Federal Human Capital Survey but is now known as the Federal Employee Viewpoint Survey. The instrument is administered online, and hence participation in it is anonymous and voluntary; several hundred thousand employees respond but a great many do not, meaning its results are noteworthy but not necessarily representative. The survey asks about eighty questions that cover many issues. Of primary interest to us are responses that shed light on personal work motivation and assessments of agencies and leaders. Table 3.7 summarizes the responses to eighteen questions from the 2013 survey.

With respect to motivation, we see that large majorities of respondents say they like the work they do, find it important, and derive satisfaction

TABLE 3.7	Perceptions Reflected in Federal Employee Viewpoint Survey of 2013 (in percent)		
Question	Agree	Disagree	Neither
Personal Motivation			
I like the work I do.	82.8	6.2	11.0
The work I do is important.	90.0	3.1	6.9
My work gives me a feeling of personal accomplishment.	70.3	14.6	15.1
My talents are used well in the workplace.	57.3	25.4	17.3
I am constantly looking for ways to do my job better.	90.4	1.8	7.8
When needed I am willing to put in the extra effort to get a job done.	95.6	1.5	2.8
Agency Assessment			
My agency is successful at accomplishing its mission.	74.4	17.6	8.0
Awards in my work unit depend on how well employees perform their jobs.	37.7	36.0	26.3
Arbitrary action, personal favoritism and coercion for partisan political purposes are not tolerated.	50.7	26.0	23.4
I have sufficient resources to get my job done.	43.8	39.5	16.7
I feel encouraged to come up with new and better ways of doing things.	55.7	25.2	19.2
I can disclose a suspected violation of any law, rule or regulation without fear of reprisal.	62.2	19.5	19.4
Leader Assessment			
I have a high level of respect for my organization's senior leaders.	52.3	23.9	23.8
Employees have a feeling of personal empowerment with respect to work processes.	42.9	31.1	26.0

(Continued)

(Continued)

Question	Agree	Disagree	Neither
In my organization, leaders generate high levels of motivation and commitment in the workforce.	40.8	33.0	26.2
In my work unit, steps are taken to deal with a poor performer who cannot or will not improve.	28.0	44.5	27.5
My organization's leaders maintain high standards of honesty and integrity.	53.6	22.8	24.5
My supervisor/team leader is committed to a workforce representative of all segments of society.	64.6	10.9	24.5

Source: US Office of Personnel Management, "Federal Employee Viewpoint Survey Results: Employees Influencing Change," government-wide results for 2013. Accessed November 19, 2013 at www.fedview.opm.gov.

Note: "agree" combines strongly agree and agree percentages, and "disagree" combines disagree and strongly disagree percentages. Survey items listed for Personal Motivation are questions number 4, 5, 7, 8, 11, and 13. Items for Agency Assessment are 3, 9, 17, 25, 37, and 39. Those for Leader Assessment are 23, 30, 45, 53, 54, and 61. Statistically weighted calculations are provided.

from doing it. The two behavior queries that assess motivation indirectly, looking for ways to do the job better and willingness to expend extra effort on it, are positive in the 90s range. These data strongly suggest that federal bureaucrats are substantially dedicated to work that is integral to agency's mission. The one item in this group that draws a more modest degree of agreement concerns making full use of the respondent's talents, apparently reflecting some restlessness on not having more of a chance to serve the cause.

The second group of questions assesses the agency itself. Nearly three-quarters agree with the proposition that it achieves its mission successfully. This response seems remarkable in that many government missions are never finished by their nature. Majority but weaker agreement is registered on the absence of favoritism or partisan coercion, the presence of encouraged innovation, and a fear-free climate for reporting illegality—in all cases a good sign. Two other questions in the group fall below majority agreement. The one on fairness of rewards suggests little enthusiasm for a performance approach to management. The response on sufficient resources is not surprising in this era of budget reduction.

Responses to the leader assessment group of questions are less reassuring. Only a bare majority indicates a high level of respect for senior leaders. The same is true for high standards of honesty and integrity on the part of leaders in general. Supervisors and team leaders come out looking better, although the question directed to them concerns commitment to diversity. Furthermore all leaders fail to garner much approval for making workers feel empowered, generating motivation and commitment, and—in particular—dealing with poor performers. The first two of these lesser assessments are indeed disappointing; the last-named may in part be the consequence of merit protections against dismissal.

To sum up, federal employees seem, on a personal basis, highly invested in the mission of their agencies. They definitely like their work, are willing to put extra effort into it, and look for better ways to do it. As for the organizational conditions and leaders they deal with in performing their work, respondents are accepting of their individual situations but not wildly pleased.

Public Service Motivation. The advantage of quantitative social science is that it can go beyond descriptive statistics like these and explore the possibilities of causation. A line of such research directly connected to the interests of this book is on Public Service Motivation, or PSM. In 1990 James Perry, the prime mover in this work, and his colleague Lois Wise developed a theory that postulates that bureaucrats more than private sector employees possess four attitudinal traits: (1) attraction to the possibility of shaping public policy; (2) commitment to ideals of public interest and civic duty; (3) being personally compassionate; and (4) being willing to sacrifice self-interest. They then advance three hypotheses to test PSM: (1) high-PSM individuals are especially attracted to working for government; (2) such individuals perform there with a high degree of motivation and commitment; and (3) organizations employing PSM-oriented persons will be less dependent on extrinsic incentives such as pay to motivate them.[47]

Perry later went on to formulate a 24-item survey scale to measure the four characteristics of PSM precisely so that further scholarship on the concept would be encouraged. Since 1990 more than 150 studies have been published that are anchored in the concept. Some researchers expanded and modified the original version of PSM. The nonprofit sector was added as a venue in which PSM would be expected to be present, a step Perry himself became involved in. Additional traits were put forward for inclusion, such as sensitivity to concerns of social justice, devotion to democratic processes, and commitment to the public service. Some scholars not only tested PSM as an independent causal variable but a resultant dependent one.

In 2010 Perry and colleagues reviewed the scholarly verdict of twenty years of research on PSM's initial three hypotheses. As for being attracted to policymaking, several studies did indeed establish positive correlations between PSM and a preference for working in government (and the nonprofit sector as well), especially on the part of young people. Also PSM has been linked to higher retention rates in organizations and lower turnover, although these relationships depend, too, on degree of job satisfaction. Other findings are less conclusive: effects on performance seem present from respondent self-reports but are not validated independently; and while it has been shown that financial rewards are less important to government workers than those of business, PSM's effect on this difference is unclear.[48]

I have selected from this large body of scholarship three studies to describe here. Danish scholars Lotte Bøgh Anderson and Søren Serritzlew conducted a study of the possible effects of PSM on the practice of physiotherapists in their country's system of national health care. Danish physical therapy divides patients into two categories, those who need only occasional help and the permanently disabled that receive long-term treatment. Continuing cases are considered less desirable because they are medically more demanding and call for more time-consuming visits. Although therapy providers are obliged to treat all comers, it is possible to influence the composition of intake by selectively lengthening wait times and advertising proactively for easier patients. After surveying the service providers for their degree of personal commitment to the concept of public interest, Anderson and Serritzlew examined the Health Insurance Register to see if high PSM therapists treated a significantly higher proportion of permanently disabled patients. This was found to be true, and moreover they did not cut corners with them or leave out any available forms of treatment.[49]

Randall Davis investigated whether PSM exists among unionized employees of two Midwestern cities. To find out whether union member-ship promotes PSM, he had first to identify members highly socialized into union values. This was done by noting who attended meetings and interacted with prounion colleagues. Davis had no idea how his study would turn out, because these men and women belong to a shared ben-efit association that lobbies for liberal public policy causes yet also nego-tiates hard with management for higher pay. The outcome was mixed: union socialization correlated positively with the value of public service and, to a lesser extent, with self-sacrifice; negatively to compassion; and had no significant relationship to policymaking.[50]

Finally, Leisha DeHart-Davis, whom we have already met more than once, joined Justin Marlowe and Sanjay Pandey to analyze PSM among women. Much feminist theory would predict that women should score high on compassion since that trait is seen as an essence of being female. However commitment to public service is contrary to the traditional image of women remaining in the home and not engaging the external world. As for attraction to policymaking, the competitive nature of that activity would seem to go against a female disposition for collaboration. The dimension of self-sacrifice was omitted from consideration. As it turned out, using national survey data on staff attitudes within pubic health and social survey agencies, DeHart-Davis and colleagues found that women respondents are 57 percent more likely than men to score high on compassion. Policymaking and public service possess the same high degree of attraction for both genders, an outcome that no doubt pleases many contemporary women.[51]

Agency Commitment. In PSM, analysis is at the level of the individual. Other academic research on bureaucratic motivation is at the level of the organization. In practice, of course, the two levels operate in tandem, and early writers on public administrative success conceded this point. For example, in Hal Rainey and Paula Steinbauer's classic theoretic pro-file of exceptionally well-performing government agencies they call "galloping elephants," such creatures are energized not merely by per-sonal altruism but also a "mission motivation" generated by shared belief in the institution's inherent purpose.[52]

To illustrate, Bradley Wright developed a concept of mission motivation based on goal theory. It is induced when a job is perceived as important because it contributes to an agency goal perceived of high value. Wright then goes on to argue that if the job task is clearly specified, attention is sharply focused and performance expectations are well understood. If the job is difficult, failure can cause demoralization but success can generate deeper satisfaction. Contributing personally and successfully to a well-defined, albeit difficult goal, Wright reasons, then leads to a sense of self-efficacy, which—when applied in behalf of a worthy mission—helps send the elephant off galloping. Wright tested his model with a large-N survey of employees of a major New York State agency, and he found that these joined elements accounted for two-thirds of variance in employee work motivation.[53]

In another model focusing on felt contribution, Craig Boardman and Eric Sundquist propose for consideration the concept of "perceived public service efficacy," or PPSE. They argue that if public employees are convinced their agency does in fact provide important benefits to citizens, they will be more committed to working for that agency. At the same time, this perception leads to greater personal satisfaction with the job they hold. These effects are then reinforced when agency loyalty and personal satisfaction combine to encourage members to define more concisely their personal role and hence identify more closely with the overall enterprise. Collectively, these factors cause workers to apply themselves diligently to their tasks and take pride in their work. When Boardman and Sundquist tested the model using national survey data on state public health and social service managers, all key relationships were statistically significant when holding the others constant, yielding for the model an R^2 of .442.[54]

It was mentioned above that interest has been aroused in whether PSM applies to nonprofit organizations. A chronic problem with nonprofits, especially small ones, is that they cannot pay their employees well or offer them a secure future. Hence they must depend even more on the inherent attraction of their cause to retain personnel. It is probably not an accident, then, that scholars of nonprofits use the term mission "attachment" when considering the organization's ability to "gallop."

A survey instrument has been developed for screening job applicants in this field. It asks four questions, each one of which addresses an attribute consciously sought in the hired worker: (1) Awareness: "I am well aware of the direction and mission of this organization"; (2) Support: "The programs and staff at my work unit support the mission of this organization"; (3) Agreement: "I like to work for this organization because I believe in its mission and values"; and (4) Alignment: "My work contributes to carrying out the mission of this organization."[55]

Empirical studies of nonprofits have shown, however, that even when levels of mission attachment so measured are high, staff retention problems are merely lessened and not solved because of relatively low pay and less job security. The brutal reality is that to motivate human beings properly, intrinsic rewards based on belief must be accompanied by adequate material rewards as well. This point should never be lost sight of in our field.

Deeper Institutional Study. Agency-based motivational forces are not always reducible to quantified variables. Institutions emerge organically and uniquely over time. To understand what goes on motivationally in each one we must, I believe, look deeper into individual cases.

What follow are summaries of the factors I found at work in the six agencies I covered in my book *Mission Mystique*. I see them as a kind of "reverse engineering" exercise whereby the task of predicting motivating factors is foregone and instead analysis is conducted that looks for what seem to be the shaping forces of what is clearly an established high degree of dedication.[56]

National Park Service (NPS) rangers regard themselves as guardians of natural and cultural resources that constitute treasures of the nation. Hence they feel a personal responsibility to keep them safe, even while making it possible for the broad public to visit and experience them. Many rangers initially become socialized to this attitude during childhood experiences when their parents took them camping. Over their careers, they share memorable and sometimes harsh experiences with fellow rangers around the country with whom they keep in touch the rest of their lives.

National Weather Service (NWS) forecasters are fascinated by the intricacies of the science of meteorology. Often introduced to the field by training in the military, they are nerdish "geeks" who are propelled in their jobs by fascination with the equipment and the challenge of predicting how the thin and fluid envelope of air and water that surrounds the earth's service will behave several days in advance. When a serious storm or flood approaches, all hands gather for lengthy shifts in the forecast operations room, forming a sense of comradeship not unlike that of soldiers at war.

Centers for Disease Control (CDC) research scientists and epidemiologists work at the confluence of two streams of aspiration: the medical doctor's desire to alleviate the effects of human suffering and the public health administrator's hope of achieving this goal on the grand scale of human populations. The most important entryway to this role is two years of service in the Epidemic Intelligence Service, a rotating group of young MDs who are sent at a moment's notice to the scene of disease breakouts anywhere in the world to diagnose what's going on and devise a response. Fellow EIS classmates frequently keep in touch for the balance of their careers.

Protective social workers of the Mecklenburg County Department of Social Services (DSS) are motivated not by heady abstractions, but by the immediate need for quick intervention and help in response to frantic calls from persons who experience or observe domestic abuse. These workers are on standby at all times of the day and night to rush alone anywhere in the city, including to low-income neighborhoods. The work is dangerous; and each instance is different and must be approached with great skill and care, with a readiness to take precisely the right steps on the spot.

Troopers of the Virginia State Police are attracted to their dangerous profession by a desire to be a part of the most respected law enforcement agency in the state and region. They apply in the hundreds for a few available positions despite a starting annual salary of only $32,200 and an arduous training cycle of 44 months. A paramilitary organization, the agency issues badges, assigns ranks, flies an institutional flag, and has its own museum and a portrait gallery of the fallen. In addition to the name of the agency, the initials VSP stand for Valor, Service, and Pride. Off-duty social occasions reinforce personal and organizational ties.

Peace Corps volunteers and professional staff have no match in US public administration. Despite civil service regulations, all are employed temporarily. Volunteers are limited to two years and staff to five, occasionally renewable after an absence. Volunteer motivation springs from an opportunity for unforgettable overseas adventure coupled with the task of developing a mentality whereby they can help needy and culturally different people help themselves. As for members of the staff, who are often former volunteers, they abandon the role of innocents abroad in order to strengthen the institution during their five years.

What generalizations, if any, can be made about motivation within these six diverse institutions? While in all of them both individual and corporate dedication is strong, different kinds of source are discernable. In some, the appeal of broad social causes is evident, as with preserving national parks and enhancing the public's health. In other instances, the drawing card is a chance to serve other human beings on a person-to-person basis, found in protective social workers and Peace Corps volunteers. Still another source of inducement is an opportunity for personal vocational fulfillment, the operant influence for weather forecasters and state troopers.

As for other patterns, the Park Service and State Police possess aspects of what sociologists call "total" organizations. In big Western parks, rangers live in clustered, agency-provided housing; and Virginia state troopers are provided all clothing and tools for the job, including a highly symbolic weapon and new police cruiser. Socialization processes vary as well. The VSP, CDC, and Peace Corps utilize formal entry socialization processes: that is, police academy training, the EIS experience, and three months of in-country acculturation and language training respectively. The NPS and NWS rely on preservice orientation experiences, topped off by in-service training at centralized facilities. DSS is special in that the director personally conducted all socialization exercises.

In all instances I observed that organizational members seemed to bond well with each other, although ties at the VSP, NWS, and NPS are reinforced by the closely interactive nature of the work itself. Bonding among CDC scientists and DSS social workers is based on specialized professional interests and hence not as agency wide. What brings Peace Corps volunteers together is facing unprecedented situations and looking back on unforgettable experiences. A commonality that seems universal to all six agencies is the feeling that the cause has a moral dimension, whether in fighting evil or battling for the good. The evils are dangerous weather, epidemics, and domestic abuse. The goods are educating Americans about their natural and cultural treasures, keeping the highways as safe as possible, and advancing world peace and understanding.

PASSING IN REVIEW

This chapter began by metaphorically ordering American bureaucrats front and center for special scrutiny. It ends with another military ritual, the passing in review, whereby the reassembled formation marches past those in command, leaving evaluative impressions behind. Three stand out.

First, a cultural revolution has swept through American bureaucracy. The days of white male predominance within its exclusive executive and professional strata have come to a close. In recent decades the proportions of minorities and women have grown significantly throughout the public service at all three levels of government. The task of equalizing the demographics of bureaucracy is not over, however. For the most part, minorities and women do not yet occupy positions of power in equal degree. This is a most important goal in that it is the only way agencies can incorporate into their constructions of social reality the full range of values held within our society.

Second, critics have overblown the faults and misdeeds of our bureaucrats. By no means are all government employees big-spending liberals who eagerly vote for left-leaning candidates. Red tape as a bureaucratic disease is not as common as we think. More rules are needed in government than business because of the extra scrutiny bureaucrats receive. Yet bureaucrats who work with clients also exercise discretion as well as just follow rules, and do so the more they gain work experience. Evidence shows that these men and women are not imperious or more authority oriented than other people, but are just as thoughtful and creative as the rest of us. For the most part, they carry out the law as well as they can and follow legitimate political instructions. An extra bonus for citizens is that those who serve them are better educated than their private sector counterparts.

Third, government workers deserve more than being exonerated from nonexistent sins. They deserve also being recognized for the extent to which they embody principles essential to effective governance. One principle is being dedicated in their work to a major public policy goal enshrined in law. It is enunciated in the mission assigned to the agency for which they work, and it becomes the touchstone for their actions. A second principle is a willingness to serve others, by which I mean the interests of the broader public. Bureaucrats are of course human beings with selfish needs, but they have chosen to spend years of their life in public service at modest pay rather than try to get rich. A final principle is that they are willing to make a personal commitment to that career. They become loyal to their agency and its purpose. They like being charged with individual responsibility to perform their duty, and they derive satisfaction when able to do so.

ENDNOTES

1. Factoid data from the *Statistical Abstract of the United States*, 2012 at the following pages: government level employment, 267; work domains, 300; age and tenure of bureaucrats, 300; race percentages, 9, 301, 327; male-female ratios, 301, 327; veteran employment, 327; union membership, 429. Tax delinquency figures are from the *Washington Post*, March 24, 2002.
2. Eric Yoder, "Panel: Federal Workers' Salary Gap Grows," *Washington Post*, October 20, 2012.
3. Congressional Budget Office, "Comparing the Compensation of Federal and Private-Sector Employees," January 2010, retrieved online July 26, 2012.
4. Frank Mauro, "Are Public Employees Overpaid?" *Public Administration Review* 72, no. 5 (September–October 2012): 637.
5. Keith A. Bender and John S. Heywood, "Out of Balance? Comparing Public and Private Sector Compensation over 20 Years," report of the Center for State & Local Government Excellence and National Institute on Retirement Security, April 2010, p. 7.
6. *Statistical Abstract*, 2012, pp. 10, 301, 327.
7. *Statistical Abstract*, 1978, pp. 283, 320.
8. Vernon Greene and Sally Coleman Selden, "Measuring Power and Presence: Bureaucratic Representation in the American States," *Journal of Public Administration Research and Theory* 11, no. 3 (July 2001): 379–402.

9. Ed O'Keefe, "Study: Percentage of Minority Federal Workers Up Slightly," *Washington Post*, June 14, 2011. Joe Davidson, Federal Worker column, *Washington Post*, August 9, 2012. The reference to more top positions for Hispanics refers to membership in the Senior Executive Service.

10. J. Donald Kingsley, *Representative Bureaucracy: An Interpretation of the British Civil Service* (Yellow Springs, OH: Antioch Press, 1944). Quote taken from *Representative Bureaucracy: Classic Readings and Continuing Controversies*, Julie Dolan and David H. Rosenbloom, eds. (Armonk, NY: M.E. Sharpe, 2003), p. 18.

11. Norton E. Long, "Bureaucracy and Constitutionalism," *American Political Science Review* 46, no. 3 (September 1952): 814.

12. Jessica E. Sowa and Sally Coleman Selden, "Administrative Discretion and Active Representation: An Expansion of the Theory of Representative Bureaucracy," *Public Administration Review* 63, no. 6 (November/December 2003): 701.

13. Sally Coleman Selden, *The Promise of Representative Bureaucracy: Diversity and Responsiveness in a Government Agency* (Armonk, NY: M.E. Sharpe, 1997).

14. Sylvester Murray, Larry D. Terry, Charles A. Washington, and Lawrence F. Keller, "The Role Demands and Dilemmas of Minority Public Administrators: The Herbert Thesis Revisited," *Public Administration Review* 54, no. 5 (September/October 1994): 409–417.

15. Kenneth J. Meier and Kevin B. Smith, "Representative Democracy and Representative Bureaucracy: Examining the Top-Down and Bottom-Up Linkages," *Social Science Quarterly* 75, no. 4 (December 1994): 790–803.

16. Vicky M. Wilkins and Brian N. Williams, "Black or Blue: Racial Profiling and Representative Bureaucracy," *Public Administration Review* 68, no. 4 (July/August 2008): 654–664.

17. *Statistical Abstract*, 2012, p. 10, 377.

18. *Statistical Abstract*, 2012, pp. 301, 327, 377.

19. *Statistical Abstract*, 1962, p. 406; 1970, p. 395; 1978, pp. 278, 320; 1982–1983, p. 268; 1991, pp. 306, 330; 2001, p. 295; 2002, pp. 297, 321; 2012, pp. 301, 327.

20. *Statistical Abstract*, 2012, p. 399.

21. Stephen Losey, "Women Make Progress in the Federal Workplace," *Federal Times*, May 24, 2011. Jitinder Kahli, John Gans, and James Hairston, "A Better, More Diverse Senior Executive Service in 2050," report of Center for American Progress, September 2011.

22. Joe Davidson, "EEOC Chides Government For Not Reflecting 'Tapestry of America,'" *Washington Post*, August 10, 2010. EEOC Diversity Task Force of Federally Employed Women, "Barriers to Women Working in the Federal Government," accessed online August 23, 2012.

23. *Statistical Abstract*, 2012, p. 301.

24. Cynthia J. Bowling, Christine A. Kelleher, Jennifer Jones, and Deil S. Wright, "Cracked Ceilings, Firmer Floors, and Weakening Walls: Trends and Patterns in Gender Representation Among Executives Leading American State Agencies, 1970–2000," *Public Administration Review* 66, no. 6 (November–December 2006): 823–836.

25. Amy E. Smith and Karen R. Monaghan, "Some Ceilings Have More Cracks: Representative Bureaucracy in Federal Regulatory Agencies," *American Review of Public Administration* 43, no. 1 (January 2013): 50–71.

26. See, for example, Kathy E. Ferguson, *The Feminist Case Against Bureaucracy* (Philadelphia: Temple University Press, 1984); J. Acker, "Hierarchies, Jobs, Bodies: A Theory of Gendered Organization," *Gender & Society* 4 (1990): 139–158; and Georgia Duerst-Lahti and Rita Mae Kelly, *Gender Power, Leadership, and Governance* (Ann Arbor: University of Michigan Press, 1995).

27. Leisha DeHart-Davis, "Can Bureaucracy Benefit Organizational Women? An Exploratory Study," *Administration & Society* 41, no. 3 (May 2009): 340–363.

28. Shannon Portillo and Leisha DeHart-Davis, "Gender and Organizational Rule Abidance," *Public Administration Review* 69, no. 2 (March–April 2009): 339–347.

29. Shannon Portillo, "The Paradox of Rules: Rules as Resources and Constraints," *Administration & Society* 44, no. 1 (January 2012): 87–108.

30. Judith R. Saidel and Karyn Loscocco, "Agency Leaders, Gendered Institutions, and Representative Bureaucracy," *Public Administration Review* 65, no. 2 (March–April 2005): 158–170.

31. Vicky M. Wilkins, "Exploring the Causal Story: Gender, Active Representation, and Bureaucratic Priorities," *Journal of Public Administration Research and Theory*, 17, no. 1 (January 2007): 77–94.

32. Kenneth J. Meier and Jill Nicholson-Crotty, "Gender, Representative Bureaucracy, and Law Enforcement: The Case of Sexual Assault," *Public Administration Review* 66, no. 6 (November–December 2006): 850–860.

33. James C. Garand, Catherine T. Parkhurst, and Rusanne Jourdan Seoud, "Bureaucrats, Policy Attitudes, and Political Behavior: Extension of the

Bureau Voting Model of Government Growth," *Journal of Public Administration Research and Theory* 1, no. 2 (April 1991): 177–212, 195.

34. Gregory B. Lewis, "In Search of the Machiavellian Milquetoasts: Comparing Attitudes of Bureaucrats and Ordinary People," *Public Administration Review* 50, no. 2 (March–April 1990): 220–227.

35. David M. Konisky, "Bureaucratic and Public Attitudes Toward Environment Regulation and the Economy," *State and Local Government Review* 40, no. 3 (2008): 139–149.

36. Jason L. Jensen, Paul E. Sum, and David T. Flynn, "Political Orientations and Behavior of Public Employees: A Cross-National Comparison," *Journal of Public Administration Research and Theory* 19 (2009): 709–730.

37. Barry Bozeman, *Bureaucracy and Red Tape* (Upper Saddle River, NJ: Prentice-Hall, 2000). See also Bozeman and Mary K. Feeney, *Rules and Red Tape: A Prism for Public Administration Theory and Research* (Armonk, NY: M.E. Sharpe, 2011).

38. John L. Foster, "Bureaucratic Rigidity Revisited," *Social Science Quarterly* 71 (June 1990): 223–238.

39. Charles T. Goodsell, "Looking Once Again at Human Service Bureaucracy," *Journal of Politics* 43, no. 3 (August 1981): 763–778.

40. Zachary W. Oberfield, "Rule Following and Discretion at Government's Front Lines: Continuity and Change during Organization Socialization," *Journal of Public Administration Research and Theory* 20, no. 4 (October 2010): 735–755.

41. Leisha DeHart-Davis, "Green Tape: A Theory of Effective Organizational Rules," *Journal of Public Administration Research and Theory* 19, no. 2 (2009): 361–384. See also "Green Tape and Employee Rule Abidance: Why Organizational Rule Attributes Matter," *Public Administration Review* 69, no. 5 (September–October 2009): 901–910.

42. Ralph P. Hummel, *The Bureaucratic Experience: The Post-Modern Challenge*, 5th ed. (Armonk, NY: M.E. Sharpe, 2008), chs. 4 and 6.

43. Melvin L. Kohn, "Bureaucratic Man: A Portrait and an Interpretation," *American Sociological Review:* 36 (June 1971): 461–474.

44. Claire Mostel, "Finding the Heart and Soul of Bureaucrats: A Practitioner Talks Back," *Public Administration Review* 69, no. 3 (May–June 2009): 544–547, quotes at 544, 546.

45. Carole Kennedy Chaney and Grace Hall Saltzstein, "Democratic Control and Bureaucratic Responsiveness: The Police and Domestic Violence," *American Journal of Political Science* 42, no. 3 (July 1998): 745–768, 763.

46. John Brehm and Scott Gates, *Working, Shirking and Sabotage: Bureaucratic Response to a Democratic Public* (Ann Arbor: University of Michigan Press, 1997), quote at p. 202.

47. James L. Perry and Lois Recascino Wise, "The Motivational Bases of Public Service," *Public Administration Review* 50, no. 3 (May–June 1990): 367–373.

48. James L. Perry, Annie Hondeghem, and Lois Recascino Wise, "Revisiting the Motivational Bases of Public Service: Twenty Years of Research and an Agenda for the Future," *Public Administration Review* 70, no. 5 (September–October 2010): 681–690.

49. Lotte Bøgh Anderson and Søren Serritzlew, "Does Public Service Motivation Affect the Behavior of Professionals?" *International Journal of Public Administration* 35, no. 1 (January 2012): 19–29.

50. Randall S. Davis, "Blue-Collar Public Servants: How Union Membership Influences Public Service Motivation," *American Review of Public Administration* 41, no. 6 (November 2011): 705–723.

51. Leisha DeHart-Davis, Justin Marlowe, and Sanjay K. Pandey, "Gender Dimensions of Public Service Motivation," *Public Administration Review* 66, no. 6 (November–December 2006): 873–887.

52. Hal G. Rainey and Paula Steinbauer, "Galloping Elephants: Developing Elements of a Theory of Effective Government Organizations," *Journal of Public Administration Research and Theory* 9, no. 1 (January 1999): 1–32, 25–26.

53. Bradley E. Wright," Public Service and Motivation: Does Mission Matter?" *Public Administration Review* 67, no. 1 (January–February 2007): 54–64.

54. Craig Boardman and Eric Sundquist, "Toward Understanding Work Motivation: Worker Attitudes and the Perception of Effective Public Service," *American Review of Public Administration* 39, no. 5 (September 2009): 519–535.

55. William A. Brown and Carlton F. Yoshioka, "Mission Attachment and Satisfaction as Factors in Employee Retention," *Nonprofit Management & Leadership* 14, no. 1 (Fall 2003): 5–18, 10. Seok Eun Kim and Jung Wook Lee, "Is Mission Attachment an Effective Management Tool for Employee Retention?" *Review of Public Personnel Administration* 27, no. 3 (September 2007): 227–248. 244. I have taken the liberty of labeling the second component "support" instead of "awareness."

56. Goodsell, *Mission Mystique: Belief Systems in Public Agencies* (Washington, DC: CQ Press, 2011), chs. 2–7.

4

INSIDE BUREAUCRATIC GOVERNANCE

The phrase "bureaucratic governance" is almost never used. If you Google it, references come up on authoritarian organizations. Hence in common usage this terminology points to ominous implications for public administration.

In my own perverse way, however, I take a different view. I find the words not alarming but rather a stimulating verbal doorway through which to pass as we engage the topic of this chapter. It is, no less, the *power* of bureaucracy. What power do bureaucracies possess? What do they do with it? What forces, if any, check it? To what extent is it monopolized or shared? After thinking about these matters, you can decide for yourself whether bureaucratic governance is indeed dangerous—or possibly essential.

BUREAUCRATIC GOVERNANCE DEFINED

The root meaning of "governance" is to steer or pilot. In popular discourse this control is primarily thought of as exercised by elected officials; but as we know, the biggest part of government in both people and budgets is administration.

I recall vividly when I first appreciated this fact. It was when, as a sophomore in college, I accidentally picked up a little book called *Big Democracy*, by Paul Appleby. As a top administrative official in the US Department of Agriculture for many years, Appleby commented on what we call bureaucracy this way: "The organized government comprehends in some way, it impinges upon and is affected by, practically everything that exists or moves in our society." As a consequence, "big democracy is different from little democracy. The difference is the difference between the simple and the complex."[1]

All too often we oversimplify this complexity by means of what is called in public administration classrooms the politics-administration dichotomy. This is the notion that governance policies are made by elected officials and that administration's role is merely their implementation. While a measure of truth lies in this formulation, it can lead us to overlook the combined effects of thousands if not millions of discretionary decisions made every day by public administrators all across the country at all levels of government.

In an effort to counteract the misconceptions generated by the politics-administration dichotomy, I have suggested elsewhere that a conceptual antidote is to rotate the dichotomy's cross section 90 degrees. What this exposes is what I call a distinction between "Rule" and "Response." Both of these functions of governance are carried out in administration as well as politics. Rule refers to all actions of initiation, direction, guidance, and rulemaking that take place in the public sector, no matter what the level of authority. Response denotes all actions of questioning, disputing, countering, and replacement that arise in opposition to Rule, both from inside the government and from the external society. While the most visible confrontations between Rule and Response take place in legislatures and the public media, numerically the vast majority of acts by which Rule and Response *are resolved* occur in the responsible bureaucracies.[2]

In addition to discussing in this chapter bureaucracy's Rule and Response roles, we would be amiss in not giving considerable attention to these functions when devolved upon and transferred to nongovernmental third parties. United States public administration has long been known for this dispersed feature, and in some ways it is becoming more pronounced as time goes by. It includes contracting out tasks, collaboration and joint action, and the engagement of citizens in administration.

GOVERNANCE AS RULE

Bureaucracy's "Legislation." We begin our inquiry into the Rule aspect of bureaucratic governance by examining it from the standpoint of its literal rulemaking powers. The *U.S. Code of Federal Regulations* or CFR is a series of books published by the Government Printing Office in

Washington that is so voluminous it occupies 9 linear yards of shelf space. In it are thousands of pages of rules that have been adopted by federal agencies. They are promulgated under authority of statute and take on the full power of law. Thus the CFR may be thought of as a compilation of the federal bureaucracy's "legislation," so to speak. Most state governments publish equivalent administrative codes.[3]

Box 4.1 lists the fifty topics—or "titles"—covered in the body of federal administrative legislation. Depending on the material, titles are subdivided by subtitle, chapter, subchapter, part, subpart, and section. In citations of rules, the custom is that the secondary unit of identification is part; hence "15 CFR 241" refers to Title 15, Part 241. Each title requires at least one volume and often several. Around 4,500 rules are published each year, roughly a third of which are of substantive importance. The only CFR volume not produced by the bureaucracy proper is title No. 3, issued by the Executive Office of the President. The biggest titles in terms of number of volumes are Nos. 4 (24 volumes), 7 (15), 12 (9), 26 (18), 40 (31), 46 (9), 48 (7), 49 (9), and 50 (10). Title 35 is vacant to be available for future use.

BOX 4.1	Numbered Titles in the Code of Federal Regulations

1. General Provisions	13. Business Credit and Assistance
2. Grants and Agreements	14. Aeronautics and Space
3. President	15. Commerce and Foreign Trade
4. Accounts	16. Commercial Practices
5. Administrative Personnel	17. Commodity and Security
6. Domestic Security	18. Conservation of Power
7. Agriculture	19. Customs Duties
8. Aliens and Nationality	20. Employees' Benefits
9. Animals and Animal Products	21. Food and Drugs
10. Energy	22. Foreign Relations
11. Federal Elections	23. Highways
12. Banks and Banking	24. Housing and Urban Development

(Continued)

(Continued)

25. Indians	38. Pensions, Bonuses, and Veterans' Relief
26. Internal Revenue	39. Postal Service
27. Alcohol, Tobacco Products and Firearms	40. Protection of Environment
28. Judicial Administration	41. Public Contracts and Property Management
29. Labor	42. Public Health Exchanges
30. Mineral Resources	43. Public Lands: Interior and Water Resources
31. Money and Finance: Treasury	44. Emergency Management and Assistance
32. National Defense	45. Public Welfare
33. Navigation and Navigable Waters	46. Shipping
34. Education	47. Telecommunications
35. Reserved	48. Federal Acquisition Regulation System
36. Parks, Forests, and Public Property	49. Transportation
37. Patents, Trademarks, and Copyrights	50. Wildlife and Fisheries

Source: United States Code of Federal Regulations (Washington, DC: Government Printing Office, 2011 [nos. 42–50], 2012 [nos. 1–41]).

Much rulemaking deals with the finest conceivable details of program administration. A Department of Agriculture rule, for example, defines Georgia's Vidalia onions as any variety of *allium cepa* of the hybrid yellow granex or similar variety (7 CFR 955.5). A Department of Commerce rule says "barrels" (for measurement purposes) of fruits, vegetables, and other dry commodities must have the capacity of 3.281 bushels, 105 quarts, or 7,056 cubic inches (15 CFR 241.1). In the interests of sea turtle preservation, the National Oceanic and Atmospheric Administration requires that comatose specimens taken unintentionally while fishing be resuscitated by elevating their hindquarters at least 6 inches and rocking them gently for 4–24 hours (15 CFR 223–226).

The triviality of these examples may give the impression that the CFR is a giant rule monster disgorging countless absurd bureaucratic demands. Yet, as with other instruments of law in a civilized society, thoughtfully drawn and thoroughly clear administrative rules are essential to meeting major public goals in a competent and fair manner. In highly complex subject matter areas where elected officials are loathe or unable to write such rules, bureaucracies have to do the job.

And, in many instances, this task is absolutely crucial. An example is rules issued in behalf of environmental protection. To realize this, we need only mention how the city of Beijing is beset by such bad air pollution that facemasks must be worn outside and the very old and very young need remain indoors. With the city's level of fine particulates exceeding 700 micrograms per cubic meter, sunlight is largely blocked out and one cannot see any distance. Obviously, China's bureaucracy has been unable to produce and enforce adequate rules on air quality.[4]

Actually it took a long time for America to recognize the full extent of the problem. For years Los Angeles suffered from terrible smog, and drinking water was poisoned by mercury and lead. Only Rachel Carson's *Silent Spring* and the discovery that Love Canal was a burial ground for toxic chemicals began to wake us up. Beginning in the 1950s and continuing through the 1970s, Congress enacted several environmental laws and created an Environmental Protection Agency that has been effectively proactive in many, but not all, presidencies since. This is why we have 31 volumes in Title 40 of the CFR.

Their effects on America's air quality are visible in Table 4.1. All of the measures shown are declining and are within established standards. The level

TABLE 4.1	National Ambient Air Pollution Concentrations, 2003–2009				
Type of Pollutant	Air Quality Standard	2003	2005	2007	2009
Carbon monoxide	9.0	2.7	2.3	2.0	1.8
Ozone	.075	.080	.079	.077	.069
Sulfur dioxide	.0300	.0043	.0041	.0035	.0027
Fine particulates	35.0	31.1	33.6	31.3	24.9
Nitrogen dioxide	.053	.014	.013	.012	.011
Lead	.15	.16	.15	.15	.11

Source: *Statistical Abstract of the United States*, 2012, p. 229.

Note: Fine particulates are daily average. Units are parts per million except for particulates and lead, which are micrograms per cubic meter.

of fine particulates is a small fraction of that in Beijing. Emissions of all green-house gases (not shown in the table) dropped over 500 million metric tons between 2005 and 2009.[5] The rule text of three of the standards that enabled achievement of this degree of air pollution progress is shown in Box 4.2.

BOX 4.2	Texts of Three National Air Quality Standards Set by the Environmental Protection Agency Pursuant to the Clean Air Act

Sec. 50.8 National Primary Ambient Air Quality Standards for Carbon Monoxide

(a) The national primary ambient air quality standards for carbon monoxide are:

  (1) 9 parts per million (10 milligrams per cubic meter) for an 8-hour aver-age concentration not to be exceeded more than once per year and

  (2) 35 parts per million (40 milligrams per cubic meter) for a 1-hour average concentration not to be exceeded more than once per year.

Sec. 50.4. National Primary Ambient Air Quality Standards for Sulfur Oxides (Sulfur Dioxide)

(a) The level of the annual standard is 0.030 parts per million (ppm), not to be exceeded in a calendar year. The annual arithmetic mean shall be rounded to three decimal places (fractional parts equal to or greater than 0.0005 ppm shall be rounded up).

(b) The level of the 24-hour standard is 0.14 parts per million (ppm), not to be exceeded more than once per calendar year. The 24-hour averages shall be determined from successive non-overlapping 24-hour blocks starting at midnight each calendar day and shall be rounded to two decimal places (fractional parts equal to or greater than 0.005 ppm shall be rounded up).

Sec. 50.11. National Primary and Secondary Ambient Air Quality Standards for Oxides of Nitrogen (with Nitrogen Dioxide as the Indicator)

(a) The level of the national primary annual ambient air quality standard for oxides of nitrogen is 53 parts per billion (ppb, which is 1 part in

1,000,000,000), annual average concentration, measured in the ambient air as nitrogen dioxide.

(b) The level of the national primary 1-hour ambient air quality standard for oxides of nitrogen is 100 ppb, 1-hour average concentration, measured in the ambient air as nitrogen dioxide.

(c) The level of the national secondary ambient air quality standard for nitrogen dioxide is 0.053 parts per million (100 micrograms per cubic meter), annual arithmetic mean concentration.

Source: Code of Federal Regulations, Title 40, Protection of Environment, Parts 50–51 (pp. 7–9), revised as of July 1, 2012.

The Process of Rulemaking. We turn now to how these rules of administrative law are enacted. The book *Regulation and Public Interest*, by University of Michigan law professor Steven Croley, is informative. His thesis is that the intricately legalized character of agency rulemaking helps make it lead to "public-interested" outcomes more often than does the legislative process in Congress.[6]

The nature and requirements of rulemaking are stipulated in the Administrative Procedure Act (APA) of 1946, the "constitution" of US administrative law. Assuming that a statute has already been passed by Congress that authorizes rulemaking in a given area, the following five steps take place. (1) The agency's staff studies a pertinent problem closely over a period of time and drafts a tentative rule on the matter. (2) The draft rule is made available to the public by being published in a government periodical known as the *Federal Register*. (3) Comments from all interested parties are invited on the draft and when received are examined by staff for usefulness in improving the draft. Sometimes these run in the thousands. (4) Thirty days before the completed rule takes effect, a "concise general statement" is published by the agency that explains why the rule's text has taken a modified form, if this is the case. If, as a result, new information or compelling new objections then come to the agency's attention, repeated iterations of the process are ordered. (5) The final version of the rule is submitted to the Office of Information and Regulatory Policy, a unit of the Office of Management and Budget in the Executive Office of the President. If approved, it is published as part of the next update of the appropriate title in the CFR.

Croley points out that these procedures lessen greatly the possibility that special interests are able to influence the outcome by means of informal lobbying activity, as happens in Congress and state legislatures. This was one of the prime purposes for enacting the APA in 1946 in the first place. Success has been met in many respects, says Croley. With published records and hearings open to all parties, proceedings are transparent and secret deals or the exercise of backdoor influence are difficult to consummate. All interested parties must be heard on an equal basis, and all proposals for change must be given impartial consideration. The very explicitness of APA rules is such that parties angered by their final content will look for minor procedural violations as a basis for challenging a rule in court. Both politically appointed regulators and professional administrative law judges are careful to watch for any irregularity that could be construed as violating the principles of due process and equal protection of the laws.

A second advantage of administrative rulemaking seen by Croley is that the substantive quality and timeliness of decisions can be superior to that produced by legislatures. The currency of influence in affecting these outcomes is not political power, private contacts, or campaign contributions, but information—relevant, accurate, and verifiable data that enhance understanding of the problem. Formally submitted evidence comprises "the facts" on which decisions must be based. All feasible alternative ideas and approaches to follow are sought and considered. Public hearings are not choreographed to support a point of view as happens in Congress, but to give all interested parties an equal chance to testify in a way that reflects their position. Another advantage is that because of the APA's strict time deadlines, the rulemaking process cannot be inordinately delayed. At the same time, the fact that the procedural cycle can be repeated an indefinite number of times before closure means it is unnecessary to act hastily but instead wait until the best possible language is worked out.

Croley contends that this kind of open, fair, and informed process of governance by an independent and relatively autonomous authority has contributed significantly to elevating much American public policy to higher levels of public interest attainment than would otherwise be the case. He describes in detail several cases in point. In 1995 the Federal Trade Commission promulgated the Telemarketing Sales Rule, which limited the use of automatic telephone dialers for commercial calls and required sellers to identify themselves. In 2003 the agency amended the rule to establish a "Do Not Call" registry that became immensely popular. In 1996 the Food and Drug Administration, despite outcries of opposition from the tobacco industry, brazenly asserted jurisdiction over cigarette advertising, sales, and distribution by citing the "drugs" and "devices" authority mentioned in the Food, Drug and Cosmetic Act. Although in 2000 the US Supreme Court denied this claim by a 5–4 decision, the effort became a pivotal point for reduction of cigarette smoking in this country.

An example of where the rulemaking process involved particularly exhaustive negotiations is the "roadless rule" that applies to forest management by the Forest Service. In the face of immense opposition from Western timber and mining interests, it banned all but primitive and temporary roads in approximately a third of national forest land. To reach this outcome, endless meetings were held with groups of all kinds; detailed studies were conducted of effects on flooding, landslides, stream sedimentation, and wildlife; a reoriented forest transportation inventory and plan was developed; and a formal Environmental Impact Statement was prepared and submitted. Although lengthy court litigation took place and successive presidents both supported and opposed it, the rule finally went into effect with broad public support.

The Craft of Problem Solving. Another inside look at bureaucracy's Rule function, offered by Malcolm Sparrow, reminds us that bureaucracy's directive activity is not confined to policymaking but also infuses policy implementation. A former British police officer turned public management consultant, Sparrow wrote *The Regulatory Craft* to emphasize that managers cannot be content to think of administrative operations as running themselves. They need always to be ready to intervene when concrete, unplanned barriers to program success arise and proceed to attack them pointedly and proactively.[7]

Sparrow urges that a specific strategy of six stages be followed in such problem solving. He illustrates its use by a number of actual cases, and I draw on one of them to aid in their depiction. The problem at hand arose when the Boston police department was, in the early 1990s, suddenly confronted by a surge of child and teen homicides. Sparrow's first stage is to confirm for sure that the problem is unusual rather than frequent or typical, for to address it requires taking the major step of going outside the normal organizational hierarchy to form a cross-departmental study team. Moreover the team must be given free rein to explore possibilities and experiment with solutions. The Boston chief of police signed off to this degree of independence, provided he would receive a briefing on the outcome.

Second, care must be taken to define the problem precisely. In this instance the team established how frequently the murders were occurring, how they compared with historical crime statistics, and where in the city the outbreaks were most serious. After analyzing these data, the team concluded that the problem came from the activities of particular named gangs that operated in specific neighborhoods.

The third stage is to consider, through team brainstorming, possible interventions. Bringing in outside experts for this purpose is possible. When weighing options the team takes a fourth step, which is to isolate benchmarks by which success or failure could be established. The team decided to track localized crime rates but also to conduct interviews with individual gang members. A fifth stage is to work out the tactical details of how to carry out the chosen course of action, making sure to think creatively "outside the box" as well as consider standard police procedures.

In implementing the plan for stage five, the team initiated a project named Operation Ceasefire. Its essence was to launch an all-out law enforcement assault on the gang that seemed responsible for the next identified wave of killing. When one did in fact break out, every effort was made to conduct a swift investigation and move as fast as possible with arrests, trials, convictions, and sentencing. It turned out that after a few weeks, another spike of homicides occurred in a different neighborhood. The team then arranged for a similar, swift, all-out law enforcement hit. Much to the team's satisfaction, after this second assault the level of neighborhood murders dropped way down. Interviews within the gang community indicated that two successive enforcement "surges" had convinced the youth that bloody wars with rivals had become too costly. Sparrow's sixth stage was reached when the team determined that the crime wave had actually stopped. It then briefed the mayor on what they had done, filed an extensive report on Operation Ceasefire for future possible use, and declared itself dissolved.

GOVERNANCE AS RESPONSE

The Response side of bureaucratic governance refers to ways in which bureaus react to direction from the three branches of government and to signals from the electorate and elsewhere. Agencies must be ready to absorb new information, stop doing something if unnecessary, adjust policies in view of changed circumstances, or even take on new tasks when necessary. At this point I discuss administrative responses to other components of the governmental system; responses to voices outside government are treated later.

The legal setting for Response within government is America's constitutional separation of powers. In this ingenious arrangement, the three branches check each other by exercising authority that intervenes in the others' realm, illustrated by legislative confirmation of executive appointments, executive veto of legislative bills, and judicial review of the actions of both political branches. While most bureaucracies serve under the ultimate direction of the elected chief executive—whether president, governor, or mayor—they are authorized, funded, and overseen by the elected legislative bodies and subject to judicial scrutiny and appeal in all they do. Hence bureaucracy is not a "fourth branch of government" as sometimes touted, but a set of institutions that is responsible in different ways to all three constitutional branches.

Two Governing Perspectives. Within this setting of separation of powers, two distinct viewpoints on bureaucracy's status are found among scholars in political science and public administration. One respects the importance of administrative discretion and the other does not. This difference is famously reflected in a "debate"—actually a published and not oral exchange—between two leading scholars that occurred more than seventy years ago.

On one side is Carl J. Friedrich, long-time professor of government at Harvard known for his much-quoted assertion that bureaucracy is "the core of modern government." In an article titled "Public Policy and the Nature of Administrative Responsibility" appearing in the first issue of *Public Policy* in 1940, Friedrich argued that because of the inevitable complexity of administrative problems and the continuously changing conditions surrounding them, it is impossible for administrators to receive prior instructions for everything they do. As a consequence, to be responsible for outcomes means acting frequently on their own, utilizing all available knowledge that can be acquired through specialized expertise, while at the same time giving proper regard to existing community preferences. The way to assure fulfillment of such responsibility is that the highest values of public service must be nurtured among civil servants, namely integrity, impartiality, and prudent consideration of all interests.[8]

On the opposite side stands Herman Finer, a British political scientist who taught at the University of Chicago for many years. He, by contrast, is partial to parliamentary authority and skeptical of bureaucratic power. In a lengthy rebuttal to Friedrich's piece, published in the first volume of *Public Administration Review*, Finer insisted that external control of administrators by an elected legislature is the only way that administrative responsibilities can be adequately defined and met. Responsible action comes not from a bureaucrat's personal sense of right and wrong, but from adequate ways to correct and punish any wayward bureaucrats that step out of line. Speaking of Friedrich, Finer wrote, "I do not think for a minute that he really is antidemocratic, but his line of argument presses him to enunciate views which might lead to this suspicion."[9]

It can fairly be said that Finer won the debate, for his position has remained the dominant one, both in the broader political culture and in most of academic political science. Because of the nonelected and continuing tenure of civil servants, their influence must be kept at a minimum, it is often said. Given bureaucracy's large size and hierarchical nature compared to the other branches of government, this logic seems irrefutable to many. Consequently the prime consideration in contemplating bureaucracy's status is to keep it firmly under control by all three branches: that is, executive, legislative, and judicial. Indeed,

I confess that as a young instructor in a political science department, I repeated this mantra regularly in my American government classes.

Enunciation of the mantra is then accompanied by claims its demands are seldom met. Authors writing on the presidency lament that US presidents, even though head of state in history's most potent super-power, cannot reliably control their own executive branch. Students of Congress worry that congressional committees fail to exercise adequately their constitutional responsibility of overseeing the bureaucracy. Another theme often encountered is that when bureaucratic power melds with that of allied economic institutions, the result is uncontrollable combined power. A favorite image expressing this idea is the "iron triangle," a pre-sumably unstoppable nexus of advocatory bureau, collusive legislative subcommittee, and a privileged industry that together dominate a specific realm of public policy.

Even sophisticated researchers who see themselves as systematically analyzing the operations of executive-legislative relationships as a whole, lean heavily toward the dangerous bureaucracy idea. A common format for this critique is to demonstrate, one at a time, the inadequacy of each constitutional branch to face down bureaucratic power. A more arcane approach is to construct numerical spatial models of policy making, whose mathematics purportedly conclude that a paucity of external opportunities exist to ever intervene in bureaucratic action.[10]

Hence it is rather rare to encounter in the literature the Friedrich frame of mind. Scholars and citizens alike in this individualist, auto-matically suspicious-of-government society of ours seem automatically reluctant to place themselves in the shoes of public administrators, charged as they are with pursuing difficult and even impossible missions. They forget that inspectors general, political appointees, legislators, lob-byists, media commentators, and whistleblowers are constantly looking over their shoulders to uncover something to blame the bureaucrats for.

Patterns of Inside Influence. Two books are helpful in sorting this situa-tion out. The first is *Bureaucratic Dynamics* by Dan Wood and Richard Waterman. They examine the interactive relationships of eight federal agencies to their external political environments in the 1970s and 1980s, namely the Interstate Commerce Commission (ICC), Equal Employment

Opportunity Commission (EEOC), Federal Trade Commission (FTC), Nuclear Regulatory Commission (NRC), Food and Drug Administration (FDA), National Highway Traffic Safety Administration (NHTSA), Office of Surface Mining (OSM), and Environmental Protection Agency.[11] Wood and Waterman measure the policy behavior of these organizations by a number of specific actions, such as operating certificates issued by the ICC, litigation actions taken by the EEOC, consent decrees obtained by the FTC, safety violations found by the NRC, inspections done by the FDA, engineering evaluations completed by the NHTSA, cessation orders given by OSM, and litigation referrals made by the EPA. The data were analyzed on a monthly or quarterly basis and account for lag time, permitting a fine-tuned longitudinal study. The external stimuli held against these measures for possible causal effects are from the presidency, Congress, courts, and other entities in the larger political environment. Both one-time stimuli were identified, such as the appointment of a new administrator or passage of a new law, and developments over time, like a trend in budget reductions, a spate of congressional investigations, or a rise in press attention. The researchers modeled dynamic interactive effects between the agency and these signals, repeating the equations until the best statistical fit emerges. Follow-up interviews supplemented the statistical analysis.

Wood and Waterman conclude that typically instructions received from these sources come from more than one place at a time, especially when both the president and Congress are involved. Agency responses to them definitely take place, often very fast and usually positive in tone. A common theme in the reactions is to bring to elected officials' attention the precedents at stake with regard to the issue's historical background. As a result, much of the interaction has the function of integrating past and current preferences of the public and its representatives.

Yet the bureaucrats send out their own policy signals as well, note Wood and Waterman. Bureaucracy's main effect on the policy process was to press decision makers to frame democratically induced initiatives within schemes of rational action, and to do so relatively fast. Administrators "are not slow, omnipotent, or unresponsive to public preferences," the researchers found. Far from being out of control, they routinely respond to both top-down and bottom-up stimuli, integrate past and present understandings, and respond faithfully to changes in presidential administration. As a result, Wood and Waterman depict the eight bureaucracies as "eminently moldable instruments of policy implementation."[12]

A second book from which we can learn is *The Craft of Bureaucratic Neutrality* by Gregory Huber. In it he examines one federal agency, the Occupational Safety and Health Administration, or OSHA. A combination of quantitative and qualitative research was used to conduct the study, incorporating agency histories, statistical data, and field interviews.[13]

OSHA was established by Congress in 1970 and placed in the US Department of Labor. Early in the agency's lifetime it became something of a punching bag in terms of our Response category, in that the affected business community and Republicans in general berated it for being excessively aggressive, picky, and hardnosed in safety inspections and follow-up enforcement. Yet over time, Huber notes, the bureau replied to this criticism by developing an operating philosophy that earned it a reputation for being both tough enough to save lives and injuries while being reasonable in enforcement conduct.

The way this was done was to forget about any understanding implied by the OSHA statute that all places of employment needed to be inspected on a uniform and equal basis. Instead, the agency prioritized its safety assessment and improvement activities in order to concentrate on two kinds of situations: organizations having large numbers of employees and industries where the very nature of the work inevitably involves high safety risks, such as petrochemicals and construction. OSHA contended this strategy allowed it to achieve the Act's purposes to the highest net degree possible within limited resources. A second strategy was to take advantage of our federal system and delegate the function of enforcing occupational safety standards to 20 state governments that agreed to establish their own "OSHAs" while abiding by national standards and procedures.

Huber describes this response by OSHA as a holistic one in which multiple features are combined into a unified posture of "strategic neutrality." These elements include conformity to the agency's core mission, acceptance of policy directives from executive and legislative sources, and evenhanded enforcement independent of partisan pressure or demands of plant managers and unions. Also the approach is demonstrably cost efficient, decentralized to the extent possible, and unified by centralized policy making with consistent procedures. The strategy was neutral in the sense that it was developed in consultation with safety professionals and, Huber argues, did not constitute an illegal or obviously "political" move—yet it entailed having the agency initiate its own altered policy.

Huber concludes his book with the general observation that in taking such reasoned measures, bureaucracies need not be controlled in a total and absolute manner within the constitutional separation of powers. Rather, they should be free to create implementation approaches that satisfy the institution's self-image and thus make it effective.[14]

Bureaucracy's Place in the Sun. I end this section on bureaucracy's Response function by proffering for consideration some thoughts on our subject that embrace the Friedrich viewpoint but go beyond.

In 1982 the Virginia Tech faculty to which I belonged met for a retreat at Federal Executive Institute in Charlottesville, Virginia. After dinner and a glass of wine or two, we exchanged views on the state of public administration in the United States. Much to our surprise, despite highly disparate intellectual orientations, much common ground was evident among us. The next morning we began brainstorming with the eventual result being a common declaration known as the Blacksburg Manifesto.[15]

The Blacksburg position visualizes bureaucratic work as being carried out in the society by an organic collective known as the "The Public Administration." It springs from the spirit of the US constitutional order that anticipated creation of America's first viable nationwide governing system. Although it is often mentioned that the 1787 document does not contain the word "administration," it makes it clear in other ways that public agencies are contemplated. Article I, Section 7 empowers Congress to create post offices, an army, a navy, and militias. It also calls for numerous activities to be performed that would be impossible for Congress to do, such as collect taxes, borrow money, coin money, and operate a patent system. Moreover, Article II, Section 2 allows the president to request opinions from the heads of "each of the executive departments." Since most members of the constitutional convention had themselves been leaders in their own state's government or members of the Continental Congress, they were undoubtedly familiar with the administrative organizations of their day, which included individuals commissioned to deal with Indians, state agents to procure supplies, boards of confiscated property, land offices, and in Virginia a State Medical Department headed by a Surgeon-in-Chief who coordinated all military hospitals.[16]

The Manifesto advances what is called an "agential perspective." This refers to a focus on government agencies as the heart of effective public administration. They are also in a position to be prime promoters of the public interest in that they are "repositories of, and their staffs are trustees of, specialized knowledge, historical experience, time-tested wisdom, and most importantly, some degree of consensus as to the public interest relevant to a particular society function." As for their position in the separation of powers where they face three different constitutional masters, the Blacksburg solution—offered by John Rohr—is to have them perform as a "balance wheel." In that role, when differences occur among them as to what should be done, the agency needs to work out a solution that properly resolves the matter and—if possible—becomes a commonly agreed on solution.[17]

In the years since the Manifesto was published, some members of the Blacksburg faculty went beyond the balance wheel notion to chart out their own theories of proper exercise of administrative power. Your author was one of these. As stated in chapter 1 of my book *Mission Mystique,* I stipulate that the ideal government agency is endowed with an aura of mystique by which it can assert "qualified policy autonomy" so as to provide room for experimentation with new measures. The adjective "qualified" in this instance means within reason and in the absence of instructions to the contrary.[18]

I proposed another concept in a 2006 article that advances the idea of a mission trajectory. It is based on the assumption that, when Congress or a state legislature establishes an agency, the organization has received a standing commitment—unless explicitly withdrawn—that it can and should chart a pathway forward whereby the mission is not compromised by the passage of time. As conditions and technology undergo change, adjustments must be made. This is done with the assumption that, in the absence of authoritative censure, tacit support exists for such renewal without receiving permission every step of the way. The conditions required for such "trajectory management" are creative and sensitive leadership, conscious organizational learning, and an ongoing reservoir of public support for the mission.[19]

My later faculty colleague Brian Cook had, in the meantime, developed an intellectual perspective on public administration that takes the additional step of reconceptualizing its total role in the governance of a democratic polity. It is found in his book *Bureaucracy and Self-Development*, published in 1996. He views administration's role as not merely the instrumental one of carrying out laws and policies settled by others. It is as well a *constitutive* one of engaging in a myriad of educative, informative, representative, and shaping activities within the society. Cook believes that by the nature of its work, administration is in the position to acknowledge and absorb what goes on in the daily experiences of citizens more fully than other organs of government. Hence it possesses a unique capacity to define public problems and formulate strategies to address them. Although bureaucracy's operating world is the immediate present and proximate future, agencies have stored within them an understanding of past laws, agreements, and attempts to act. This allows public administration to inject well-grounded practical reasoning into the charting of the polity's future course.[20]

GOVERNANCE AS ACQUISITION

We now direct our attention to aspects of bureaucratic governance that involve relationships with private parties. The first one is the seemingly simple act of acquiring goods and services—which in practice turns out to be quite complicated.

Inside Government Contracting. Obviously governments must buy things. It would be a waste of time for a bureau to manufacture its own desks, so as a result it buys them on the open market. The same would be true for possessing a fleet of moving vans to be on hand for the occasional transfer of office locations. This has always been the case in our country; and with America's vibrant private enterprise economy, the lure of government outsourcing is especially strong.

Yet in recent times the scale, scope, and import of private outsourcing has expanded to the extent that it has altered the nature of bureaucratic governance. Whereas in most countries the term "privatization" refers to the divestiture of government enterprises, in the United States the term usually means removing from government many of its normal duties and handing them over to for-profit contractors. The consequence is a significant shift to the ideological right within the public sector's structure, heralded by its supporters as contributing to a more nimble new governance and attacked by its critics as leading to hollowed out government.

The total amounts of money spent on government procurement are huge. In 2011 the value of all federal contracts together was $537 billion, or 14 percent of federal outlays.[21] For some years this amount had been expanding fast: $146 billion in 1984, $171 in 1990, $388 in 2005, and $550 in 2009.[22] At the present time federal outsourcing is so extensive that three out of four civilians working in behalf of the federal government receive their paycheck from private corporations rather than the US treasury.[23] As for states and local governments, growth in aggregate procurement expenditures has risen greatly as well: $960 billion in 1989, $1,221 in 1994, and $1,750 in 1999. Approximately 40 percent of all state and local government spending is accounted for this way.[24]

With this rapid quantitative growth in the sheer amount of outsourcing has come a proliferation of types of activities that are privatized. By a statute named the Federal Activities Inventory Reform Act (or FAIR), Congress effectively said that anything and everything is acceptable except "inherently governmental" activities. These are defined as exercising discretion to bind the United States, taking diplomatic or military action, conducting judicial proceedings, managing government contracts, affecting significantly the life, liberty, or property of citizens, or controlling government personnel or property.[25]

Yet even these quite explicit boundaries can be violated. With respect to military action, more than 100 private contractors supplied an estimated 85,000 men to Iraq during the 2003–2011 war. Although most performed support functions, a number—most notoriously those employed by Blackwater USA—carried weapons, wore body armor, accompanied troops on patrol, and guarded prisons in which torture took place. And like the overstressed troops, at times contractor personnel shot unarmed civilians in cold blood and were themselves kidnapped or murdered.

As for the FAIR prohibition against privatizing the management of contracts, in the aftermath of Katrina FEMA found itself facing a severe shortage of trained contract management personnel. Only about 100,000 trained contract mangers are available to oversee the government's non-defense outsourcing each year, and they were all busy.[26] Hence one of the first emergency steps taken after the storm was to hire the Acquisition Solutions company to manage the bidding, writing, and monitoring of largely open-ended contracts to scores of unvetted vendors.

As to the inherently governmental act of controlling government personnel and property, in defense and national security agencies particularly, it has been the habit for years to supplement available civil servants with ex-military people and retirees hired under contract. These individuals wear security badges, attend regular staff meetings, participate in planning sessions, write reports, and conduct staff duties such as training and the maintenance of equipment.

Meanwhile state and local governments are free to contract out any governmental duties their lawmakers do not forbid. The degree to which this is done varies by jurisdiction, as one might expect. Box 4.3 lists commonly outsourced activity at the local level. Note that some activities are routine, such as building repair, day care, operation of parking lots, tree trimming and utility billing, but others are decidedly not—for example, crime prevention, cultural programs, hospital operation, and legal systems.

BOX 4.3	Activities Commonly Contracted Out by Local Government

Architectural services	Library operations
Building repair	Mental health facilities
Crime prevention	Parking lots
Cultural programs	Street construction
Data processing	Transit systems
Day care	Trash collection
Drug/alcohol treatment	Tree trimming
Hospital operation	Utility billing
Legal services	Vehicle towing

Source: John A. Rehfuss, *Contracting Out in Government: A Guide to Working with Outside Contractors to Supply Public Services* (San Francisco: Jossey-Bass, 1989), pp. 11–12.

This almost unbounded spread of government outsourcing has led scholars to develop criteria as to what functions of government should and should not be turned over to contractors. John Donahue, taking an economics-oriented position, says outsourcing is acceptable (1) if bids can be tendered competitively and (2) when a task's outcome can be specified in advance and evaluated afterwards.[27] Steven Kelman offers criteria more sympathetic with government's responsibilities: (1) when not core to the agency mission, (2) when capabilities are needed only occasionally, (3) when the needed talent is more easily found in the private sector, and (4) when sufficient scale is achieved to lower costs.[28]

The prime political impetus for privatization by contract is to make government smaller on the ideological plane and cheaper at the instrumental level. As mentioned in chapter 2, considerable evidence exists that shows outsourcing can be marginally less costly than in-house provision for repetitive services. For more complex, discretion-requiring tasks, this is not necessarily the case—in fact, the opposite may be true. For long-running contracts, especially in areas like IT where evolving systems and shifting technology are commonplace, unanticipated external factors often require change orders to be negotiated. Because of the original contractor's inside position in the situation, the outcome typically benefits that firm, leading to cost overruns and delay.

The other built-in negative side of contracting out is the difficulty of monitoring with regard to outcomes. Even if strict, measurable goals are set, frequently it is the contracting organization that does most post hoc evaluation. In that instance, the bureau that is paying for the work simply receives a report rather than engaging in independent auditing. The matter is made worse by the need on big jobs to have subcontractors—and they too may wish to subcontract down still yet another layer or two. In this byzantine multilayered situation, the only means by which the responsible authorities may find out about a problem is when the press breaks news of a scandal.

When the Stakes Are High. In probably his most memorable speech, when President Dwight Eisenhower gave his farewell address in January 1961, he warned against the influence of the "military-industrial complex." His phrase refers to a concentration of power created by the union of interest that draws together the nation's military establishment and the big contractors that make its weapons—particularly sophisticated aircraft and ships, and now missiles, drones, and space vehicles. The lion's share of the half trillion dollars spent each year in federal contracting is directed to meeting national security goals—$374 billion for the Defense Department's top 100 contractors alone in 2011.[29] Does this mean that Eisenhower's warning has come true?

In his book *Governing by Contract*, Phillip Cooper does not use Eisenhower's language but nonetheless points to the intimate contractor-government relationships that form around defense and similar big-money contracts. This happens despite the great institutional differences that separate the civilian departments that let the contracts and the large corporations that win them. On one side, government bureaucracy, with its legal grounding, hierarchical organization, and civil service culture, depends on these features to pursue a public mission. On the other side, the private corporation, with its organizational independence, flexible structure, and right to fire, adopts an entrepreneurial culture to make money. But, Cooper states, once a marriage of the two is certified by placing signatures on a contract, the couple begins to build an institutional relationship that eventually morphs into a political alliance, whose main purpose is defense against threats posed by the external environment.[30]

Box 4.4 provides data on the top five federal contractors in terms of dollar magnitude and contract activities. Together, these firms receive revenues well in excess of $100 billion annually from the US government. A figure of this magnitude exceeds the GNP of nearly fifty of the world's national economies.[31] Most of the amount comes from the Department of

BOX 4.4	The Top Five Federal Contractors and Their Work			
Rank	Name	HQ City	$ (in billions)	Sample Projects or Products
1	Lockheed Martin	Bethesda, MD	40.0	F-35 Lightning Fighter, Strategic Missiles, Terminal High Altitude Area Missile Defense, Space Vehicles and Launch Systems, Airlift Capability, Joint Light Tactical Vehicle

Rank	Name	HQ City	$ (in billions)	Sample Projects or Products
2	Boeing	Chicago	21.5	Civilian and Military Fixed-Wing Aircraft, Airframe Structural Components, Navy F/A-18F Super Hornet Fighter, 747-8 Jet Aircraft Engine, Landing Approach Systems, GPS Systems
3	General Dynamics	Charlotte, NC	19.5	Aegis Control Systems, Rockets, Aircraft Gun Systems, Naval Gun Barrels, Tank Armor, Hummer Armament, Remote Control Land Guns, Truck Axles and Suspension Systems
4	Northrop Grumman	Falls Church, VA	16.8	Aircraft Supercarriers, Nuclear Submarines, B-2 Sprint Strategic Bomber, RQ-4 Global Hawk Fighter, C41 Radar Air Defense Systems, Satellites for Air Force, NASA and NOAA
5	Raytheon	Waltham, MA	14.8	Integrated Air and Missile Defense Systems, Naval Combat Ship Electronic Systems, Integrated Sensor Systems, Polar-Orbiting Satellites, Cybersecurity Threat Protection

Sources: CNBC 10 Biggest U.S. Government Contractors; Wikipedia Top 100 Contractors of U.S. Government; and company websites. Accessed March 13, 2013.

Note: Contract amounts are for 2011, except for Northrop Grumman, which is for 2010.

Defense but also from the budgets of NASA, NOAA, and the Department of Homeland Security. When looking over the projects indicated, we see that most concern the national security of the country in a direct way, with the remainder constituting other high stakes for a twenty-first-century superpower. Also most of them provide substantial portions of their contractors' revenue streams.

The implications of this particular kind of outsourcing go beyond the political alliances mentioned by Cooper. I suggest instead a closeness that perhaps can best be described as *functional fusion*. By this I do not mean becoming one entity in a legal sense, but rather possessing a close unity of purpose. This happens on three levels.

One is that of the dual workforces. I have already mentioned how in the Defense Department and other security agencies contractor personnel and agency employees mix closely on the job. Think for a moment what the culture of that joint activity must be when the individuals involved are working on something as intricate and urgent as an Aegis control system's firing accuracy in rough seas. At these times the team is worrying about life-or-death matters and each member is equally responsible; the importance of the task transcends such minutia as who signs my paycheck.

A second level is organizational interdependence. Neither the government nor the company can achieve its core goals without its opposite number doing so as well. For complex weapons or IT systems, no real alternative exists to the continued symbiosis: the private seller is a monopolist for whom the government has no other source, and the public buyer is a monopsonist for whom the contractor has no other customer.

The third level is a common economic and political environment. Both parties are equally helped or hurt by the same external factors. If war breaks out, both benefit; if a recession hits, both are in trouble. Hence they are united by common risks that arise from any economic or political event that creates a parallel threat that must be defended against—exactly what Ike was talking about in regard to the power of the military-industrial complex.

The presence of such large high-stakes outsourcing in our field of public administration has significant implications. We are talking about great opportunities to serve the nation as well as great responsibilities in wielding political power. Intellectually, the phenomenon calls into question cherished boundaries we have always assumed to exist, such as public administration versus corporate management, public sector versus private sector, and even state versus society. Perhaps even the concept of bureaucratic governance itself loses some of its clarity.

When Coercion Is Great. It was mentioned earlier that the FAIR statute prohibits outsourcing that affects the life, liberty, and property of citizens. Aside from the rendering of justice by the courts, the most likely area to cross the line in this regard is incarceration. Almost always we assume that prisons are owned and operated by government because of their large responsibility for and intimate embrace of human life. Yet in many instances—especially at the state level—they are managed under contract or even owned by private enterprise. While outsourcing appropriateness is usually debated in terms of the economics of monetary cost, many students of this subject have doubts about its moral rightness.

The practice of gaining profit from the incarceration of criminals goes back at least 150 years. After the Civil War many Southern states, bankrupt and their penitentiaries in ruins, leased convicts to entrepreneurs for cheap labor so as to obtain cash and not to have to pay for their confinement. As a legacy of this practice, the leasing out of chain gangs continued in Alabama up until 1995. During the latter nineteenth and early twentieth centuries, many states owned houses of correction but contracted their management to private parties or engaged in other forms of prison privatization, usually to save money. The trend came to a standstill in 1950, however, when reports of rampant abuse of inmates came to the public's attention.[32]

In the 1980s, an era when President Reagan's antigovernment conservatism was influencing the country, a return to the practice occurred. The context at that time was soaring crime rates, a newly fashionable get-tough attitude toward criminals, and reports of dangerously overcrowded state prisons. Beginning with Tennessee's negotiation of a privatization contract with a newly formed prison company, Corrections Corporation of America (CCA), the states of California, Connecticut, Florida, Massachusetts, Minnesota, Nevada, Utah, and Virginia initiated or restarted the practice.

As this new penal market blossomed, several other firms entered it, such as RCA, General Electric, Westinghouse, and the Wackenhut security firm. Eventually CAA and Wackenhut merged as the Geo Group, and it now controls 74 percent of private-sector prison beds in 126 facilities. At last word the industry operates 264 prisons that house approximately

129,000 inmates, 9 percent of the total state prison population in the United States.[33]

Penal privatization exists in three main forms. One is to market the fruits of prison labor. Although the days of convict chain gangs are a thing of the past, in some states the corrections department contracts out the use of incarcerated inmates to work for private firms. John Rehfuss reported in 1989 that a Utah graphic arts company had prisoners do work for them in the state print shop. In Utah, Best Western hotels employed Arizona women in a prerelease center to staff a nationwide reservation service.[34]

The second and most pervasive form of privatization is contracting out the management of state houses of correction. This accounts for most of the bed capacity mentioned above. Typically the contract makes the company responsible for hiring, training, and evaluating staff; guarding against escape; intervening when riots occur; and providing for food service, health care, and education programs. In many instances the contract also calls for the in-house presence of government monitors from the state department of corrections.

The third form is a practice whereby prison companies construct new penitentiary buildings and then lease them to the state for a period of usually ninety-nine years, after which time ownership reverts to the state. In the meantime the firm operates the facility under a profitable management contract. These "speculative" prison investments, as they are called, are usually made in poor rural areas where community leaders are anxious to attract new jobs. If the new prison does not fill sufficiently, the corporation scans the national inmate market for overcrowded penitentiaries from which to import convicts.

Advocates of prison privatization argue that the practice has many economic advantages, including making available low-cost prison labor and postponing state capital outlays for new facilities. The principal selling point is budgetary cost savings, however. Some studies verify this aspect while others say that economies are largely achieved by lower pay to guards.

As to the quality of contract management, an extensive study of the privately operated Hamilton Country prison in Silverdale, Tennessee, found that costs were reduced by 4–8 percent, but the quality of services as evaluated in inmate surveys was affected. Convicts rated the institution high on upkeep and staff competence; low on recreational programs and release procedures; and mixed on physical safety, food, and medical care. Secondary interview analysis by the investigators concluded that actually "the inmates could not care less about who runs the prison . . . their paramount interest is much simpler: decent conditions and decent treatment."[35]

Many students of this subject argue that the privatization of punishment is not a matter of costs or inmate service at all but one of ethics and morality. Penitentiaries are complete total institutions in that every aspect of inmates' lives is controlled, over long periods of years and even lifetimes. Large numbers of dangerous persons are concentrated in a closed space. Discipline is meted out formally and informally with little or no external accountability. At night the strongest and most brutal inmates attack the weaker and more pitiful. A society that allows the most hallowed values of fairness, justice, and human decency to be placed at the mercy of commercial interests seeking material profits is not, critics say, in accord with the standards of a civilized community.

GOVERNANCE AS ENGAGEMENT

Other external relationships than outsourcing exist in bureaucratic governing. These include organizational linkages within our system of federalism, service agreements with nonprofit organizations, and the direct involvement of citizens in governing.

Joint Bureaucratic Action. The New Governance school of thought in our field does not share my concern for making a case for bureaucracy. This is because its adherents believe stand-alone bureaucracy is outdated and unable to address the twenty-first century's complex and multifaceted public problems. Isolated organizational "silos," as they call government agencies, are not sufficiently innovative, outreaching, flexible, and nimble. Bureaucracy by its nature is seen as inward in outlook, top-down in hierarchy, overspecialized in competence, and status quo in attitude. Instead, what is needed is joint action by a number of collaborating nonprofit, commercial, and governmental actors that work together not within one institutional framework but a multimember network.[36]

This book is not on the subject of collaboration or networking, hence it does not address this paradigm of public action in any detail. Suffice it to point out, however, that the government agency is the only public policy actor available that *simultaneously* combines the following elements: legal authority, integrated effort, stable workforce, dedicated resources, coherent culture, and clear accountability to our democratic system. When public missions that are sizable in scale and vital in importance are taken on by the political system, my recommendation is to keep depending upon bureaucracy as the centerpiece of the public sector. This does not mean, however, that collaboration and joint action with numerous outside groups is not needed or should not happen; in fact this is true much more often than not for most government agencies. But I would go on to assert my belief that if clear accountability to the electorate is necessary, the bureaucracies involved in these arrangements should be the *lead* collaborators.

In my study of the six mission mystique agencies, I encountered numerous examples of just this kind of joint action among governments and other parties. National park rangers routinely join with their state counterparts and local law enforcement in search and rescue operations. The Weather Service convenes crisis meetings of state governors, city mayors, and local emergency managers when a hurricane is brewing. Epidemiologists from the CDC assist local public health officials as they diagnose diseases that break out. The Mecklenburg Department of Social Services brings psychologists, police officers, private attorneys, and members of the clergy into evaluations of custody cases. Virginia state police detectives participate in drug task forces continuously that include representatives from all affected law enforcement jurisdictions. As a standard practice, the Peace Corps supports volunteer projects with the help of local business firms, schools, community groups, and diplomatic offices.[37]

Any mention of administrative joint action should also take note that our federal system *requires* interorganizational collaboration within government. Originally the Founding Fathers conceived of their invention as a stark, two-level system of sovereign authority. As it turned out, however, American federalism eventually became an interwoven swirl of programmatic activity that ties together thousands of bureaucracies from national, state, and local levels.

The centerpiece of "cooperative federalism," as it is called, is the federal grant-in-aid. With its earliest ancestor being a nationwide series of land-grant universities (at one of which I worked), in the 150 years since that time intergovernmental interaction has evolved into a vast collection of joint-action enterprises covering a multitude of governmental activities. At present approximately 550 federal grant programs remit $625 billion to states and localities each year for governing purposes. While most of this funding is sent directly to individuals, over a third is intergovernmental in that it funds state and local bureaucracies. Some goes to states for their own use, some is redistributed by the states to their cities and counties, and some is sent to local authorities directly. Overall, the intergovernmental grant flow constitutes 16.4 percent of federal outlays and augments state and local revenues by 37.5 percent.[38] Along with our earlier topic of contracting out, the magnitude of this practice is also a reason why the per capita number of federal bureaucrats has sunk so low. Table 4.2 lists the fourteen biggest program areas by funding level.

TABLE 4.2	Outlays for the Largest Categories of Federal Grants to State and Local Governments, 2011 (estimated amount in billions of dollars)
Category	**Outlay**
Highway construction and maintenance	$35.0
Special education	17.4
Urban mass transportation	13.2
Child and family services programs	11.0
Community development fund	8.1
Agriculture programs	6.5
Environmental protection	6.5
Energy programs	5.7
Administration of justice	5.6
Training and employment services	4.1
Disaster relief	3.9
Grants for airports	3.3
Homeland security state and local programs	2.0
Social services block grant	2.0

Source: Statistical Abstract of the United States, 2012, p. 269.

The underlying rationale of the federal grant-in-aid system is to funnel down to the 50 states, about 20,000 municipalities, and 3,000 counties some of the fruits of the highly productive US Tax Code. This arrangement not merely corrects a fiscal imbalance within the federal system but also possesses the advantage of decentralizing national policy implementation. This in itself is politically attractive in a huge and diverse country whose political culture varies greatly by section. America would not be well served if public administration were exclusively in the hands of an all-powerful central state. At the same time, most of the funds come with strings attached in the form of mandates or conditions of acceptance. In other instances they are block grants for a general purpose that allow wide latitude of use, examples being mental health, drug addition education, and community development. Hence this form of joint bureaucratic action helps make viable all of America's thousands of governments and, at the same time, unites their purposes more fully than would otherwise be the case.

Cooperative federalism is not without its problems. Recipient governments can employ proffered dollars to free up local monies already dedicated to the funded task and are thus "fungible" in terms of use. Inevitably, transaction costs must be borne, such as taking valuable staff time to prepare and review applications and conduct evaluations and file reports. Another issue is the uncertainty as to when and how much funding will be received; decisions at the state and local level must often be made at the last minute, and jurisdictions can be left hanging if severe budget cuts occur in Washington. Fragmented administration can moreover be slow acting because of the number of procedural steps involved, as Pressman and Wildavsky classically document in their book *Implementation*.[39] Also centralized national control can be superimposed on state administering offices with stultifying effects, as occurs in employment services and disability claims. Unfunded mandates may consume local resources without community approval and displace other higher priority needs. In short, this giant maze of joint action is a blessing from the standpoint of avoiding centralized statist administration in a continent-sized country—but it requires constant tinkering and improvement.

The Purchase of Care. A second area of governance as engagement is the devolution of social service programs to nonprofit organizations. The topic belongs here rather than under governance as acquisition for two reasons. First, it does not involve buying things for government's own use but for the benefit of needy citizens. Second, the purchase of care transcends the commercial-type contract in that it affects the survival and dignity of individual human lives, a matter of inherent importance and not instrumental usefulness.

Bureaucracies at the state, city, and county levels enter into agreements with nonprofit organizations (and occasionally for-profit companies) to render services for a fee to members of the public. Common examples are foster care for children, the mentoring of troubled youth, and daycare for failing seniors living alone. Other illustrations are family abuse counseling, substance abuse counseling, pre-employment training, and assistance with sheltering opportunities and health insurance.

As Ruth Hoogland DeHoog and Lester Salamon explain in a comprehensive review of the subject, this form of bureaucratic devolution requires *relational* ties, not just contractual ones. Governments and third parties together enter social service realms where long-term institutional ties and mutual trust are essential for success in attending to the welfare of individuals not capable of helping themselves. The work requires case-by-case services over time and calls for a holistic approach in each instance. Hence outcomes are always uncertain. Quantitative measures of "performance success" are largely meaningless. Personal care is by its very nature labor intensive. Because of unpredictable workload demands, costs are impossible to predict or control. Caregivers must have discretion in prioritizing and treating cases. Hired professionals cannot be commanded as is done to employees in a factory; instead management must develop close personal relationships with the staff, who can themselves try to form close bonds with their clients: children, senior citizens, abused women, counselees, foster parents, and juvenile delinquents among others.

This image of close working ties reminds us of the functional fusion found between large corporate contractors and national security agencies. The stakes here are not the security and future of the nation but the security and future of troubled individuals. In both instances fusion takes place; but while one is based on common self-interest the other is founded on a shared caring ethos—a kind of "altruistic fusion," perhaps.

This point leads to behavioral consequences. Bids are not tendered publicly; rather, institutions approach each other privately and negotiate terms bilaterally. Ideally agreements are not based on cost considerations alone but on the assurance of competence and dependability. DeHoog and Salamon emphasize that the purchasing agency must invest significant time and expense in reaching purchase agreements. The dominant normative theme in the process is not entering a competitive market to get the best deal, but engaging in cooperative action so as to produce adequate trust. This means that nonprofits with whom the agency has successfully worked with in the past are usually preferable. At the same time, continued independent monitoring of the quality of the purchased care is necessary. It is important for the government body to retain enough in-house professional expertise to make sound judgments in this regard.[40]

Wolfgang Bielefeld, James Perry and Ann Marie Thompson detect possible tendencies for dysfunctions to develop in government-nonprofit collaboration. One is that since its success depends on the establishment of prior conditions of trust, subsequent changes and reforms are made difficult and must proceed incrementally. Persistence of the status quo has its own built-in justification. Moreover the fundamental human values at the heart of care purchase can be compromised by economic motives on each side of the relationship: the agency wants to save money and thus outsources on the cheap, while the nonprofit—hungry for contract dollars—may stand ready to sell its mission soul to get them.[41]

Another danger is that the informal relationships inherent in nonprofit purchase of care make this mode of service delivery more susceptible to perversions than the formal rules of a bureaucracy would permit. In an earlier book on bureaucracy, I described one such situation described by a *Washington Post* reporter as "bordered on the incestuous" and a product of being "wired into the system." A bankrupt company cofounded by a social worker employed by the District of Columbia government and a private consultant who served on the agency's contract review board was granted a contract to house convicted juveniles. Conditions in the home were so terrible that the conflicts of interest were uncovered only after six of its youth inmates had been murdered and a seventh had committed murder.[42]

Elsewhere in my research I have run into creative arrangements that are not only solid ethically but belie the pessimism of Bielefeld and associates that not much innovation in this field can be expected. The Department of Social Services in Mecklenburg County developed a "Wiping Out Poverty" program whose goal was to "create an environment where all Mecklenburg residents can become self-sufficient and have equal access to services." Employing savvy political skills and indefatigable outreach efforts, a ten-sided "decagon" of networked interacting entities was formed to this end. Their top leaders met monthly to discuss common problems and hear reports on matters of mutual interest (see Figure 4.1).

The decagon became the emblem for an extensive antipoverty effort throughout the Charlotte metro area. Starting at the top were the governments involved: the two local jurisdictions strongly committed to the campaign along with state social service authorities that were unfortunately lukewarm. The range of their ties with community organizations can be appreciated by going around the figure clockwise. Members of the chamber of commerce promised to hire welfare-to-work graduates. The local community college agreed to conduct literacy and vocational training classes. Hundreds of area nonprofits participated in a telephone service–referral system whereby clients could be given appointments on the spot. Two local hospitals stood ready to employ former welfare clients in nonmedical support jobs and also make health care accessible to the uninsured poor. The local housing authority provided backup shelter in public housing and subsidized apartments. Numerous churches joined a Faith Initiative that furnished volunteers and cash donations. The public schools advised and supported enrolled foster care children and hired ex-welfare clients as custodians and teacher's aides. A report on the effort concluded, "While poverty cannot be eliminated, the hardship it causes can still be relieved."[43]

Citizen Engagement. Direct citizen participation in program governance and operation has been widely accepted as desirable in the field of public administration. Nancy Roberts of the Naval Postgraduate School provides a helpful overview of this large subject. She reminds us that the basic concept is not new but has long been present in this country in one

| FIGURE 4.1 | "Wiping Out Poverty" Decagon, Mecklenburg County Department of Social Services |

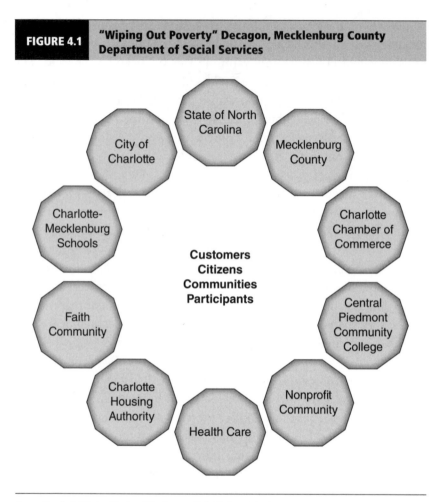

Source: Goodsell, *Mission Mystique* (Washington, DC: CQ Press, 2011), p. 169.

form or another. In Franklin Roosevelt's New Deal, farmers voted in referenda on commodity support programs. In Lyndon Johnson's Fair Deal, the affected citizens helped staff the War on Poverty and plan urban renewal projects under the Model Cities program.

Since those times, the extent and variety of citizen engagement has grown exponentially. Roberts cites the effects of the Federal Advisory Committee Act of 1972 as just one example of what has happened. More than 1,000 advisory committees are attached to agencies throughout the national government. They must hold open, preannounced meetings and provide public access to their discussions and documents. In addition their membership must be balanced so as to represent a cross-section of those directly affected or interested and qualified.

In a very different vein, Roberts cites an electronic "town meeting" convened in New York City to collect ideas on how to rebuild the site once occupied by Manhattan's World Trade Towers prior to 9/11. Some 4,300 people of all types and backgrounds from around the metropolitan area participated, offering what she describes as a stunning example of mass public participation. The task taken on was large scale, both physically and in the breadth of opinion as to what of major urban infrastructure best memorializes a profoundly tragic national event. A jaded New York columnist who covered the process was moved to exclaim, "We have a word for what they were doing. The word is democracy."[44]

While clearly favorable to the concept, Roberts is also aware of its shortcomings. Almost all authorities on this subject propose different dos and don'ts regarding citizen participation, and few see it as a panacea. My own view is that the notion should be regarded as a big chest full of different tools for selective use in particular circumstances. Roberts draws up a list of pros and cons, and I have expanded her analysis in Box 4.5. I invite you to study this summary and consider what it means for different kinds of applications.

BOX 4.5	Reasons Given For and Against Direct Citizen Participation in Governance

Reasons For

1. The active role of citizens in governance is an important ideal in American life and should be fulfilled to the extent possible.

2. Direct participation in the decisions of our democracy helps keep community life vital and public institutions accountable.

3. Such participation helps transform private residents into free and active citizens concerned for the future of the country.

(Continued)

(Continued)

4. It helps to balance a cultural mentality based on material self-interest and consumption of private goods.

5. Citizens have more ability than we imagine to help guide policy decisions and program activities.

6. Such participation is one of the fundamental rights of Americans, that is, to be engaged in collective decisions that affect their lives.

7. Direct participation performs an important educational function by acquainting citizens with issues and problems of public importance.

8. Direct participation allows less educated citizens not members of "the establishment" a voice in deciding community and national issues.

Reasons Against

1. Representative government and the voting franchise is the method intended by the Constitution for citizen influence over public policy.

2. Electoral representation has the advantage of buffering government from uninformed public opinion or tyranny of the majority.

3. Direct action by bureaucracies that are supervised by elected officials makes it possible for governance to be conducted by expert professionals monitored by the people's representatives.

4. Unlike paid officials and civil servants, most citizens do not have the time or interest to deliberate on matters of public policy.

5. Competent and enduring public agencies responsive to external opinion are best suited to conduct the public's business over time.

6. The rule of law and the maintenance of accountability require that collective public decisions be made by those legally responsible.

7. Direct citizen participation may work in localities of modest size, but is less feasible in large urban areas.

8. Participation is dominated by the outspoken middle class without proportionate numbers of the poor and disadvantaged, creating a new elite.

Source: Adapted and extended from Nancy Roberts, "Public Deliberation in an Age of Direct Citizen Participation," *American Review of Public Administration*, 34, no. 4 (December 2004): 315–316.

A form of citizen involvement I have encountered in my own field-work on bureaucracy is the concept of the city neighborhood association. Such organizations are chartered by municipalities to operate semi-autonomously within a community's separate geographic subdivisions. Typically residents adopt bylaws by which the associations are governed. Then, in accord with these rules, residents elect members of an association council that represents them. This council in turn elects a president and vice president of the association.

This leadership team invites all neighborhood residents to meet periodically in a school or home. An agenda is formed to discuss such matters as amelioration of local problems, improvement of the security or appearance of the neighborhood, or accomplishment of long-term goals such as establishing new facilities or programs. After those present arrive at a consensus, a committee is formed to study the matter. It may see fit to meet with appropriate city departments to receive their suggestions and or offers of cooperation. On matters requiring formal city approval, the association arranges for who will meet with the mayor or testify before city council.

In cities strongly committed to the neighborhood association idea, reasonable neighborhood ideas are likely to get serious consideration and perhaps offers of in-kind agency assistance. The police department may offer to mount extra patrols, for example, and the public works department could make available heavy equipment. Alternatively, the association may wish to carry out a project like a new park on its own terms, drawing on the skills and sweat equity of association members themselves, possibly supplemented by private donations. The hoped-for outcome is that citizens improve their neighborhood but at the same time learn how to mobilize community support and work with the city administration. The process can, for those who participate actively, confer a sense of empowerment, ownership, identity, and pride.

An extensive study of neighborhood associations in the United States was conducted by Jeffrey Berry, Kent Portney, and Ken Thomson. They evaluated in detail arrangements existing in Birmingham, Alabama; Dayton, Ohio; Portland, Oregon; St. Paul, Minnesota; and San Antonio, Texas. Using surveys, interviews, and focus groups, the researchers assessed the five associations against two criteria. The first was breadth of participation, defined as having large numbers of citizens involved and thus enlarging democratic representation in city affairs. The second criterion was depth of participation, meaning the extent to which council proposals were given serious consideration by authorities with subsequent action. The finding of Berry and coauthors was that for the most part these five associations did well regarding depth but not breadth; while many projects were brought to fruition, lower income residents tended not to participate in either dialog or action. The reason seemed to be that they felt intimidated by the prospect of attending and speaking at meetings. Nevertheless, Berry and associates believe, the very presence of the associations is a promising way to elevate the median level of civic participation well beyond the mere voting-and-complaining level so common to the urban environment.[45]

SO WHAT'S INSIDE THERE?

The late author and journalist John Gunther wrote *Inside Asia* and *Inside Latin America* and several more "inside" books. In them he gave readers a closer look at places we have heard about but do not know in depth. The unifying theme of this chapter has been bureaucratic power and how it is used. What did we learn from going inside bureaucratic governance on this subject?

All students have heard of the politics-administration dichotomy. However its implied placement of public administration in a subordinate role is misleading. Bureaus too "legislate" via rulemaking, far more often than do legislative bodies. At the federal level this is done in accord with a "constitution," the Administrative Procedure Act of 1946; its procedures require extensive consultation with affected parties and repeated opportunities to register objection and make modifications.

An ongoing debate is whether bureaucracies should be making policy or even influencing it. One side contends that it is undemocratic to give nonelected civil servants that much power. The other side says that administrators must have discretion to act appropriately under changing conditions and that bureaucracy was in effect contemplated by the Founding Fathers.

The evidence obtained by scholars in this area shows that agencies generally are responsive to their political masters while at the same time can be creative in modifying their mission to make it practical to carry out as conditions change. Some theorists of administration propose that agencies use a combination of reason and prudence to maintain the integrity of their missions when they are threatened.

Much administration in American is done outside the bureaucracy itself by contracting out to private firms and nonprofit organizations. In the defense and aerospace areas this can result in a nearly unified functioning of public and private organizations. The contracting out of management of state penitentiaries is controversial in view of human rights implications.

A school of thought known as the New Public Governance argues that the bureau as a unit of administration should now take a back seat to networks of public and private collaborators. This idea would seem to counter the importance of having legally accountable public organizations on the job to perform the public's most vital business.

Arranging with nonprofit organizations to provide services to endangered groups in the population is a longstanding practice. To be successful, the state and local bureaucracies that make the arrangements must be certain of the competence and integrity of these organizations. Establishing close ties of mutual trust between agencies and nonprofits is essential but should not prohibit introducing change.

Direct citizen participation in the direction and operation of governmental services has become quite common in this country. The notion is highly congruent with democratic ideals but should be applied where it will actually work. One area of considerable success is the city neighborhood association, whose advantage is to unite civic activism and governmental authority without infringing on either.

ENDNOTES

1. Paul H. Appleby, *Big Democracy* (New York: Knopf, 1945), pp. vi, 118. Appleby was Under Secretary of USDA from 1940 to 1944 and later Dean of the Maxwell School at Syracuse University.
2. Charles T. Goodsell, "A New Vision for Public Administration," *Public Administration Review*: 66, no. 4 (July–August 2006), pp. 623–635, 629–630.
3. Examples are the California Code of Regulations, Rules and Regulations of the State of New York, the Code of Massachusetts Regulations, and the Virginia Register of Regulations.
4. Didi Tang, "Beijing Air Pollution Reaches Hazardous Levels," *Roanoke Times*, January 13, 2013.

5. *Statistical Abstract of the United States*, 2012, p. 230. On a worldwide basis, however, CO_2 levels are alarmingly high at 400 parts per million, the worst in millions of years.

6. Steven P. Croley, *Regulation and Public Interests: The Possibility of Good Regulatory Government* (Princeton, NJ: Princeton University Press, 2008).

7. Malcolm K. Sparrow, *The Regulatory Craft: Controlling Risks, Solving Problems, and Managing Compliance* (Washington, DC: Brookings Institution Press, 2000).

8. Carl J. Friedrich, "Public Policy and the Nature of Administrative Responsibility," *Public Policy*: 1 (1940): 3–14. For the "core of modern government" phrase, see his *Constitutional Government and Democracy*, rev. ed. (Boston: Ginn and Co., 1950), p. 37.

9. Herman Finer, "Administrative Responsibility in Democratic Government," *Public Administration Review* 1, no. 2 (1941): 335–350, 346.

10. William F. West, *Controlling the Bureaucracy: Institutional Constraints in Theory and Practice* (Armonk, NY: M.E. Sharpe, 1995). *Politics, Policy, and Organizations: Frontiers in the Scientific Study of Bureaucracy*, George A. Krause and Kenneth J. Meier, eds. (Ann Arbor: University of Michigan Press, 2003).

11. B. Dan Wood and Richard W. Waterman, *Bureaucratic Dynamics: The Role of Bureaucracy in America* (Boulder, CO: Westview Press, 1994).

12. Ibid., pp. 150–151.

13. Gregory A. Huber, *The Craft of Bureaucratic Neutrality: Interests and Influence in Governmental Regulation of Occupational Safety* (Cambridge: Cambridge University Press, 2007).

14. Ibid., pp. 236–238.

15. Gary L. Wamsley, Robert N. Bacher, Charles T. Goodsell, Philip S. Kronenberg, John A. Rohr, Camilla M. Stivers, Orion F. White, and James F. Wolf, *Refounding Public Administration* (Newbury Park, CA: Sage, 1990). See pp. 31–51 for the text of the manifesto.

16. John C. Beach et al., "State Administration and the Founding Fathers During the Critical Period," *Administration & Society* 28, no. 4 (February 1997): 511–530.

17. Wamsley et al., *Refounding Public Administration*, pp. 37, 81.

18. Charles T. Goodsell, *Mission Mystique: Belief Systems in Public Agencies* (Washington, DC: CQ Press, 2011), pp. 23–24, 258–260.

19. Goodsell, "A New Vision for Public Administration," pp. 631–632. To illustrate this thinking, in 2013 the administrator of NASA, Charles Bolden,

spoke to the press about his agency's plans for an unmanned mission to Mars. "NASA doesn't have the capability to do that right now. But we're on the path to be able to do it in the 2030s." Joel Achenbach, "NASA Outlines Vision for Mission to Mars," *Washington Post*, May 7, 2013.

20. Brian J. Cook, *Bureaucracy and Self-Development: Reconsidering the Role of Public Administration in American Politics* (Baltimore: Johns Hopkins University Press, 1996), ch. 6.

21. CNBC.com, citing USAspending.gov. Accessed March 11, 2013.

22. John A. Rehfuss, *Contracting Out in Government: A Guide to Working with Outside Contractors to Supply Public Services* (San Francisco: Jossey-Bass, 1989), p. 15. Steven J. Kelman, "Contracting," ch. 9 in *The Tools of Government: A Guide to the New Governance*, Lester M. Salamon, ed. (New York: Oxford University Press, 2002), p. 287. Griff Witte and Renae Merle, "Contractors Face More Scrutiny, Pinched Purses," *Washington Post*, November 28, 2006. Ed O'Keefe, "OMB Reports $15 Billion in Government Contracting Cuts," *Washington Post*, February 4, 2011.

23. Paul C. Light, *The True Size of Government* (Washington, DC: Brookings Institution, 1999), p. 38. Joselyn M. Johnston and Barbara S. Romzek, "The Promises, Performance, and Pitfalls of Government Contracting," ch. 17 in *The Oxford Handbook of American Bureaucracy*, Robert F. Durant, ed. (New York: Oxford University Press, 2010), p. 399.

24. Kelman, "Contracting," p. 288.

25. Federal Activities Inventory Reform (FAIR) Act of 1998, sec. 5.

26. Johnston and Romzek, "The Promises, Performance, and Pitfalls of Government Contracting," p. 412.

27. John Donahue, *The Privatization Decision* (New York: Basic Books, 1989), chs. 3, 5.

28. Kelman, "Contracting," p. 307.

29. "The Top 100 Contractors of the U.S. Federal Government," Wikipedia, retrieved March 13, 2013. Figure is for 2011.

30. Phillip J. Cooper, *Governing by Contract: Challenges and Opportunities for Public Managers* (Washington, DC: CQ Press, 2003), chs. 1, 3.

31. *Statistical Abstract*, 2012, p. 846.

32. Byron Eugene Price, *Merchandising Prisoners: Who Really Pays for Prison Privatization?* (Westport, CT: Praeger, 2006), pp. 2–10.

33. "Private Prison," Wikipedia article accessed February 15, 2013. *Statistical Abstract of the United States*, 2012, p. 217.

34. Rehfuss, *Contracting Out in Government*, p. 32.

35. David Shichor, *Punishment for Profit: Private Prisons/Public Concerns* (Thousand Oaks, CA: Sage, 1995), pp. 160–163, 210–231. Price, *Merchandising Prisoners*, p. 150.
36. See the following chapters in *The Oxford Handbook of American Bureaucracy*, Robert F. Durant, ed. (New York: Oxford University Press, 2010): Michael McGuire and Robert Agranoff, "Networking in the Shadow of Bureaucracy," pp. 372–395; Beryl A. Radin and Paul Posner, "Policy Tools, Mandates, and Intergovernmental Relations," pp., 447–471; and Laurence E. Lynn, Jr., "Has Governance Eclipsed Government?" pp. 669–690.
37. Goodsell, *Mission Mystique* (Washington, DC: CQ Press, 2011), pp. 49, 66, 105, 167, 203, 229.
38. *Statistical Abstract*, 2012, pp. 268–269.
39. Jeffrey M. Pressman and Aaron Wildavsky, *Implementation: How Great Expectations in Washington Are Dashed in Oakland; Or, Why It's Amazing that Federal Programs Work at All—This Being a Saga of the Economic Development Administration as Told by Two Sympathetic Observers Who Seek to Build Morals on a Foundation of Ruined Hopes* (Berkeley, CA: University of California Press, 1973).
40. Ruth Hoogland DeHoog and Lester M. Salamon, "Purchase-of-Service Contracting," in *The Tools of Government: A Guide to the New Governance*, Salamon, ed. (New York: Oxford University Press, 2002), ch. 10.
41. Wolfgang Bielefeld, James L. Perry, and Ann Marie Thompson, "Reluctant Partners? Nonprofit Collaboration, Social Entrepreneurship, and Leveraged Volunteerism," in *The Oxford Handbook of American Bureaucracy* (New York: Oxford University Press, 2010), ch. 18.
42. Goodsell, *The Case for Bureaucracy: A Public Administration Polemic*, 4th ed. (Washington, DC: CQ Press, 2004), p. 76.
43. Goodsell, *Mission Mystique*, pp. 168–169.
44. Nancy Roberts, "Public Deliberation in an Age of Direct Citizen Participation," *American Review of Public Administration* 34, no. 4 (December 2004): 315–353, 337–338, 344.
45. Jeffrey M. Berry, Kent E. Portney, and Ken Thomson, *The Rebirth of Urban Democracy* (Washington, DC: Brookings Institution, 1993).

EARNING AND RETAINING THE PUBLIC TRUST

In the article I cite in chapter 4 which offers the distinction of Rule and Response as over against politics and administration, I ventured another departure from public administration orthodoxy. This was to contend that the ultimate goal of bureaucracy in a democratic society is to build and maintain the public trust in its government. I made the point using a pyramidal diagram labeled "the mountain of public administration purpose." The lower half of the pyramid shows a set of penultimate "foothill goals" of legality, integrity, efficiency, effectiveness, public involvement, dependability, transparency and fairness. These reach upward to support an ultimate "pinnacle byproduct" designated as PUBLIC TRUST. The point I was making is that successful attainment in the mountain foothills produces, without conscious intention but nonetheless great import, the foundations of an orderly and peaceable polity in which democracy and freedom can flourish.[1]

In this chapter I explore the possibilities for American bureaucracy, especially at the national level, to fulfill the mountain's pinnacle ideal at this present moment in time. First, I review briefly the prior findings of this book in regard to making the substantive case that a quite positive basis for US public agencies to be considered trustworthy themselves exists. Second, I analyze four events labeled by the press as major scandals on the part of federal agencies. My purpose here is to back into the issue of bureaucratic trustworthiness by assessing temporary barriers that crop up from time to time to the maintenance of public trust. Third, I recount several instances in which federal agencies have in effect attempted to counter two kinds of damage partisan stalemate has inflicted on bureaucracy: inflexible deep funding cuts and creeping erosion of the integrity of agency missions. The need for this kind of action is my new normative case for bureaucracy. Finally, I examine two incidents that occurred at an identical time just as the final sentences in the book were being written. One is the partial federal shutdown, which laid bare the loss felt when federal agencies stopped operating. The other is the unsatisfactory rollout of Obamacare and the extent to which it might have been caused by a lack of bureaucratic underpinning.

A TRUSTWORTHY BUREAUCRACY?

What about administration as a potential bastion of trustworthiness? I dare say "bureaucracy" as a pejorative abstraction would be ranked by survey respondents just as low in the minds of citizens as Congress. Needless to say, to make it even a candidate for popular confidence, we must redefine the word as the actual people and institutions of US administrative governance, as done in this book. Is our bureaucracy so conceived capable of building and retaining the public's trust?

A Positive Basis for Trust. The information and ideas I have presented so far in this book are my interpretation of what already exists as a basis for public administration to act as a support for public trust in ways the gridlocked portions of government do not.

In the book's first chapter that asks, "What, Defend Bureaucracy?" several preliminary points were made. Gallup polls indicate that Americans trust the federal executive and state and local government considerably more than they do Congress. The Battlefield polling arranged by Adams and Infeld found that federal civil servants generate a great deal or a lot of confidence from 20 percent of respondents and "some" from 50 percent, with only 25 percent saying very little.

A "microscopic" examination of bureaucracy in chapter 2 showed that when citizens are asked about their own direct experiences with public agencies and their programs, their levels of satisfaction are surprisingly high. Bureaucracy is capable of significant productivity gains, and its programs can be quite successful over the long haul despite the impossibility of total success. While private businesses are often less costly than government bureaucracies in doing repetitive work, they can fall short on quality and accountability. Administrative bureaus do not necessarily "age" into decrepitude and are capable of creative renewal.

When bureaucrats were summoned "front and center" in chapter 3, we learned they are better educated than their private sector counterparts. On a purely numbers basis, government employment has over the years been a boon to bringing African Americans into the middle class. While minority populations and women have not yet attained full equality with white men with respect to rank, the movement away from white male dominance at the apex of power has constituted a veritable cultural revolution. Among other benefits, this change has brought new multicultural sensitivities into the workplaces of US public administration. Another plus is that online surveys of federal employees exhibit impressively high levels of work commitment and mission dedication.

Chapter 4's look "inside" bureaucratic governance brought to the fore the point that bureaucracy makes rules with the force of law in most every policy field imaginable. As a result of strictures laid down by the Administrative Procedure Act, the bureaucrats in some respects do a better job of "legislating" than legislators. Furthermore these unelected civic servants respond quickly to political and judicial instructions received from the three branches of government and add important insight to policy discussions. The shaping influences of bureaucracy are particularly crucial in the administration of high-stakes weapons contracts and in managing agreements with nonprofit organizations to render social services. Bureaucracy cannot govern alone without joint action with other entities, but neither can networks of private entities govern in an accountable way without bureaucracy. Curiously, actions by government organizations were indispensable in inventing the Internet that makes today's networks possible.

Regardless of whether or not bureaucracy has the capacity to compensate for partisan deadlock, any serious setback in its operational abilities will damage public trust. Imagine what would happen if meat inspectors began missing the presence of contamination beef. Or if overworked air traffic controllers caused a succession of airliners to crash. In the wake of such disasters public trust in the entire governance regime would begin to disintegrate. What this tells us is that because of bureaucracy's indispensible role in carrying out the work of government, it possesses a hidden residual value to the society of almost limitless proportions. Without it, no public trust at all in government would be possible. The challenge to bureaucracy in these perilous times of political division and public distrust is therefore as follows: if it falters significantly with respect to obtaining adequate funds or keeping alive core missions, the outcome is not just a continuation of the disturbing status quo of partisan deadlock but a readiness to slide into even deeper levels of distrust.

HOW BAD ARE THE SCANDALS?

Four major scandals broke out in federal government agencies between 2010 and 2013, the years in which this book was written. I clipped files on them in order to be in a position to assess their degree of seriousness after media attention quieted and investigations were conducted. My aim in describing them is to lay out the facts that will help you (and me) to determine the extent to which they do or do not deserve to erode seriously the degree of trust we should place in the organizations involved.

General Services Administration. In the late 1970s Jeffrey E. Neely joined the General Services Administration, the agency that provides most of the supplies and buildings for the civilian side of the federal government. In 2003 Neely was named chief of its Public Buildings Service for Region 9, also called the Pacific Rim Region. It serves the states of California, Arizona, Nevada, and Hawaii; the islands of American Samoa, Diego Garcia, Guam, and Okinawa; and US facilities in Japan and South Korea.

In 2009 Neely became acting GSA administrator for Pacific Rim. Two months later the region was scheduled to be host for the agency's 2010 Western Region Conference, to be held in Las Vegas. Traditionally a big splash for Regions 7, 8, 9, and 10, its last meeting had been in New Orleans at a cost of $600,000. Just to get ready for the 2010 meeting, a large travel budget was needed to house and feed conference planners in luxury hotels. After personally exploring possibilities, Neely selected as the conference site the upscale M Resort Spa Casino just outside Las Vegas. He prided himself as a big "out of the box" thinker and was determined to have an "over the top" event that was even better than the previous one.

Accordingly, spending on the conference itself was liberal to say the least. Several contracts were let for frills and entertainment, all without competitive bidding. Color-themed tags and programs were printed at a cost of $9,000; $8,130 was spent on souvenir books and $6,325 to strike commemorative coins. A fee of $75,000 obtained the services of a one-day, team-building exercise in which participants assembled bicycles. A clown was hired to provide poolside fun, and a mind reader was brought in to mystify guests.

At a "Red Carpet" awards ceremony on the last night of the conference, a video clip was shown that featured the award winner, an employee who was named GSA Administrator of the Day. It showed the person boasting about the considerable travel expenses he would file for reimbursement. Afterwards Neely stood up and joked about a lavish private party that had been held the night before in the suite of agency head Robert Peck. The total cost of the conference—attended by only 300 — was $823,000.

The Inspector General (IG) for GSA, Brian D. Miller, got wind of the Las Vegas bash and launched what became a two-year investigation. His preliminary findings warned of excessive conference spending. It also pointed out that Neely had been given a $9,000 bonus for his work that year. It was learned that Neely's wife had attended the conference as a registered guest without paying the steep registration fee and wore the badge of a female GSA official.

Word began leaking out of these actions, and a storm of media coverage resulted. Peck was quickly dismissed and replaced on a temporary basis by Martha N. Johnson. On the day the final IG report was submitted, she too was forced out. Subsequently two other headquarters officials left, followed by all four western regional commissioners, including Neely. Committees of both houses of Congress held hearings in which Democrats as well as Republicans expressed shock. Neely asserted his Fifth Amendment rights and refused to testify. A veteran executive at Treasury not previously associated with GSA, Dan M. Tangherlini, became Administrator. After becoming familiar with the agency, he declared it had "lost its focus."[2]

Secret Service. On April 13, 2012, President Obama flew to Cartagena, Columbia to attend the 6th Summit of the Americas. As always, advance "jump teams" composed of Secret Service agents and a group of military personnel arrived several days ahead of time to arrange for security. After the work was done but before the President arrived, the men in both teams went out on the town to relax. One stop was the Pleyboy Club, where they consumed alcohol and solicited women to take back to their rooms at the Hotel Caribe.

Before leaving early the next morning, one of the women got in an argument with a Secret Service agent over a "gift" of $800 allegedly promised to her the night before. He refused to hand over the money and ejected her brusquely from the room. The hotel staff became aware of the matter. The police were called, even though prostitution is not illegal in Columbia. Paula Reid, the ranking Secret Service officer on duty for the conference, was notified and ordered all of the involved agents home immediately, to be replaced by a substitute team.

When Mr. Obama arrived on the scene the next day, he held a press conference at which he planned to discuss policy issues facing the Americas. However, all the reporters wanted to ask about was the hotel incident. After being peppered with questions about the integrity of his protective security detail, the President said that Secret Service agents must always conduct themselves with "dignity and probity." In general, he added, all US government personnel must "observe the highest standards" when on duty abroad. If the allegations prove true, he told a questioner, "of course I'll be angry."

Mark Sullivan, director of the Secret Service back in Washington, was furious when he heard about the matter and he ordered an internal inquiry. Members of Congress declared the agency's reputation had been sullied and promised that committee hearings would follow. Selective Service employees and agency retirees living around the country were quoted in the media as saying they were irate about the damage that had been done to the agency's image.

The thirteen Selective Service members involved defended themselves on grounds that they had been off duty, had broken no laws, had violated no agency regulations, and had not compromised the safety of the President. They also pointed out that bored agents awaiting arrival of the chief executive had engaged in such diversions in the past without serious recrimination.

By the end of the month, eight of the men had been forced out of the organization and another had his security clearance lifted. Four others were declared free of serious misconduct. By contrast, disciplinary actions taken against the military personnel were less serious; eleven had their security clearances suspended and one was reassigned.

In the following weeks the Secret Service issued a new code of conduct for agents serving out of the country. It prohibited visits to "non-reputable establishments." No foreigners are to be allowed in hotel rooms except hotel staff and the police. Any consumption of alcohol is banned ten hours before going on duty, and no drinking is permitted while the protective action is in progress. The code also mandates prior and in-country briefings on agent conduct.

President Obama later summed up the situation this way: "The Secret Service, these guys are incredible. They protect me, they protect our girls. A couple of knuckleheads shouldn't detract from what they do. What they were thinking, I don't know. That's why they're not there anymore." Less than a year later the President appointed the first female director in the history of this 89-percent-male institution, Julia Pierson.[3]

Bureau of Alcohol, Tobacco, Firearms and Explosives. In 2006 during the Bush administration, ATF launched a gun-running sting designed to snare Mexican drug dealers. Illegal weapons were purposely sold in US markets to persons suspected of being straw buyers for Mexican drug cartels. The idea was to track these individuals across the Mexican border, allowing agents to intercept the transit of the firearms later and apprehend the cartel members who sought them. For a time the practice was carried out on a limited basis. Care was taken not to delay the interceptions too long for fear the trail would peter out and the weapons would disappear. Several arrests were made of straw buyers and middlemen, but not high-level gang leaders.

Members of Congress complained that the tactic was being employed on such a limited scale that it was not making a serious dent in US drug smuggling. Only little fish were being caught, not cartel kingpins. In response, the head of the Phoenix office of ATF took it upon himself to develop an expanded tracking plan. He presented it to top people at Justice and the heads of the ATF, DEA, and FBI. After a lengthy teleconference, it was approved and given the code name "Operation Fast and Furious."

The plan envisioned deceptive sale of thousands of illegally bought weapons, among them AK-47 assault rifles. Their movement into Mexico was to be delayed long enough for agents to arrest top cartel leaders, enabling solid arrests and the crushing of entire gun distribution networks.

ATF agents working the Phoenix office were, however, worried about the soundness of the plan. By allowing a lengthy period of time for the guns to "walk," they could become lost in the distribution chain without producing significant apprehensions. They furthermore had grave doubts about permitting so many illegal weapons to fall into criminal hands generally. To make the plan even more questionable, Mexican law enforcement authorities were not to be notified about what was going on.

Operation Fast and Furious went ahead anyway. Large quantities of high-powered weapons were allowed on the market, and agents tried to follow their movement to ultimate buyers. When they got uneasy about the amount of time elapsing, they insisted that their superiors in Phoenix and Washington give the go-ahead for interception-and-arrest actions. Time after time they were told to wait longer, possibly because some targeted cartel leaders were undercover DEA informants. The increasingly disillusioned agents were also suspicious that Washington was eager to avoid a flurry of gun-related arrests that would arouse the ire of Fourth Amendment supporters.

On December 14, 2010, the operation began to unravel when a much admired Border Patrol agent, Terry Brian, was caught in a firefight 10 miles inside Mexico, armed only with a type of nonlethal beanbag shooter used to detain illegal immigrants. Terry was fatally shot just before planning to join his family for Christmas. Two AK-47 rifles that had been identified for Fast and Furious tracing were found on the scene.

A group of ATF agents mutinied and brought their concerns to Senator Charles Grassley, senior Republican on the Senate Judiciary Committee. He responded quickly, and the failures of the project were soon in the headlines. In time it was discovered that thousands of illegal weapons had been put into circulation with no significant arrests made. Operation Fast and Furious was immediately terminated. Several congressional investigations ensued, and Republican Congressman Darrell Issa characterized the scandal as being of Watergate proportions. At the Justice Department several top political appointees were forced out. It came to light that over 1,400 weapons had not been recovered, although 179 were found at fatal-shooting crime scenes in Mexico and 130 in the United States. For all this, not a single drug lord was arrested.[4]

Internal Revenue Service. The accusations of special "targeting" by the IRS of Tea Party applications for tax exemption is the most significant recent bureaucratic scandal in our group. It is also a complicated matter. For both reasons, I give more attention to this case than the others.

Section 501(c) provision of the Internal Revenue Code relates to special tax treatment of nonprofit organizations, a concept as old as the federal income tax itself. Generally speaking, nonprofits are exempt from the US corporate income tax and the federal unemployment tax. Many subtypes of 501(c) organization exist. Section 501(c)(3) applies to gifts to religious, educational, and charitable organizations. These are deductible from the donor's tax liability; at the same time, such entities are forbidden from participating in any form of political activity.

Another section, 501(c)(4), applies to "Civic Leagues, Social Welfare Organizations, and Local Associations of Employees." In practice, the "social welfare" piece of this classification has become a catchall category for groups that promote the public good. Unlike (c)(3) organizations, donations to them are not tax deductible. However, over time, it has been interpreted that (c)(4)s can fund political activity, if at the same time they are *primarily* engaged in social benefit work. The formal tax rules provide no more specific guidance other than this, requiring IRS personnel to examine the specific facts and circumstances of each case to decide on eligibility. Important for our subject, such groups are under no obligation to report the identity of their donors, including contributors who are affiliated with political parties or ideological causes.

After the US Supreme Court decision *Citizens United v. Federal Election Commission* was handed down in January 2010, restrictions no longer exist on private donations to political causes or candidates. During the 2010 and 2012 election campaigns, both sides of the political spectrum formed groups and hired bundlers to channel funds to favored candidates for national as well as state office. This was particularly the case for groups on the right, which suddenly began filing scores of applications to the IRS for 501(c)(4) status. Although this gave them a tax break and a form of official recognition, the move was doubtless motivated by being able to keep secret the identity of donors.

Several Democratic Senators expressed concern that this sudden growth in such applications indicated applicants were attempting to abuse the underlying purpose of this exemption. They wrote letters to IRS Commissioner Douglas Shulman asking him to investigate this possibility and take steps to clarify the rules regarding eligibility. Republican Senators, however, warned that any attempt by the agency to violate the privacy of applicant organizations and their affairs would not be tolerated.

All IRS field offices conduct routine exemption-determination reviews. Borderline cases and issues that surround them are handled by a central office. This is the Tax Exempt and Government Entities Division (TEGE), whose 900 employees work in a downtown building in Cincinnati, along with the regional IRS field office. It is here where the flood of new applications was sent that seemed to have much more on their agendas than social welfare. The task was not easy. The standard for being "primarily" engaged in such social welfare activity had already been narrowed in practice to the thinnest possible edge of eligibility, that of being at least 51 percent. This meant that TEGE employees had to decide whether political activity exceeded 49 percent. Moreover they were required to analyze each case separately, going into as much detail as needed.

In order to make a start in getting hold of the problem, IRS workers devised a rough decision tool to isolate from the start which applications were likely to have political intent and thus require extra scrutiny. This was known as the "Be On the Look Out" list, or BOLO. It consisted of multipage spread sheets on which it was checked whether the organizations have certain key words in their titles or applications. The BOLO project was developed in two stages between August 2010 and August 2012. The ultimate outcome was 15 lists of numerous search terms. The items did not cover the right wing alone, but rhetoric coming from all points on the political spectrum. For example: "Occupy Wall Street" and "Medical marijuana" on the far left; "Progressive," "Blue," "Healthcare legislation," and "Green energy organization" in the liberal camp; "Open-source software," "Israel," "Newspaper entities," and "Paying the national debt" for conservatives; and "Patriot," "9/12," and "Tea Party" for the far right.[5]

In addition to using these terms to spot hard cases, the Division struggled with its own criteria for making final decisions. These changed over time. In July 2011 a standard was adopted to reject exemption if evidence exists that the organization had lobbied to change the law to end the ban on political engagement. In January 2012 a criterion with substantive policy content was circulated: "political action type organizations involved in limiting/expanding Government, education on the Constitution and Bill of Rights, social economic reform/movement." Then, in May of that year, a third very vague rejection standard was given out: "organizations with indicators of significant amounts of political campaign intervention."

Because of the spurt in right-wing applications, a special team was set up to deal specifically with them. It took its task very seriously, which in retrospect led to the initial appearance of far-right "targeting." One step the group took was to supplement the criteria of excessive politicization with a six-point profile of conservative activism: a focus on government spending, debt, or taxes; use of phrases like making America a better place to live; criticism of how the country is being run; wider education on the Constitution and Bill of Rights; attacks on the Affordable Health Care Act; and a belief that federal election results lack integrity.

A second step was to send out lengthy queries to applicants and questionnaires for them to fill out. They asked about ties to candidates, data on members and contributors, lists of event speakers, press releases, and transcripts of interviews. This aroused the ire of these groups as they felt they were being singled out for extra scrutiny, which in this respect was true. Delays of months or even years in receiving an answer from the IRS were experienced, maddening the applicants no end. Long silences on the part of the IRS stemmed from intensified information gathering and an ability only to reject an application or to approve it. Eventually not a single Tea Party application was turned down, but approvals came forth with painful slowness. One was approved in 2009, two in 2010, and none in 2011. Finally in 2012 things broke loose, and twenty-seven were granted. Eight applications from Patriot groups were approved in 2011 and twenty-eight in 2012. Although one liberal-progressive application was rejected, approvals of them came more steadily: seventeen in 2009, twenty-one in 2009, twenty-eight in 2011, and thirty in 2012.[6]

The rightist groups did not take this treatment sitting down. They contacted Republican members of Congress repeatedly to express outrage over being singled out for delay and interrogation. Representative Darrel Issa was most sympathetic to their cause and urged J. Russell George, the Inspector General for Treasury who covered the IRS, to investigate. He launched what became a lengthy inquiry; later it was discovered that he focused specifically on treatment of Tea Party–related applications rather than the entire picture.

Meanwhile Lois G. Lerner, manager of the determinations unit in Cincinnati was becoming very uneasy about the situation. A 34-year veteran of the federal civil service, she knew full well what could happen if Tea Party exemption review were publicized in the national media. She told her staff not to do anything that cannot be reasonably explained before a congressional committee. She asked her superiors at IRS headquarters what to do, and they failed to respond with any specific instructions. Although by law the IRS was required to monitor the applications for political activity, just how this should be done was uncharted territory. Probably, in addition, no one at the top ranks in either IRS or Treasury wanted the matter to become a political liability that would step in the way of Obama's reelection. It would appear that Lerner felt she could not handle the ticking time bomb alone, so the best thing to do was to let it go off.[7]

On May 10, 2013, Lerner was scheduled to speak at a meeting of the American Bar Association in Washington. She asked a member of her internal exemptions advisory board who was also an ABA member to be in the audience and raise the issue in the question period. When that was done, she responded by denouncing the practice as "absolutely inappropriate" for "front-line people" to do. In the days that followed she made a personal apology for what had happened and went on to say the actions were not driven by anti-right sentiment within her division. Moreover, she insisted, the tactics had not been ordered by IRS headquarters, Treasury, or White House officials.

As the scandal unfolded President Obama denounced what was first believed to be deliberate partisan targeting, characterizing it as "inexcusable." "I'm angry about it," he said, and "will not tolerate this kind of behavior in any agency, but especially in the IRS, given the power that it has and the reach that it has." Democratic as well as Republican Members of Congress joined the condemnation in the strongest terms, saying it constitutes a threat to citizen trust in government in general. Some GOP members of the House made comparisons to the "enemies" list of President Nixon. Speaker John Boehner declared, "My question isn't about who's going to resign, my question is who's going to jail over this scandal."

Several congressional investigations were launched, complete with well-publicized hearings. Douglas Shulman, IRS Commissioner from March 2008 to November 2012, admitted being aware of the problem but denied bearing personal responsibility. Shulman's deputy, Steven T. Miller—who took over the agency on an acting basis after the election— was also evasive about accepting responsibility. Treasury Secretary Jack Lew immediately demanded Miller's resignation. In a hearing before Issa's House Oversight and Government Reform Committee, Lerner surprised her interrogators by saying she and her colleagues had done nothing wrong, but then she took the Fifth and refused to answer any questions.

In early May 2013, Treasury Inspector General George issued his final report. He testified before the Issa committee that the targeting was prejudicial against rightist applicants but was not the result of manipulation by the White House, which had been the assumption of the anti-Obama media and conservatives in general. Instead, the problem was bad management, he said; TEGE employees were insufficiently informed on the tax laws, defiant of their superiors, and blind to the appearance of impropriety. Former TEGE workers since retired painted a similar picture. They described the unit as not infected with malice, but not forcefully led—and trying to get the work done as best they could without rocking the boat.[8]

President Obama seemed surprised by the onset of the incident. White House staff members had seen it coming and were irate that Lerner had blown the whistle before they could get control of the issue. It appears that the White House Counsel made a conscious decision not to bring the matter to the President's attention earlier. Upon the dismissal of Miller, Daniel Werfel was named acting IRS director. He conducted his own internal inquiry and terminated further use of the BOLO lists; but at the same time, he pointed out that they were not confined to the right wing but covered all points of view.

Led by Congressman Issa, a drumbeat of criticism emanated from the Republicans for months, rivaling Benghazi as the main issue by which to attack the Obama administration. Even though the notion of an intentional conspiracy to hurt Republican chances in the presidential election eventually began to lose traction, Issa and Dave Camp, chair of the House Committee on Ways and Means, took to the op-ed pages of the *Washington Post* in a piece headlined "Holes in the IRS Narrative." They alleged that the "blame Cincinnati" thesis was unraveling and the White House and its allies had been "engaged in a flailing effort to put this scandal behind them." Representatives Elijah Cummings and Sander Levin, ranking Democrats on the Oversight and Government Reform and Ways and Means committees respectively, replied a week later by saying not "a scintilla of evidence" has been uncovered to back claims that the procedures were intentionally aimed at targeting the President's enemies during an election year.[9]

Commentary. Looking at these four incidents as a whole, several types of misdeeds can be seen: rogue administrator arrogance and blatant waste; a failure to observe appropriate personal conduct abroad; programmatic error and dismissal of compelling policy objections from the field; and a failure to recognize and correct an unintended appearance of alarming partisanship. What we did *not* find, it is important to note, is intentional violation of law, bribery, conflict of interest, refusal to obey orders, or cover-up of wrongdoing.

You will form your own opinions on how serious are these missteps. It is my view the GSA and Secret Service incidents were certainly regrettable but not of earthshaking proportions. GSA waste was in the hundreds of thousands but not the millions. Secret Service agents exercised poor judgment but did not endanger the president. In these kinds of instances it is unlikely any serious public backlash occurred after the media stir died out.

The ATF weapon sting program is at another level of importance. The agency failed to meet its objectives and its failure to halt the program had tragic side effects of a vivid and sickening nature. It is likely that ATF's reputation will continue to be burdened by Fast and Furious for some years, particularly in the law enforcement community.

The IRS matter is even more serious. It reinforced the rhetoric and confirmed the belief of antigovernment skeptics that the regime in power in America can and did use the authority and weight of the bureaucracy to perpetuate its existence by assisting the reelection of the President. This is serious indeed; any evidence thereto, whether definitive or deceiving, poisons the assumptions that underlie the acceptability of electoral outcomes of a modern democracy. Moreover, the part of the bureaucracy in question was the nation's tax collector, an institution that must retain the public's trust more than most any other. True, the White House was not guilty of a Watergate-level political crime. Moreover the singling out of Tea Party applications was not a conscious partisan act. Management ineptitude at the operations level, in IRS Washington head-quarters and to some extent among White House staff—along with unworkable exemption standards in the law—was the problem. Nonethe-less, the damage done to the image of the federal government in the minds of millions of Americans will likely linger a long time. In short, the barriers created to public trust by scandal can be both fleeting chimeras and penetrating images; hopefully agencies can learn to minimize the first and overcome the second.

BATTLING FOR RESOURCES

The substantive case I have been making for bureaucracy in this book is that our administrative institutions are far more effective in serving the public weal than most people think. My "new" normative case is that we need our government agencies to be proactive in building and maintain-ing public trust during this crisis of deadlock—even as they are them-selves suffering because of it. What we now examine is ways in which agencies handled (1) a severe lack of funding and (2) a deterioration of mission effectiveness. In both instances, we will assess how they could or could not seek to uphold public trust by circumnavigating inaction by a stalemated Congress.

An Era of Adversity. Political conditions prevailing in the twenty-first century's first decades explain why this is true. Largely in reaction to Obama's first term, a new force arose in 2010 to push the antigovernment agenda farther to the right and thereby split conservative ranks wide open. Moderate probusiness forces among Republicans found themselves competing with a right-wing Tea Party movement, whose project is to dismantle the federal government as much as possible. Meanwhile another wave of distrust has emerged on the political left in the wake of the IRS affair, the Justice Department's actions to find reporters' sources of press leaks, and revelations that the National Security Agency has been secretly gaining access to Americans' telephone and Internet information.

Following the 2010 election, a policy deadlock developed between a Democratic-controlled Senate and a House dominated by the Republicans beholden to its Tea Party faction. Budgets of the national government could not be passed. In order to get the national debt limit raised, a "sequester" was set in motion that imposed an arbitrary 8 percent cut to most federal appropriations. Prime items on Obama's domestic agenda stalled, and Senate confirmation of executive appointments was inordinately delayed. The House majority turned most of its attention from passing laws to investigating the bureaucracy. Political division within the nation became more bitter than usual because of unlimited anonymous political contributions; computer-assisted redistricting to make legislative districts safe for extremists; a 24-hour television news cycle that instantly sensationalizes events; a profuse set of social media that has created a free-for-all public discourse echo chamber; and permanently unresolved hot-button issues like abortion, gay rights, gun control, immigration, and global warming.

Looking back in history, the challenge for American public administration in the nineteenth century was creating professionalized agencies to replace partisan patronage and machine politics. The twentieth century's challenge to bureaucracy was to overcome depression and to wage war, both requiring highly capable administration at the national level. The comparable challenges for this century, to this point, are equally massive: to defend the nation against terrorists and to overcome a storm of antigovernment sentiment that threatens essential public services and the public trust.

The Squeeze on Spending. When I was interviewing National Park Service rangers for my *Mission Mystique* book a few years ago, they would joke with gallows humor that the only supplies they had money to order were bullets and toilet paper. Considering the effects of inflation, mandated salary changes, and new security measures, allocations for park operations dropped by $10 million between 2001 and 2005—even while new parks were created. During this period, 868 career positions were lost; and to keep the organization going, it had to rely on 1,400 park foundation employees, 500 interns, and 137,000 volunteers. In 2008 the National Academy of Public Administration found that interpretive staffing in the parks had fallen to its lowest level in years and that 2,811 historic structures were in poor condition. The GAO reported that Bryce and Yellowstone had curtailed backcountry patrols; Yosemite had cut the number of law enforcement rangers; and Zion had reduced restroom cleaning from twice a day to once, causing visitor complaints.[10]

Since that time, funding conditions for federal agencies have worsened. More than one million jobs were cut from public sector payrolls in the United States between 2011 and 2012. The annual pay raise for federal workers was reduced from 4 percent in 2009 to zero percent in 2011–2013. Examples of the consequences include delaying the completion of cleanup projects at Superfund sites and causing several states to cut back free AIDS/HIV medications for low-income patients. The Navy postponed the rebuilding of its fleet by 16 ships, and a naval air station in Virginia stopped mowing the grass on its grounds until it was a foot high. At the subnational level, state support for the country's major public research universities fell 20 percent, and the public libraries of Fairfax County, Virginia, dumped all books not checked out for two years—for example, *The Works of Aristotle* and *The Rise and Fall of the Roman Empire.*[11]

Early in 2013, I published a short article in *Public Administration Review* in which I advanced the notion of "self-stewardship" during these dark times for government agencies.[12] My idea was that as stewards of their own mission and of the institution that pursues it, they should not simply endure this fiscal starvation but do something about it. One of the points I made was that agencies should take the initiative and make smart budget cuts of their own. Not only would this help the larger cause, it would earn them political points with the appropriators. I urged, for example, that outdated programs and units of peripheral importance to the mission be terminated. Also support positions not essential to the core mission should be cut to the bone. However—to make this strategy possible—across-the-board, nondiscriminatory reductions must be avoided, I added. Unfortunately, the sequester set in motion by the Budget Control Act of 2011 took precisely the opposite course and dictated an approximate 8 percent reduction across in all accounts, with very few exceptions.

Some agencies actually did achieve budget cuts in addition to absorbing the 8-percent loss, but that was triggered not by self-stewardship but to defuse the adverse impact of scandal. GSA's new director Dan Tangherlini cancelled planned agency conferences and reduced executive bonuses. In addition he trimmed spending for computer systems and printing by 43 percent. While this helped him gain confirmation votes in the Senate, it did nothing to make his agency more efficient. Under similar circumstances, acting director at IRS Daniel Werfel cancelled nearly $98 million in employee bonuses. Since the IRS was also found by investigators to be sponsoring conference extravaganzas, he cut travel and hotel expenses. The same happened at Veterans Affairs, under criticism for lengthy delays in making veteran disability decisions caused by difficulties in digitizing its record system.[13]

In 2011 the White House attempted the strategy of trying to score a few points of its own by calling for nonessential expenditure cuts across the executive branch. An executive order was issued that set the goal of reducing government-paid travel by 20 percent. Future out-of-town conferences were to be minimized and held in government-owned facilities if possible. The privilege of riding around Washington in a government car was to be restricted to highest ranking officials only. Also to be curtailed were technology and equipment outlays, multiple employee laptops and cell phones, and inactive wireless accounts. The directive even included a ban on free agency baseball caps, T shirts, mugs, mouse pads, and lapel pins.[14]

The principal tool used by federal administrators to survive sequestration was the furlough, by which is meant taking one day off a week without pay over a temporary period. This was a way to cut big dollars out of personnel accounts without having to terminate people and thereby lose talent and capacity permanently. The exact number of furlough weeks stipulated could be adjusted flexibly to meet shifting circumstances. Unfortunately the realities of administering the tool turned out to be more complicated and anxiety producing than anticipated. Because of legal requirements to serve notice, thirty-day advance-warning letters had to be delivered for furloughs up to twenty-one days, with more days needing sixty-day notice. This meant that employees and their families had plenty of time to worry about household finances long before their actual extent and timing was known. As it turned out, overall furlough use was less than feared; nonetheless another emotion-laden impact hit when some agencies had to take more days than others, creating feelings of inequity. Several agencies also utilized the elimination of overtime pay to save money, contributing to anxiety among wage employees.

The biggest employee group affected was the 800,000 civilians working for the Department of Defense. Initially they were told twenty-two furlough days would be imposed, a figure later reduced to fourteen and ultimately to eleven. Then a subgroup of 118,000 was exempted entirely because their duties were categorized as particularly crucial and/or sensitive. Those remaining were slated to sacrifice one day of pay per week over three months, reducing their salary by a full 20 percent for the equivalent of one season per year. This was a hard blow to thousands of middle-class families saddled with house mortgages and college expenses. A frustrated Secretary Chuck Hagel burst out, "I can't run this institution into the ditch!"[15]

Savvy Spending Politics. Another admonition I gave for agency self-stewardship in my PAR article was to play smooth, wise, and savvy politics. What that means depends, of course, on the particular situation. Hence I cannot offer any general guidelines in this regard; by reviewing some actual cases, however, readers may think of possibilities for a given instance they have in mind.

Prior to the sequester's start-up date, a few agencies were able to have influential friends on the Hill intervene in their behalf as negotiations leading to the Budget Control Act were underway. Democrats were able to get the Social Security Administration exempted, and the Republicans did the same for one of their few favored bureaucracies, the US Border Patrol. Both parties felt obliged to demonstrate sympathy for service men and women returning from war, hence the huge Department of Veterans Affairs was entirely excluded. Although this certainly helped the VA, veterans' services performed in other departments were still sequestered; this included mental health counseling in Defense, training programs at Labor, and housing vouchers administered by the Department of Housing and Urban Development.[16]

Other federal agencies gave good reasons to be excused from sequestration, but were not able to generate the political backing needed to get it. The Census Bureau said it needed three forthcoming strong budgets to conduct the 2020 census properly. They tried to attain leverage by pointing out they had already closed half of their regional offices through consolidation, however the tactic did not win any sympathy. The CDC said its laboratories must keep up with new advances in medical science, but they failed to convince dealmakers exactly how the nation's health would thereby suffer. The National Transportation Safety Board contended that ongoing deterioration in the country's transportation infrastructure requires it to receive more funding to make buses and trains safe for the public. The agency did not lay out sufficient frightening scenarios, and the appeal fell on deaf ears.[17]

In the PAR article I urged agencies to get their constituents to organize joint publicity campaigns to pressure Congress. This turned out to be a useless idea. The Forest Service stressed how the ravaging wildfire season of 2012 totally consumed that year's funds for crews and aircraft. However the even worse 2013 season had not yet begun, so the tactic did not help. National Park Service Director Jon Jarvis outlined how deep cuts to the NPS budget over the years had hobbled services to the visiting public, and evidence was plentiful that this was the case. Unfortunately Representative Issa chose to make ridicule of the implication that trash is now piling up and bathrooms are filthy, so that effort went nowhere. The only reprieve obtained by the Park Service was a cessation of furloughs for officers of its Park Police, which patrols the National Mall. This was achieved after they pressed their case to Eleanor Holmes Norton, District of Columbia delegate to the House of Representatives. She reminded her colleagues that in exactly one week a hoard of tourists would be arriving on the Mall for the Memorial Day weekend, with 400,000 Rolling Thunder motorcycles in the forefront. The Park Police furlough problem was immediately solved.[18]

In my article I counseled against aggressive moves, such as threatening to close down an indispensable function of government. After examining the two most successful instances of savvy sequester politics, I realize I was wrong. Clearly skillful hardball *can* work in Washington. The trick is to play the public game and the insider game simultaneously. We have two good examples before us.

Two Political Victories. Secretary of Agriculture Tom Vilsack began early to convince Congress that USDA meat plant inspectors be exempted. He said food safety would be compromised if inspectors were not present at all times. If they were subject to sequester and furloughs or some other way to diminish their presence, the public interest would demand that processing plants would have to be shut down, probably for 11 days. The consequence of this would be a $10 billion loss to the economy. Furthermore, the relevant employees would lose $400 million in wages. These messages were carried to Members of Congress from agricultural states by a flotilla of lobbyists representing the National Chicken Council, National Turkey Federation, American Meat Institute, and National Cattlemen's Beef Association. Soon an additional appropriation of $55 million in new money was appropriated that made meat inspector furloughs unnecessary.[19]

An even more intricate strategy was employed in behalf of air traffic controllers. From news reports on the sequence of events, we can be led to assume that early on Secretary of Transportation Ray LaHood convinced the White House staff that long delays at airports would be so abhorrent to the flying public that this disgust might serve as a gun to shoot down sequester itself.

Without prior public notice, LaHood suddenly announced the furloughing of air traffic controllers at 149 lesser, but significant, airports. For all practical purposes, this meant they would be shut down entirely. Because LaHood had privately notified the entire aviation community of his plan, all affected transportation and economic interests were aware of what was going to happen and were primed for protest. Sure enough, a barrage of objection erupted from the cities affected, joined by protests from the Air Line Pilots Association and National Air Traffic Controller Association. Members of Congress representing the cities designated for an airport shutdown expressed grave concern. The economic implications were obvious to the aviation industry as well, and several big airlines banded together to seek a court restraining order. They argued that closing these airports would delay 6,700 flights a day across the country because of accumulated hub buildups.

On a Friday two weeks later, LaHood announced that the tower closures would take place on the following Monday. But then he delayed actual implementation for a few days, probably to let the implications sink in. Then, on April 22, 2013, 1,500 controllers—a tenth of the force—did not show up for work. Delays of 1–3 hours occurred in airports across the country, including Reagan Airport in Washington where members of Congress go to fly. As the media covered the situation over the following four days, long lines, lengthy delays, and rising traveler anger were vividly reported.

Republican leaders in the House insisted the crisis was being artificially manufactured by Obama and the Democrats to build up opposition to needed cutbacks in government spending. In the Senate, majority leader Harry Reid acted on cue and introduced a bill that would delay all sequester cuts until the following year. This got nowhere, but a measure quickly passed both houses that ended the crisis. It did not provide additional money as in the meat inspector case, but authorized fund transfers among Department of Transportation appropriation accounts so that Federal Aviation Administration furloughing could end. Fund flexibility was also instituted to stop long airport lines at Transportation Security Administration gates and Custom checkpoints. White House spokesman Jay Carney said the President would sign the measure even though it was a "Band Aid solution" that failed to repeal the sequester as a whole.[20]

Commentary. I suppose sequestration and the furloughs and other disruptions that followed constituted a success story in the eyes of Tea Party conservatives. The federal bureaucracy was temporarily cut back and billions of taxpayer dollars were not spent. A blow was definitely struck upon the federal bureaucratic beast!

Yet I also suspect that reasonable Americans will admit there were costs. The national parks continued to fall behind. Warships needed to back the nation's foreign policy will be built later. Citizens of Fairfax County will not find Aristotle or Gibbons on their library shelves. The 2020 census will not be as well executed as it could be. Research advances in epidemiology will be slowed, the nation's transportation infrastructure will not get the safety attention it needs, and funds for fighting forest fires could run out. Do these actions help build public trust in government? I doubt it.

Your author claimed he had good advice for public administrators in these dark times for public administration, packaged as "self-stewardship." My recommendations were largely useless, but I was right on one point. This was the mistake of using across-the-board cuts as a way to bring bureaucracy to its knees. A fixed percentage figure convinces casual observers that this step will clearly make the federal sector smaller—and since all of government is equally bad, we might as well lop off as big an overall slice as possible. What this strategy amounts to, however, is a blind attack on long-time, lawful, even distinguished institutions willy-nilly without bothering to find out which of their activities are essential and which are not. While the furlough device was probably the best way to minimize the damage wrought by this know-nothing approach, it created serious erosion of morale among millions of middle-class Americans who, as the federal government's civil servants, are a key to rebuilding the public trust—if that can be done.

BATTLING FOR THE MISSION

A necessary, but not sufficient, condition for good public administration is adequate funding. A strong sense of mission goes far to cover what's also necessary. *Great* public administration, I would submit, incorporates a readiness to do battle for that mission when it is threatened.

My position on this subject derives from the key importance of a sense of core purpose in motivating bureaucrats and propelling their agencies forward. In chapter 1 and elsewhere in this book, I have stated my thoughts on how a mission's "mystique" can energize bureaucracy. In chapter 3 we learned of the galloping elephant theories of Rainey-Steinbauer and the empirical studies of Wright and Boardman-Sundquist on mission motivation and public service efficacy.

Hence, as we think about how bureaucracy can best sustain public trust in this time of political gridlock, we must consider how mission integrity can be maintained through the efforts of those who are committed to keeping the governance of our democracy effective despite its divided politics. At times this may require intervening—at least temporarily—in policy matters that legislatures usually assume as a prerogative of their own to act upon.

Executive Intervention. As with my previous comments on battling for resources, I do not offer specific formulas for action. Instead, I review examples of where the practice has occurred as a source of insights.

In view of where the Constitution vests the federal government's executive power, we should not be surprised that the President at times acts counter to statutes passed by Congress. President Bush had the habit of issuing signing statements that qualified the meaning of laws he did not entirely agree with. President Obama has not been reluctant to apply his own authority in opposition to legislative action. For example he chose not to interpret the military overthrow of Egypt's Morsi regime as a "coup" even though by any reasonable definition it was precisely that. The reasoning was that although foreign assistance legislation requires that aid be cut off to any government so formed, he wished to keep the option of keeping it available in this instance.

During the period of deadlock within Congress and between the two political branches of government, the White House has on several occasions brought the bureaucracy directly into efforts to counteract dysfunction on Capitol Hill. This has placed political appointees and administrators in the position of openly defying legislative intention. When Congress failed to replace the Bush administration's No Child Left Behind Act, the Education Department's Secretary Arne Duncan went ahead on his own and waived standard-testing requirements for many states. In the absence of comprehensive immigration reform, Mr. Obama directed Immigration and Customs Enforcement (ICE) within the Department of Homeland Security to stop deporting young illegal aliens. As the time came for the Affordable Care Act's full implementation, because of the hardship it would cause for larger businesses, the employer mandate to provide workers health insurance was postponed for one year by the Department of Health and Human Services. In response Representative Steve Scalise of Louisiana, chair of the conservative Republican Study Committee in the House, asserted, "We all take an oath to uphold the laws of this country and our Constitution, and that doesn't mean you pick the laws you like and you ignore the laws you don't."[21]

In another key example, when Congress refused to pass what was vilified as the "cap and trade" bill to cut greenhouse admissions, EPA was given the green light to regulate atmospheric heat-trapping gasses anyway. Because of this agency's extensive rulemaking powers, the result was that significant steps were taken to slow global warming. With the words "cap and trade" now being equated with "the war on coal" in mining states, the issue had become too hot for Congress to handle in any form.

A "carbon plan," issued by the White House in June of 2013, had many facets. The most important was to take full advantage of the 2007 US Supreme Court decision *Massachusetts v. the EPA* that explicitly declares that Clean Air Act authority applies to regulation of greenhouse gases. In fact earlier in 2013, the agency had already published a draft regulation that dealt with such emissions from new electric power generating plants. Now the administration is taking the step of applying it to existing ones as well, necessitating heavy retrofitting expenditures. In a concession to the wishes of the utility industry, different standards were contemplated for coal-fueled versus natural gas–fueled plants, in that the former would be more seriously affected.

The carbon plan also included many other steps to be carried out by executive agencies. Loan guarantees for fossil fuel projects will be made available. Wind and solar energy installations would be allowed on public lands. Fuel economy standards will be issued for trucks as well as cars. Added federal commitments are to be made to encourage energy efficient buildings, develop a comprehensive methane strategy, and protect the integrity of forests and landscapes.

As a consequence, the bureaucracy is about to enter the global warming political battlefield as an active participant. The brickbats are already flying. American Electric Power's CEO Nick Akins called Obama's rhetoric "fervent." Republican Representative Steve Daines, Montana's only House member, declared that Obama "wants to move toward shutting down the coal industry." A spokesperson for PPL Montana, owner of the giant Colstrip power plant in Montana that consumes 10 million tons of coal a year, said carbon dioxide controls will add $57 in cost for every ton of coal it burns. On the bouquet-throwing side, Sierra Club executive director Michael Brune said the President is "lacing up his gloves and getting ready" for a fight with the coal industry. Gina McCarthy, the newly confirmed EPA administrator, insists that cutting carbon pollution will not destroy jobs but will "feed the economic engine of this country." As for the coal industry, she argues its best interests lie in actively adapting to fundamental changes that have taken place in the energy marketplace.[22]

Policy actions by the Department of Justice are usually thought of as expressions of administration wishes, but it too is a bureaucracy and its actions can tread on congressional toes. In 2013 Attorney General Eric Holder directed all US Attorneys around the country to stop bringing criminal charges that carry long mandatory prison sentences against low-level, nonviolent defendants. Many voices in and out of Congress saluted the measure as a way to alleviate the massive size of the state prison population, currently at 1.3 million persons. However this view is not unanimous. Republican Senator Charles Grassley, displeased with Obama's solo initiatives of late, said such action should be taken only by Congress: "The overreach by the administration to unilaterally decide which laws to enforce and which laws to ignore is a disturbing trend."[23]

In another 2013 Justice Department action, a memo from Deputy Attorney General James Cole to US Attorneys dealt with the problem that federal law still bans the use of marijuana, even though the states of Colorado and Washington have legalized it in small quantities. Instead of outlining a plan to challenge these state actions in court, the memo resolved the dilemma by stating US enforcement will now concentrate on specific objectives of (1) keeping the substance out of the hands of minors, (2) not growing it on public land, (3) keeping drug cartels out, and (4) preventing export to states where marijuana use remains illegal. This time it was former DEA administrator Peter Bensinger who was incensed. He declared Holder is "not only abandoning the law, he's breaking the law. He's not only shirking his duty, he's not living up to his oath of office."[24]

Reacting sharply to these successive instances of presidential policy actions, conservative observers began writing op-ed pieces with headlines like "Can Obama Write His Own Laws?" (Charles Krauthammer) and "Obama's Grab for a New Power" (Ronald Rotunda). Columnist Ruth Marcus, in a responding piece that asks "How 'Lawless' Is Obama?" wrote: "Obama is not the rogue usurper of conservative imagining. Rather, he has been understandably aggressive in wielding executive power while remaining within the lines. Still, those lines bear constant watching, whichever president holds office."[25]

Actions at the Program Level. The executive interventions just discussed advanced the Obama administration's agenda despite congressional inaction in the areas of school reform, immigration reform, affordable care, global warming, prison reform, and drug enforcement. Yet translating these steps into concrete action was made possible by bureaus in the departments of Education, Homeland Security, Health and Human Services, Justice, and the EPA. In the process, the missions of these agencies were advanced and updated. We now turn to illustrations of where individual bureaus themselves have taken independent actions to keep the wheels of government turning.

In 2002, the year after 9/11, the new Customs and Border Protection agency (CBP) of Homeland Security launched a Container Security Initiative to monitor the contents of the thousands of closed cargo containers shipped daily to the twenty busiest American seaports. It involved using intelligence and automated data to identify containers that might pose a terrorist risk by prescreening with Gamma ray detectors targeted boxes received from suspicious sources. Another step was to modify container design so that it would be evident if boxes had been tampered with.

In 2007, in the wake of the 9/11 Commission report, Representative Edward Markey of Massachusetts cosponsored a measure that required the Department of Homeland Security to get much tougher. It called for establishing, within five years, a system of 100 percent prescanning of the roughly 12 million containers shipped annually to all of America's 300 sea and river ports. This was to be done at some 700 foreign ports using monitors capable of detecting the low levels of radiation emitted by nuclear devices. Moreover the screening technology to be used was at a higher and more expensive level than CBP's existing Gamma machines, which are able to detect only high levels of radiation.

On Capitol Hill, the project's progress was being tracked as the five years were going by, probably by Markey's office. It was observed as not proceeding on schedule, and the Government Accountability Office was asked to investigate. It issued a report that took the agency to task for risking nuclear blasts in port cities. For one unnamed port, it was estimated that a nuclear explosion would result in $1 trillion in damage (the human toll was not mentioned). When the statutory deadline ran out in 2012, Secretary Napolitano wrote Congress that it would not be met. She formally extended the deadline for two years but in reality she was dumping an absurdly unworkable idea. She pointed out the project would be enormously cumbersome to carry out and cost at least $16 billion. Representative Markey was unrepentant: "I personally do not believe they intend to comply with the law. This is a real terrorist threat, and it has a solution. We can't afford to wait until a catastrophic attack."[26]

In 2013, in response to the 2012 Sandy Hook School shooting, the Obama White House and gun control advocates around the country urged passage of several reforms to federal gun control legislation. With the help of strident opposition from the National Rifle Association, a measure narrowly failed to pass in the Senate. After that defeat, Vice President Biden was charged with combing the bureaucracy for small steps that could be taken without congressional action. Two were proposed by ATF.

The first was to require corporate purchasers of machine guns, sawed-off shotguns, and other such weapons to undergo a background examination before registering these especially dangerous firearms with ATF. Current law requires individual buyers to do so, but not companies or trusts. In 2012 some 39,000 such registrations were recorded without a check this way. ATF suspects that many of these entities are fronts for criminal gangs and other organized groups prone to violence. At present ATF is in the process of rulemaking on this subject.

The second initiative relates to military weapons that have been exported by US manufacturers or the Defense Department to other countries on a sale-for-purchase basis or under military assistance programs. After decades go by and the equipment becomes obsolete, private buyers in this country often buy up this materiel for import back into the United States. Over the past five years some 250,000 items have entered the country this way, ranging from rifles to heavy weapons. Such transfers are now banned outright, except for museums that wish to display them. Gun collectors ridicule the idea of prohibiting the purchase of what they consider to be relics. The National Rifle Association emphatically opposes both corporate machine gun background checks and the ban on private importation of military weapons as doing nothing to reduce crime, as one would expect.[27]

In 2010 Secretary of Agriculture Tom Vilsack launched a program initiative called StrikeForce. This was done without Hill permission or funding, in the face of unwillingness by Congress to pass a farm bill for the first time in decades. Aimed at very poor communities in rural areas, its purpose is to help them develop and improve the quality of farm life.

The program's administrators use census information to locate underserved areas with poverty rates above 20 percent. At this point, it operates in eight states. In each one a StrikeForce coordinator is named to be available to farmers, food processors, businesses, nonprofit organizations, congregations, and volunteer groups. USDA staff members stand ready to answer inquiries, make suggestions, give technical advice, and facilitate applications for federal funding. Examples of projects include soil conservation projects, home loans, the development of cooperatives, extension services, school lunch programs, and afterschool nutrition projects. The underlying premise of the program is that over 90 percent of persistently poor counties in America are in rural areas. If people can grow their own fruits and vegetables and learn to eat better, Vilsack says, they "don't have to rely on a convenience store that has a very limited set of offerings."[28]

The Postal Service Battles On. I conclude this review of efforts by bureaucracy to compensate for the inaction of Congress by examining in detail dramatic attempts by the United States Postal Service to shore up the integrity of its mission and possibly even save it. This function of government goes back to colonial times, and the Founding Fathers specifically authorized establishment of national "post offices and post roads." Prior to 1971, the organization was known as the Post Office Department, headed by a member of the president's cabinet known as the Postmaster General. In that year Congress converted the department to an independent government corporation. This permitted it to operate autonomously on its own revenue under the supervision of a Board of Governors. The board appoints a chief executive officer, still known as the Postmaster General. With a current workforce of 522,000, it is the second largest bureaucracy in the federal government, exceeded only by the Department of Defense. In that the USPS is not financed by taxes, it was not subject to the pay freeze or the sequester; this did not shield it from financial problems, however.

The magnitude of the US postal system defies the imagination. It delivers more mail to more addresses in a larger geographic area than any other postal system in the world. In 2012 it processed 160 billion pieces, 40 percent of the world's overland mail. Thirty-one thousand directly managed post offices exist in all corners of the country, and postal products are sold in 70,000 other places—forming a retail network larger than all McDonalds, Walmarts, and Starbucks combined. A fleet of 212,500 vehicles transports mail daily to 152 million homes and businesses. Modernized postal processing centers utilize optical character recognition technology to read automatically addresses on 98 percent of letters. Tradition as well as technology is honored; some 1,400 New Deal–era murals and sculptures are still visible in post office lobbies around the country.[29]

The problem before the United States Postal Service is money. At the same time when Congress established it as an independent corporation that lived on its own earnings, it undercut this business model by retaining control of its finances. A separate Postal Rate Commission was established to regulate rate increases, which could not rise faster than inflation. Riders placed annually in appropriation bills (for other agencies than USPS) require that it prefund employee health-benefit escrow accounts by 100 percent, a standard set for no federal entity and seldom done in private industry. As a consequence, these accounts build up to tens of billions of dollars, but the agency cannot use or borrow from them for operational shortfalls. Other statutory language forbids labor arbitrators from mentioning the organization's financial plight when negotiating union contracts. Some of these contracts prohibit layoffs flatly, yet by law the agency must deliver the mail six days a week to every person in the country at a reasonable price.

For several decades these restrictions did no major damage. Changes in the mail market could be dealt with by adding new product lines and introducing new technologies such as optical scanning. Yet the digital age eventually changed all that. Because most "letters" are now sent electronically, the bottom fell out of the corporation's must lucrative activity, the delivery of First-Class Mail. Also major declines occurred in the volume of advertising mail and of customer purchases at post offices. Heavy competition in the parcel post market emerged from FedEx and UPS.

At the same time the number of delivery points within a growing and spreading population kept increasing. Successive attempts to close or consolidate small post offices were blocked by Congress for the most part. Since 2006 the USPS has cut its workforce by 28 percent. Although it was able to return briefly to the black in 2003–2005, since that time it has been losing money and going into debt just to keep operating. In 2012 a deficit of $16 billion was experienced. A *Washington Post* editorial opined, "The U.S. Postal Service faces a financial death spiral."[30]

After insistent warnings from Postmaster General Patrick R. Donahoe, in 2012 both chambers of Congress finally began giving attention to the crisis. The Senate worked through and finally approved a bill that would allow the USPS to transfer $11 billion from the escrow accounts to operational use. The House voted in committee to end Saturday delivery and create a study commission to examine the issue, but the bill never reached the floor.

With further action on the Hill delayed indefinitely by deadlock, Donahoe took matters into his own hands. An opportunity presented itself when a stopgap temporary budget put in place to avert the government's closure did not mention the six-day delivery requirement. Donahoe announced on February 6, 2013, that beginning in August, letter mail would not be delivered on Saturdays. Taking this action would not solve the overall problem, but it would reduce the annual deficit by about $8 billion. USPS-sponsored surveys show that 70 percent of Americans accept the idea.

The White House, not informed in advance of the initiative, was taken aback. In the Senate, majority leader Harry Reid charged that Donahoe's unilateral actions "have damaged his reputation with congressional leaders" and complicated the possibility of comprehensive reform. Yet Senator Thomas Coburn and Representative Darrell Issa, both influential legislators on postal matters, jointly stated that this is "one solution worthy of bipartisan support." Union leaders were much displeased; the president of the National Association of Letter Carriers declared, "This maneuver by Mr. Donahoe flouts the will of Congress."[31]

It was an audacious independent act. But although it once more brought to the fore the fiscal woe facing this enormous part of the government, Saturday delivery continued. The political opposition to a seemingly positive and practical policy intervention was simply too great. It came from several directions: lobbying by the $8 billion mailing industry, drawing support from Republicans; outrage from postal unions, of concern to Democrats; and the pique felt by Members of Congress of both parties at the thought of a bureaucratic CEO trying to sidestep Congress.

In April the USPS Board of Governors met in closed session and afterwards the Postmaster General announced the plan had been canceled. Unbowed, Donahoe said the push for comprehensive reform would continue, and indeed Coburn and Issa showed every inclination of trying to orchestrate it, one way or another. As these words are being written, a compromise seems possible but is far from concluded. In addition to five-day delivery, curbside-only and cluster-box delivery are on the table. Donahoe is also proposing authority to deliver parcels containing wine and beer, which he believes would be a lucrative revenue source. In another step to make more money from package delivery, he made a deal with Amazon to deliver their packages on Sunday in major metropolitan markets. In fiscal 2013 an 8 percent increase in package revenues helped the USPS to reduce its deficit to $5 billion, a third of that for the previous year.[32]

Commentary. My argument here is that American public administration is sufficiently worthy of public trust to act as a counter to—and hopefully have the ability to compensate for—the loss of public trust being engendered by the current political gridlock in Washington. In achieving this aim it will help for bureaucracy to keep its own house in order as well as possible. Yet the current deadlock in Congress, if it persists, presents bureaucracy with the possibility of years of fiscal starvation and a weakening of vital bureaucratic missions. Individual agencies can battle for survival and integrity, but overall there is only so much the public administration establishment can do to counteract serious deterioration in bureaucracy's capabilities. This could mean that eventually only a colossal breakdown of public services would bring sanity to our nation's deep partisan and ideological division. Perhaps a foretaste of that eventuality stands before us that can actually help in this regard to a small degree. This possibility is the topic of what now takes our attention.

STRUGGLING IN A SHUTDOWN

A "moment of truth" struck along this line in the first sixteen days of October 2013 when political gridlock in Washington caused a partial shutdown of the federal government. During it the essential nature of a fully functioning national bureaucracy became inescapably visible. While the event certainly deserved being called a crisis, it seemed to make at least some contribution to a national realization that we must, after all, have a dependable central government as a component of civilized public order.

Social scientists might choose to regard these sixteen days as a "natural experiment," by which is meant a context suddenly altered by external events that unwittingly sheds light on human behavior in an unplanned way. During such an episode, a causal relationship that is otherwise obscured from view becomes visible. In this instance, the positive impact of the independent variable of a solid bureaucracy on the dependent variable of a safe, productive and satisfying polity is laid bare when the disappearance of the first correlates with the degradation of the second—the readiness of a polity to slide ever deeper into levels of distrust, as mentioned at the beginning of the chapter.

The stoppage was set in motion by the Republican majority in the House of Representatives as an attempt to defund the Affordable Care

Act. It was set in motion by demands by the Tea Party faction of the GOP to condition renewal of the sequester's funding authority on October 1 and an increase in the government's borrowing authority a few days later on termination of the entire ACA project.

The political atmosphere in Washington became increasingly tense as the October 1 deadline approached. The White House refused to back off its position of refusing to allow the nation to be "held hostage" to House Republican demands to end Obamacare. The Senate, with its Democratic majority, went on ahead and approved a continuing resolution to allow the government to continue operating at sequester levels. Majority Leader Harry Reid said, "We're not going to be extorted. The country's not going to negotiate with a gun at our heads."[33]

The House refused to consider such a resolution; and, at midnight September 30, large blocks of the federal bureaucracy closed down. The next morning hundreds of thousands of federal civil servants found themselves on furlough status, and they were ordered not to report for work or to conduct official business by telephone or e-mail. As the magnitude of this step began seeping into the national consciousness over the next few days, House Republicans attempted to ameliorate the political damage to their party (and embarrass Democrats in the process) by voting to reopen popular pieces of the government, such as the national parks, Smithsonian museums, and veterans benefits. Reporters noted the irony in this attempt at a piecemeal pullback: "The party of small government is struggling—mightily—to decide how much government it actually wants."[34]

As the shutdown wore on, House Republicans also backed off their initial condition of defunding Obamacare. Reduced demands were gradually proffered as ways to end the stalemate. These included delaying the program's implementation, repealing a medical device tax, and omitting the individual mandate for one year. The House also passed a bill that denied the lawmakers themselves from receiving government health benefit subsidies, a proposal close to the heart of Tea Party devotees. The Senate refused to consider all of these measures.[35]

In the late evening of October 16, action was finally taken that led to an end to the shutdown. A deal put together mainly by moderate female Senators of both parties was translated into a lengthy 35-page bill that funded the federal government through January 15, 2014, and raised the debt limit through February 7, 2014. Thus, it was only a temporary reprieve, but better than nothing. The measure authorized back pay for furloughed civil servants and left untouched a one percent pay increase due them in January. In addition, the bill called for creation of what became known as the "budget conference committee" to negotiate long-term plans. The Senate passed the bill by a whopping 81–18 vote, and later that night the House approved it 285–144. All 198 Democratic members voted for it, but Republicans were divided at 87 for and 144 against. John Boehner's Republican conference had been split wide open, and the only concession obtained was a requirement that the Department of Health and Human Services report that it is verifying the incomes of ACA subsidy recipients. The enrolled bill was rushed to the White House, and the President signed it early the next morning.[36]

Consequences of the Shutdown. The federal government "shutdown" was highly consequential, but not total or complete. Of the 2,724,000 civilian federal employees on duty in September 2013, approximately 800,000 or 29 percent were furloughed on October 1. The nearly 2 million exempted employees fell into two main categories. One was workers in organizations funded by fee income, such as the USPS, US Mint, Federal Reserve, Office of the Comptroller of the Currency, and Patent and Trademark Office. Workers whose jobs are considered essential to protect life or property formed the other category. Examples were air traffic controllers, nuclear security personnel, Social Security check–writing administrators, federal court personnel, security guards at prisons and airports, intelligence agents, meat inspectors, and daily weather forecasters.[37]

This left 800,000 bureaucrats whose paychecks depend on timely appropriations by Congress and whose work is, by implication, "nonessential" to the country—a label much resented by those so designated. Box 5.1 lists many of the organizations and activities staffed by these men and women. These are the people who regulate the corporations of our economy, track epidemics, safeguard the elderly and veterans, protect the environment, test drugs, provide preschool and nutritional food for poor children, manage the national parks, assist small business, and run national museums.

BOX 5.1	Status of Nondefense Federal Agencies and Activities During Shutdown of October 1–16, 2013

Mostly Shut Down	Mostly Not Affected
Antitrust regulation	Air traffic control
Banking regulation	Amtrak
Bankruptcy applications	Arlington National Cemetery
Capitol tours	Atomic arsenal security
Centers for Disease Control	Border control
Communications regulation	Entitlement payments
Energy regulation	Federal courts
Entitlement claims	Federal prisons
Environmental Protection Agency	Food stamps
Fish and Wildlife Service	Intelligence activities
Food and Drug Administration	Kennedy Center
General Services Administration	Meat and poultry inspection
Geological Survey	National Institutes of Health
Head Start	Obamacare
Housing rental assistance	Passport and visa offices
Immigration status checks	Patent Office
Internal Revenue Service	TSA airport security
Mall monuments	US Postal Service
National Archives	Washington METRO
National Park Service	Weather forecasting
National Science Foundation	
National Zoo	
Occupational health regulation	
Small Business Administration	
Smithsonian museums	
Tennessee Valley Authority	
Trade regulation	
Wage and hour enforcement	
WIC nutrition programs	

Washington Post Sources: Susan Svrluga, Tara Bahrampour, and Paul Duggan, "Local Impact: By Dawn's Early Light, a City Full of Aimless Tourists and Workers?" October 1, 2013. Brad Plumer, "Who Will Get Hurt the Most?" October 3, 2013. Dana Milbank, "Republicans Are Going to Need a Bigger Lifeboat," October 3, 2013.

For the most part, what might be called the "national security state" portion of the bureaucracy remained adequately staffed. James Clapper, Director of National Intelligence, complained on the second day that 72 percent of the intelligence community's civilian workforce was to be fur-loughed, but the other 28 percent kept vital functions going. As for the Department of Defense, on the day before the shutdown began, Congress passed and the President signed a law that appropriated whatever funds would be necessary to pay (1) members of the Armed Forces on active duty, (2) civilian Defense and Coast Guard workers interpreted as pro-viding support to the Armed Forces, and (3) employees of contractors determined to be providing such support. Secretary Hagel interpreted the term "support" liberally and on the October 5–6 weekend he recalled some 350,000 Defense civilians, nearly the entire complement. This left the number of furloughed bureaucrats at roughly 450,000, amounting to 17 percent of the total federal workforce.[38] The economic costs of the shutdown were significant. According to Standard & Poor, the sixteen days of suspended government spending with its multiplier effect pre-cipitated a $24 billion GNP loss. It is estimated that uncertainty over raising the debt limit would shave fourth-quarter economic growth by 0.2 to 0.6 percentage points. Also federal agencies directly spent many millions of dollars to cover the costs of preplanning and transition. Roughly $2 billion in productivity was lost due to post hoc payment for 6.6 million hours not worked by federal employees. Among other delete-rious economic effects, Alaska's crab fishing season was delayed by three to four days, about 1.2 million applicants for mortgages faced delays, approximately $4 billion in tax refunds were postponed, Pentagon small-business contracts were cut back by almost a third, and NTSB investiga-tions of fifty-nine air crashes were held back.[39]

Needless to say, harsh consequences were visited upon individual American citizens. Midway during the period, readers of the *Washington Post* were asked to respond online to an unscientific poll on how the shutdown was affecting them personally. Of the 2,317 responses received, 19.4 percent checked "It doesn't affect me"; 16.4 percent responded "It affects me a little"; 22.7 percent indicated "It affects me on a daily basis"; and 41.5 percent—the largest category—replied "It threat-ens my livelihood." Individual cases of the last-named consequence that caught the attention of reporters were: a fly-fishing guide who could not enter the federal wildlife refuge to practice his occupation; a micro-distiller of rum about to start is his business who needed ATF approval; a low-income mother with several young children who had to quit her job because Head Start was no longer open; a local law enforcement officer planning to advance his career by attending the FBI Academy who could not enter his training cycle; a Kansas livestock farmer unable to know when to sell his hogs because the National Agricultural Statistics Service was not reporting pork prices; and a university microbiologist who had to give up a full season of drilling to shallow lakes under Antarctic ice to study how life might survive in the dark and cold of other planets.[40]

Impacts on the Bureaucrats. Although the 450,000 civil servants who had to endure the entire 16 days of shutdown were only 17 percent of the federal workforce, these middle-class Americans nevertheless formed a huge group of families that faced sudden financial insecurity. They, like the whole country, had no idea how long the shutdown would last. Although bills were being introduced in Congress that would eventually vote them back pay, their passage was by no means guaranteed. The first pay cycle for October produced a check half the usual amount. The next one would be in zeros. Anxieties rose as the monthly bills kept piling up, leading many households to cancel automatic payments from bank accounts. Only essentials were bought at the supermarket, restaurant meals were sacrificed, and family trips were postponed. Many breadwinners applied for unemployment compensation, and many spouses looked for temporary work. In communities with large federal government populations, restaurants offered discounts and theaters gave out free tickets to anyone showing a federal ID. One furloughed individual confided to a reporter, "We love public service. We're very committed to our jobs and the mission of our agency. But it's just too unstable."[41]

This attitude of mission dedication spawned a sense of ennui during the days of forced inactivity. Busy professionals, used to being up and out early for the commute and tackling the day's work while responding to frequent electronic messages, felt empty. Doing some office work from home was tempting but was not allowed because of the Antideficiency

Act, an old law that forbids obligating the government for payments not preauthorized. A gesture by some members of Congress who offered to donate their own pay to charity out of sincere or posed sympathy to the unpaid civil servants did not help.[42]

But on October 17, the end abruptly came. This natural experiment was over. Street barriers and "closed" signs on doorways went down. Websites lit up and BlackBerrys went into action. Staff meetings were called, and colleagues greeted each other to trade furlough experiences. Jodi Hammer, manager of the Peace Corps career center in downtown Washington, spoke for many when she blurted out on that first day: "It was great spending time with my 6-month-old daughter, but the whole thing is just ridiculous. I wanted to work. I'm glad we are most likely getting back pay. But in the end, we don't lose. But the whole country does."[43]

Not only were line bureaucrats glad to be back, top executives were glad to see them back. Secretary of Education Arne Duncan walked around his large office building on Maryland Avenue and greeted employees as they arrived. Seeing desk chairs filled and copying machines finally running, he ruminated about his own shutdown feelings while being in the offices with a skeleton crew: "I never felt so helpless. You miss everything—the people, the camaraderie. You don't realize how much until something like this happens. The building was empty. It was dark, it was quiet. It felt awful."[44]

Others in Washington had comments on this notable occasion as well. Speaking on CBS's "Face the Nation," Senate Minority Leader Mitch McConnell derisively characterized the shutdown as "a two-week paid vacation for federal employees." Taking a quite different view, OMB director Sylvia Mathews Burwell said: "I think one probably needs to distinguish between trust and faith in the political system and trust and faith in the federal employees and the day-to-day running of government. I would say those probably went in opposite directions." On an even higher plane, President Obama made the following remarks on the Thursday morning after everyone had returned to work:

> I've got a simple message for all the dedicated and patriotic federal workers who've either worked without pay or have been

*forced off the job without pay these past few weeks, including
most of my own staff: Thank you. Thanks for your service.
Welcome back.*

*What you do is important. It matters. You defend our coun-
try overseas. You deliver benefits to our troops, who have earned
them, when they come home. You guard our borders. You protect our civil rights. You help businesses grow and gain footholds
in overseas markets. You protect the air we breathe and the
water our children drink, and you push the boundaries of science and space, and you guide hundreds of thousands of people
each day through the glories of this country.*

*Thank you. What you do is important, and don't let anybody
else tell you different, especially to the young people who come
to this—this city to serve, believe that it matters. Well, you know
what? You're right. It does.*[45]

An Assessment. Unlike the sequester, the partial federal shutdown of
October 2013 did not require federal agencies to battle for resources or
fight to maintain the integrity of the mission. Instead it meant bowing
out, sitting on the sidelines. It was the second such event in recent
history, the other being a set of two quickly succeeding stoppages in
1995–1996 during the first term of the Clinton administration. Then,
too, the Republicans had taken control of the House of Representatives
when a Democratic President occupied the White House.

Although the policy activism was largely impossible by a benched
bureaucracy, a few instances occurred where closed agencies took the
initiative to cover emergencies and ameliorate hardships. The CDC, for
example, called in a dozen furloughed data analysts and epidemiologists
to study a salmonella outbreak in poultry that had been spotted by
USDA's Food Safety and Inspection Service in California. With its skeleton crew of ten, the CDC's food division was unable to monitor bacteria
strains adequately or update its PulseNet data base. In another instance,
after consulting the White House, the National Park Service allowed the
governors of four states to make it possible to reopen certain parks within
their borders, provided the states provided the necessary funding with
control of the parks remaining in NPS hands.[46]

It is noteworthy that all this turmoil did very little to aid the cause of the groups and politicians who caused it to happen. According to a *Washington Post*–ABC poll conducted just after the shutdown, 81 percent of Americans disapproved of the shutdown and only 17 percent thought it was good idea. The survey found that 86 percent of the public saw it as damaging the country's image, 82 percent believed it hurt the morale of federal employees, and 80 percent speculated that it set back the economy's recovery. Three-quarters of respondents said they were dissatisfied with the way the country's political system is working. Unfavorable ratings registered in the wake of the debacle were: 59 percent for the Tea Party movement, 63 percent for the Republican party, 49 percent for the Democratic party, and 48 percent for President Obama. Conversely, in the same order favorable ratings were 26, 32, 46, and 50 percent.[47]

As for public sentiment during the shutdown period, Pew polling data collected around the middle of the event are available in Table 5.1. The approval rating for Congress is only 23 percent and its unfavorable rating 73 percent. This level of public support is considerably less than the trust and confidence levels accorded Congress in 2012, as noted in Tables 1.2 and 1.4 of chapter 1. Even Republicans agreed with this negative assessment.

In contrast, the survey reveals a strong show of support for the federal bureaucracy. Favorable-unfavorable ratings of 62 and 29 percent respectively for federal workers are not far from constituting a mirror image of the outcomes recorded for Congress. Referring again to data offered in chapter 1, the trust and confidence scores for federal bureaucrats in Tables 1.3 and 1.4 are at similar levels. This positive image of bureaucracy is found at the agency level as well in the Pew findings. All agencies on which inquiries were made except the IRS obtained approval ratings ranging from above-50 percent positive to above-70 percent positive. Democrats even admired the IRS and Republicans gave nine of the thirteen organizations majority scores.

Commentary. What these data suggest to me is that it is to the citizenry of this country that we can turn to make the normative case for bureaucracy. When push comes to shove, Americans realize how important bureaucracy is when its benefits are suddenly withdrawn. When even a

TABLE 5.1	Favorable and Unfavorable Public Opinion Toward Components of the Government During the Federal Shutdown (in percent)			
	All Public		**Republicans**	**Democrats**
Component	Favorable	Unfavorable	Favorable	Favorable
Congress	23	73	23	25
Federal Workers	62	29	46	79
Centers for Disease Control and Prevention	75	14	70	80
National Aeronautic and Space Administration	73	15	76	74
Defense Department	72	23	77	77
Veterans Administration	68	25	66	74
Homeland Security	66	30	62	76
Food and Drug Administration	65	29	66	73
Environmental Protection Agency	62	30	47	77
Health and Human Services Department	61	30	45	78
Justice Department	61	33	54	71
Federal Reserve	57	32	54	71
National Security Agency	54	35	55	64
Department of Education	53	42	43	71
Internal Revenue Service	44	51	23	65

Question: "Is your overall opinion of _____ very favorable, mostly favorable, mostly unfavorable, or very unfavorable?" The first two options are combined for "favorable" and the second two for "unfavorable." Percentages for "don't know" and "Independent" are omitted. Survey conducted October 9–13, 2013.

Source: Pew Research Center for the People & the Press, "Trust in Government Nears Record Low, but Most Federal Agencies Are Viewed Favorably," October 18, 2013, accessed online October 30, 2013.

partial federal shutdown occurs, they suddenly become more admiring of their national bureaucrats than they are of their politicians. They even seem to trust the nation's government agencies more than its political parties. At least for the moment, the radical right's cry to dismantle the bureaucracy headquartered in Washington, DC, is repudiated by a realization that functioning public agencies are vital to America as we know it. While this temporary understanding in no way quells the country's deep-seated ideological divide, it assures us that there is little likelihood that, unless shutdowns become routine, our partisan hostilities will degenerate into pitched battles in the streets. As long as government "works" on a day-to-day basis with respect to the fundamental needs of its populace, political conflict should remain at the rhetorical and electoral level—at least we hope so.

AFTERWORD ON OBAMACARE

Meanwhile the Tea Party Republicans, temporarily deflated by the outcome of the shutdown, were soon gloating over something else. This was the outcome of the launch of the Patient Protection and Affordable Care Act (ACA) enacted in 2010. Getting the program up and running was plagued by an inability to use the HealthCare.gov website, embarrassingly small numbers of initial enrollees, and White House concessions that certain features of the program had to be delayed. Obama political allies were upset about how the outcome damaged the President's poll numbers, and his political enemies were delighted to be able to claim that the program is so misguided and flawed that it is falling of its own weight. If Obamacare could not be killed by the shutdown, its demise could result from implementation failure.

Question: Does this development, a clear failure in public administration, thereby demolish the case for bureaucracy? I say no—not because the breakdown was not serious or permanent, but because bureaucracy was not the tool used for its implementation. Normally when a statute is passed that creates a brand new government program, the law also authorizes a new bureaucracy to carry it out. To illustrate, when Congress enacted the Dodd-Frank Wall Street Reform and Consumer Protection Act in 2011, the Consumer Financial Protection Bureau was established to administer it. In this instance, however, central administrative authority for the federal government was dumped on the existing Centers for Medicare and Medicaid (CMM) in the Department of Health and Human Services. The expectation was that this small agency could simply extend its mission of operating Medicare and overseeing Medicaid to directing the creation of the ACA. This small entity, however, already had its hands full and could in no way lead adequately the task of revolutionizing a very large segment of the national economy.

What happened is that all important planning, development, testing and evaluation activity was delegated to a variety of private IT contractors. Each contractor had a separate piece of the action and CMM was not even capable of bringing the individual components together into a meaningful whole. This was all the more essential because the administration of ACA requires merging multiple data systems operated by insurance companies, employers, health providers, and state exchanges into an overall workable system of systems. Eventually CMM had to hire yet added contractors to manage centrally the many repairs needed and take the lead in perfecting the HealthCare.gov website. For the government to have any chance of preparing for the launching of this program adequately it would have needed to establish a substantial Weber-style in-house bureaucracy that could oversee the multiple components, make certain their joint operations were connected, keep track of timelines and costs, and have the clout to quell demands from the White House to launch the program prematurely.

A future case study of this debacle will be needed to remind students of public administration how essential bureaucracy is to developing and executing complex, large-scale government programs. It would take its place as a classic alongside Pressman and Wildavsky's *Implementation*, magnified several times over.[48]

ENDNOTES

1. Charles T. Goodsell, "A New Vision for Public Administration," *Public Administration Review* 66:4 (July-August 2006): 632–634.
2. *Washington Post* sources: Rein, "Conference Fallout Hits Another GSA Leader," April 10, 2012. Lisa Rein, "Criminal Probe Sought in GSA Case," April 14, 2012. Rein and Timothy R. Smith, "Competitive Bidding Is Focus of Inquiry," April 16, 2012. Jonathan O'Connell, "Possible Kickbacks and Bribes at GSA," April 17, 2012. Smith, "GSA Official Accused of Running 'A Fiefdom,'" April 18, 2012. Rein, "GSA Freezes Hiring, Cancels Most Bonuses After Scandal," July 18, 2012.
3. *Washington Post* sources: David Nakamura and Ed O'Keefe, "Obama Seeks Thorough Inquiry in Secret Service Scandal," April 16, 2012. Nakamura and Scott Wilson, "Scope of Summit Scandal Expands," April 17, 2012. Julie Pace, "Director: Agents, Military Offer Inconsistent Details," April 18, 2012. Nakamura, Del Quentin Wilber and Carol D. Leonnig, "Secret Service Ousts Three in Scandal," April 19, 2012. Nakamura and O'Keefe, "Inquiry Hints at Wider Scandal in Columbia," April 20, 2012. Nakamura and O'Keefe, "Secret Service Ousts Three More Agents," April 21, 2012.

EARNING AND RETAINING THE PUBLIC TRUST **211**

Nakamura, "Out of Public Eye, Secret Service Director Seethes," April 26, 2012. Nakamura and O'Keefe, "Secret Service Issues New Rules for Foreign Trips," April 28, 2012. Nakamura and Wilson, "Secret Service Gets New Chief," March 27, 2013.

4. *Washington Post* sources: Sari Horwitz, "A Gunrunning Sting Gone Fatally Wrong," July 26, 2011. Horwitz, "Fast and Furious Creator Defends Gun Operation" June 28, 2012. Horwitz, "Report Casts Blame for 'Fast and Furious'" September 20, 2012. Wikipedia article, "ATF Gunwalking.Scandal," accessed June 6, 2013.

5. *Washington Post* sources: Zachary A. Goldfarb and Karen Tumulty, "IRS Targeted Tea Party Groups for Tax Scrutiny," May 11, 2013. Juliet Eilperin, "Report Details IRS Scrutiny," May 13, 2013. Eilperin and Goldfarb, "IRS Officials in D.C. Implicated," May 14, 2013. Goldfarb and Eilperin, Acting IRS Chief Quits in Scandal," May 16, 2013. O'Keefe, "Panel Grills IRS on Tax Targeting," May 18, 2013. Goldfarb and Kimberly Kindy, "How the IRS Seeded the Clouds for a Political Deluge," May 20, 2013. Goldfarb, "IRS Says Tax-Exemption Scrutiny Ranged Widely," June 25, 2013. Alan Fram, "Official: IRS Also Screened Liberal Groups," AP article appearing in *Roanoke Times*, June 25, 2013.

6. *Washington Post* sources: Josh Hicks and Kindy, "For Groups, and IRS 'Horror Story'," May 16, 2013. Dana Milbank, "Accuse First, Ask Questions Later," June 4, 2013. Eilperin, "Groups Targeted by IRS Cite Intrusions," June 5, 2013. Hicks, "Cummings: Cincinnati IRS Staffers Began Effort," June 11, 2013. Hicks, "Cummings Releases Full Transcript of Interview with IRS Manager," June 19, 2013. Hicks, "IRS's "BOLO' List Raises New Questions on Political Targeting," July 5, 2013.

7. *Washington Post* sources: Richard Rubin, "Watchdog Defends IRS Scrutiny Report," June 28, 2013. Hicks, "IRS's "BOLO' List Raises New Questions on Political Targeting, July 5, 2013. Stephen Ohlemacher, "Investigator Who Rebuked IRS to Testify," July 17, 2013.

8. *Washington Post* sources: Eilperin and Goldfarb, "IRS Officials in D.C. Implicated," May 14, 2013. Philip Rucker and Eilperin, "On IRS, Senior Aides Focused on Shielding Obama," May 23, 2013. O'Keefe and William Branigin, "IRS Official Takes the Fifth, Starts a Debate," May 23, 2013. Rucker and Eilperin, "On IRS, Senior Aides Focused on Shielding Obama," May 23, 2013.

9. *Washington Post* sources: Rubin, "Watchdog Defends IRS Scrutiny Report, June 28, 2013. Ohlemacher, "Investigator Who Rebuked IRS to Testify," July

17, 2013. Darrell Issa and Dave Camp, "Holes in the IRS Narrative," August 7, 2013 (op-ed piece). Elijah E. Cummings and Sander M. Levin, "Reform the IRS, but Leave Politics Out of It," August 13, 2013 (op-ed piece).

10. Charles T. Goodsell, *Mission Mystique* (Washington: CQ Press, 2011), pp. 59–60.

11. Tim Mullaney, "Local Government Budgets Stall Call for Workplace Cuts," *USA Today*, May 9, 2012. *Washington Post* sources: Joe Davidson, "Another Hand in Federal Workers' Pockets," March 13, 2012. Eilperin, "Lack of Funding Slows Cleanup of Hundreds of Superfund Sites," November 25, 2004. Shefali S. Kulkarni, "States Cutting Back Efforts to Help HIV/AIDS Patients," May 24, 2011. Craig Whitlock, "Asia Plans Give Navy Key Role, Fewer Ships," February 16, 2012. Mike Hixenbaugh, "Sequestration Cuts Navy's Lawn Mowing Funds," June 1, 2013. Associated Press, "Budget Cuts Threaten Research Universities," *Roanoke Times*, September 26, 2012. Rein, "Hello Grisham—So Long, Hemingway?" *Washington Post*, January 2, 2007.

12. Goodsell, "Public Administration as Its Own Steward in Times of Partisan Deadlock and Fiscal Stress," *Public Administration Review* 73, no. 1 (January–February 2013): 10–11.

13. *Washington Post* sources: Hicks, "Senate Panel Backs Tangherlini Selection," June 26, 2013. Rein, "IRS Says It Used Poor Judgment in Approving Lavish Conference," and Davidson, "Costly IRS Conference's Waste Undermines Everybody's Credibility," June 7, 2013. Ohlemacher, "Investigator Who Rebuked IRS to Testify," July 17, 2013. Rein, "VA Investigated Over Conference Spending," August 15, 2012; Steve Vogel, "A Boondoggle or a Vacation?" November 29, 2012.

14. O'Keefe, "Federal Agencies' Swag Latest to Go Under the Knife," *Washington Post*, November 10, 2011.

15. *Washington Post* sources: Steve Vogel, "Hagel Details Defense Department Furloughs," May 18, 2013. Vogel, "OPM Updates Furlough Rules," December 28, 2012. Ernesto Londoño, "Pentagon Could Furlough 800,000 Civilian Workers," January 1, 2013. Vogel, "Major Furloughs Spur Uncertainty at U.S. Agencies," April 22, 2013. Davidson, "Federal Workers Face Smorgasbord of Furloughs," April 23, 2013. Vogel, "Pentagon Finds That Furloughs Can't Be One-Size-Fits-All," April 29, 2013. Vogel and Rein, "Pentagon Delivers Furlough Notices," May 30, 2013.

16. Vogel, "The VA Is Exempt From Cuts, but Veterans Are Not," *Washington Post*, March 11, 2013.

17. *Washington Post* sources: Carol Morello, "Census Will Cut Six Offices, Save up to $18 Million A Year," June 30, 2011. Jim Tankersley, "Sequester Could

Increase Cost of 2020 Census, Official Warns," June 1, 2013. Bob Stein, "CDC Chief Is Concerned About Budget Reductions," June 17, 2011. Ashley Halsey III, "NTSB: Don't Sacrifice Safety in Deficit Debate," November 15, 2012.

18. *Washington Post* sources: Darryl Fears, "Burning Through Wildfire Budgets," October 8, 2012. Eilperin, "Signs of Funding Strains Surface at National Parks," August 20, 2012. Richard Lardner, "Issa Pushes Park Service Chief on Sequester Issue," April 17, 2013. Rein, "U.S. Park Police Furloughs to End: Savings Found After 'Deep Dive' into Budget," May 25, 2013. Rein, "After Furloughs, Officers Pushed Back," May 27, 2013.

19. Rein, "Stopgap Budget Retains Furloughs," *Washington Post*, March 18, 2013. David A. Fahrenthold and Rein, "Beef with the Sequester? One Agency Beat It," *Washington Post*, April 1, 2013.

20. *Washington Post* sources: Lori Aratani, "Ports and Airports Feeling Effects of Sequester Cuts," March 6, 2013. Aratani, "Sequester Prompts Tower Closures at Nearly 150 Airports," March 23, 2013. Aratani, "Closings of Nearly 150 Air-Traffic Control Towers Delayed by the FAA," April 6, 2013. Halsey, "Airlines Battle Furloughs in Federal Court," April 20, 2013. Halsey and Luz Lazo, "U.S. Flights Delayed by Furlough of Controllers," April 23, 2013. Halsey, "Sequester Sparks a Fight Over Flights," April 24, 2013. Halsey and Lori Montgomery, "Senate Votes to End Air Traffic Controllers' Furloughs," April 26, 2013.

21. Erica Werner, "Bill Critics Focus on Health Law Delay," AP article in *Roanoke Times*, August 6, 2013.

22. Eilperin, "Obama Unveils Climate Agenda," *Washington Post*, January 26, 2013. Matthew Brown, "Coal Country Put on the Defensive," AP article published in the *Roanoke Times*, July 2, 2013. Eilperin, "EPA Chief Vows to Tackle Climate Change," *Washington Post*, July 31, 2013. "Obama's Plan to Cut Pollution Forges On," AP article published in *Roanoke Times*, September 21, 2013.

23. Horwitz and Matt Zapotosky, "Holder's Order Targets Packed Prisons," *Washington Post*, August 13, 2013.

24. Brady Dennis, "Justice Dept. Won't Challenge Marijuana Laws," *Washington Post*, August 30, 2013. "Justice Department Won't Stop Marijuana Use in 2 States," AP article in *Roanoke Times*, August 30, 2013.

25. *Washington Post* sources: Charles Krauthammer, "Can Obama Write His Own Laws?" August 16, 2013. Ronald D. Rotunda, "Obama's Grab for a New Power," July 19, 2013. Ruth Marcus, "How 'Lawless' Is Obama?" August 21, 2013.

26. Douglas Frantz, "Port Security: U.S. Fails to Meet Deadline for Scanning of Cargo Containers," *Washington Post,* July 15, 2012. Wikipedia article, "Container Security Initiative," accessed July 10, 2013.
27. Eilperin, "Obama Administration Closes Two Gun Sale Loopholes," *Washington Post,* August 29, 2013.
28. Meg Kinnard, "USDA Expands Program to Help the Rural Poor," *Washington Post,* March 27, 2013. Telephone interview with Max Finberg, Strike Force Coordinator in Washington, DC, on September 17, 2013. See also StrikeForce: USDA website.
29. *Postal Facts 2013,* accessed online on July 12, 2013, pp. 4, 5, 7, 12, 16.
30. *Washington Post* sources: Christopher Lee, "2-Cent Stamp Increase Is Only Temporary Fix for Postal Woes, January 9, 2005. O'Keefe, "Postal Service Aims to Shutter 2,000 Sites," January 25, 2011. Rein, "USPS May Close Doors to Thousands of Post Offices, July 27, 2011. Rein, "Postal Service Abandons Plans for Closures, Will Reduce Hours," May 10, 2012.
31. *Washington Post* sources: Rein and O'Keefe, "Postal Service to End Saturday Mail Delivery," and Davidson, "USPS's Bold, Risky Move Draws Support, Fury," February 7, 2013. Davidson, "Reid Says Postmaster General 'Damaged Reputation,'" February 8, 2013.
32. *Washington Post* sources: Rein, "Postal Service Bows to Pressure, Won't End 6-Day Delivery," April 11, 2013. Rein, "Some Common Ground Found on Postal Service, July 18, 2013. Rein, "Bill to Sustain Postal Service Nears Passage by House Panel," July 25, 2013. Davidson, "Unions Oppose Postal Service Bill in House," July 26, 2013. Rein and Hicks, "USPS Posts Rare Revenue Increase," November 18, 2013. Cecilia Kang, "Amazon to Deliver on Sunday Using the Postal Fleet," November 11, 2013.
33. Sean Sullivan, "Between Implacable Friends, Unbending Foes," *Washington Post,* September 28, 2013.
34. *Washington Post* sources: Fahrenthold and O'Keefe, "What to Fund During Impasse Is No Open-and-Shut Case," October 9, 2013. See also Milbank, "Republicans Are Going to Need a Bigger Lifeboat," October 3, 2013.
35. *Washington Post* sources: Montgomery and Paul Kane, "Down to the Wire: Government Prepares for Shutdown," October 1, 2013. Sullivan, "Boehner May Need to Travel the Road Less Uncomfortable," October 10, 2013.
36. *Washington Post* sources: Nakamura, Montgomery, and Kane, "Shutdown Nears End: House Gets Bill Raising Debt Limit," October 17, 2013. Goldfarb, "What Would the Deal Do? What Happens Next?" October 17, 2013.
37. Floyd Norris, "Bloated Government? Federal Employment at 47-Year Low," *New York Times,* September 26, 2013. Josh Barro, "Even with the Government

Shutdown, 80% of Federal Employees Will Keep Working," Business Insider website, posted September 26, 2013, accessed October 26, 2013.

38. *Washington Post* sources: Rein, "For Defense Department, a Unique Challenge," September 28, 2013. Greg Miller, "Officials Say Furloughs Threaten U.S. Security," October 3, 2013. Ylan Q. Mui and Marjorie Censer, "Fears of Shutdown Damage Ebb," October 8, 2013. *Note:* The pay law is cited as Pay Our Military Act, H.R. 3210, signed September 30, 2013. Rein, "OMB Report Adds Up Costs of Shutdown," November 8, 2013.

39. *Washington Post* sources: Hicks, "How Much Did Closing the Government Cost?" October 26, 2013. Hicks, "Furloughed Contractors Face a Harsh Reality When Federal Shutdown Ends," October 9, 2013. Jia Lynn Yang and Tom Hamburger, "In Budget and Debt-Ceiling Fight, White House Finds an Unexpected Partner," October 12, 2013. Vanessa Small, "Nonprofit Groups Furlough Employees, Cut Services and Prepare for the Worse," October 10, 2013. Kevin Sullivan, "Some Scratch Their Heads, Others Smirk," October 1, 2013. Lenny Bernstein, "U.S. Shutdown Stalls Antarctic Research," November 18, 2013.

40. *Washington Post* sources: Davidson, "Stories of Shutdown Misery in from Across the Country, October 15, 2013. Marc Fisher and Holly Yeager, "Across the Nation Effects Ripple Out Beyond Just Those in the Federal Workforce," October 11, 2013. Roxana Hegeman, "Ag Reports Wither in Shutdown," AP article in *Roanoke Times,* October 8, 2013.

41. *Washington Post* sources: Steve Hendrix, "Shrunken Paychecks Heighten Anxiety for Furloughed Workers," October 11, 2013. Hicks, "Bills Would Grant Missed Pay to Federal Workers," October 4, 2013. Robert Samuels, Pamela Constable, and Hamil Harris, "Idled Workers Find Places to Pass the Time—and Plenty of Company," October 7, 2013. Davidson, "Soaring Jobless Claims Show Federal Shutdown's Impact," October 16, 2013.

42. *Washington Post* sources: Michael S. Rosenwald, "Lament of the Powered-Down Federal Worker: Silence," October 10, 2013. O'Keefe, "Some Lawmakers Share Pain, Donate Pay," October 3, 2013.

43. *Washington Post* sources: Paul Duggan and Leah Binkovitz, "'Closed' Signs Come Down, and Computers Are Fired Up," October 18, 2013. Emily Wax-Thibodeaux, "Wary—But Eager to Be Back at Work," October 17, 2013.

44. Lindsey Layton, "For Some, Going Back to Work Feels a Bit Like the First Day of School," *Washington Post,* October 18, 2013.

45. *Washington Post* sources: Davidson, "Federal Workers, for the Most Part, Couldn't Wait to Get Back on the Job," October 18, 2013. Davidson, "Employees' Morale Is Still Recovering from the Shutdown," October 22, 2013.

46. *Washington Post* sources: Dennis, "CDC Calls Back Those Who Are Experts on Foodborne Illnesses," October 9, 2013. Matthew Daly, "States Told They Can Reopen Parks if They Foot Bill," October 11, 2013. Eilperin and Lenny Bernstein, "Four States Pay to Reopen National Parks," October 12, 2013.

47. Dan Balz and Scott Clement, "Poll Finds Major Damage to GOP After Shutdown," *Washington Post*, October 22, 2013.

48. Jeffrey M. Pressman and Aaron Wildavsky, *Implementation*. Berkeley: University of California Press, 1973.

LIST OF BOOKS

Ansell, Christopher K. *Pragmatist Democracy: Evolutionary Learning as Public Philosophy.* Oxford: Oxford University Press, 2011.

Appleby, Paul H. *Big Democracy.* New York: Knopf, 1945.

Benveniste, Guy. *Bureaucracy,* 2nd ed. San Francisco: Boyd & Fraser, 1983.

Bernstein, Marver H. *Regulating Business by Independent Commission.* Princeton, NJ: Princeton University Press, 1955.

Berry, Jeffrey M., Kent E. Portney, and Ken Thomson. *The Rebirth of Urban Democracy.* Washington, DC: Brookings Institution Press, 1993.

Borins, Sandford. *Innovating with Integrity: How Local Heroes Are Transforming American Government.* Washington, DC: Georgetown University Press, 1998.

Bozeman, Barry. *Bureaucracy and Red Tape.* Upper Saddle River, NJ: Prentice-Hall, 2000.

Bozeman, Barry, and Mary K. Feeney. *Rules and Red Tape: A Prism for Public Administration Theory and Research.* Armonk, NY: M.E. Sharpe, 2011.

Bragaw, Louis K. *Managing a Federal Agency: The Hidden Stimulus.* Baltimore: Johns Hopkins Press, 1980.

Brehm, John, and Scott Gates. *Working, Shirking and Sabotage: Bureaucratic Response to a Democratic Public.* Ann Arbor: University of Michigan Press, 1997.

Cook, Brian J. *Bureaucracy and Self-Development: Reconsidering the Role of Public Administration in American Politics.* Baltimore: Johns Hopkins University Press, 1996.

Cooper, Phillip J. *Governing by Contract: Challenges and Opportunities for Public Managers.* Washington, DC: CQ Press, 2003.

Donahue, John D., ed. *Making Washington Work: Tales of Innovation in the Federal Sector.* Washington, DC: Brookings Institution, 1999.

Donahue, John D. *The Privatization Decision.* New York: Basic Books, 1989.

Downs, Anthony. *Inside Bureaucracy.* Boston: Little, Brown, 1967.

Du Gay, Paul. *In Praise of Bureaucracy: Weber, Organization, Ethics.* London: Sage, 2000.

Durant, Robert F. *The Oxford Handbook of American Bureaucracy.* New York: Oxford University Press, 2010.

Epstein, Richard A. *Design for Liberty: Private Property, Public Administration, and the Rule of Law.* Cambridge: Harvard University Press, 2011.

Ferguson, Kathy E. *The Feminist Case Against Bureaucracy.* Philadelphia: Temple University Press, 1984.

Friedrich, Carl J. *Constitutional Government and Democracy*, rev. ed. Boston: Ginn and Co., 1950.

Gerth, H. H., and C. Wright Mills, eds. *From Max Weber: Essays in Sociology.* New York: Oxford University Press, 1946.

Goodsell, Charles T. *The American Statehouse: Interpreting Democracy's Temples.* Lawrence: University Press of Kansas, 2001.

Goodsell, Charles T. *The Case for Bureaucracy: A Public Administration Polemic*, 3rd ed. Chatham, NJ: Chatham House, 1994; 4th ed. Washington, DC: CQ Press, 2004.

Goodsell, Charles T. *Mission Mystique: Belief Systems in Public Agencies.* Washington, DC: CQ Press, 2011.

Heclo, Hugh. *On Thinking Institutionally.* Boulder, CO: Paradigm, 2008.

Hodge, Graeme A. *Privatization: An International Review of Performance.* Boulder, CO: Westview Press, 2000.

Huber, Gregory A. *The Craft of Bureaucratic Neutrality: Interests and Influence in Governmental Regulation of Occupational Safety.* Cambridge: Cambridge University Press, 2007.

Hummel, Ralph P. *The Bureaucratic Experience: The Post-Modern Challenge*, 5th ed. Armonk, NY: M.E. Sharpe, 2008.

Jacoby, Henry. *The Bureaucratization of the World.* Berkeley: University of California Press, 1973.

Jacques, Elliott. *A General Theory of Bureaucracy.* London: Heinemann, 1976.

Kingsley, J. Donald. *Representative Bureaucracy: An Interpretation of the British Civil Service.* Yellow Springs, OH: Antioch Press, 1944.

Krause, George A., and Kenneth J. Meier, eds. *Politics, Policy, and Organizations: Frontiers in the Scientific Study of Bureaucracy.* Ann Arbor: University of Michigan Press, 2003.

Light, Paul C. *The True Size of Government.* Washington, DC: Brookings Institution Press, 1999.

Lipsky, Michael. *Street-Level Bureaucracy: Dilemmas of the Individual in Public Services.* New York: Russell Sage Foundation, 1980.

McCurdy, Howard E. *Faster, Better, Cheaper: Low-Cost Innovation in the U.S. Space Program.* Baltimore: Johns Hopkins University Press, 2001.

Osborne, David, and Ted Gaebler. *Reinventing Government: How the Entrepreneurial Spirit Is Transforming the Public Sector.* New York: Plume, 1993.

Parsons, Talcott, ed. *Max Weber: The Theory of Social and Economic Organization.* New York: The Free Press, 1947.

Pressman, Jeffrey M., and Aaron Wildavsky. *Implementation: How Great Expectations in Washington Are Dashed in Oakland; Or, Why It's Amazing that Federal Programs Work at All—This Being a Saga of the Economic Development Administration as Told by Two Sympathetic Observers Who Seek to Build Morals on a Foundation of Ruined Hopes.* Berkeley: University of California Press, 1973.

Preston, Larry M. *Freedom and the Organizational Republic.* Berlin: Walter de Gruyter, 1992.

Price, Byron Eugene. *Merchandising Prisoners: Who Really Pays for Prison Privatization?* Westport, CT: Praeger, 2006.

Rehfuss, John A. *Contracting Out in Government: A Guide to Working with Outside Contractors to Supply Public Services.* San Francisco: Jossey-Bass, 1989.

Salamon, Lester M., ed. *The Tools of Government: A Guide to the New Governance.* New York: Oxford University Press, 2002.

Seldon, Sally Coleman. *The Promise of Representative Bureaucracy: Diversity and Responsiveness in a Government Agency.* Armonk, NY: M.E. Sharpe, 1997.

Shichor, David. *Punishment for Profit: Private Prisons/Public Concerns.* Thousand Oaks, CA: Sage, 1995.

Sparrow, Malcolm K. *The Regulatory Craft: Controlling Risks, Solving Problems, and Managing Compliance.* Washington, DC: Brookings Institution Press, 2008.

Von Mises, Ludwig. *Bureaucracy.* New Haven, CT: Yale University Press, 1944.

Wamsley, Gary L., Robert N. Bacher, Charles T. Goodsell, Philip S. Kronenberg, John A. Rohr, Camilla M. Stivers, Orion F. White, and James F. Wolf. *Refounding Public Administration.* Newbury Park, CA: Sage, 1990.

West, William F. *Controlling the Bureaucracy: Institutional Constraints in Theory and Practice.* Armonk, NY: M.E. Sharpe, 1995.

Wilson, H.T. *Bureaucratic Representation: Civil Servants and the Future of Capitalist Democracies.* Leiden: Brill, 2001.

Wood, B. Dan, and Richard W. Waterman. *Bureaucratic Dynamics: The Role of Bureaucracy in America.* Boulder, CO: Westview Press, 1994.

INDEX

ABOUT THE AUTHOR

Charles T. Goodsell is Professor Emeritus at the Center for Public Administration and Policy at Virginia Polytechnic Institute and State University. His other books include *The American Statehouse*; *Public Administration Illuminated and Inspired by the Arts*, co-edited with Nancy Murray; *The Social Meaning of Civic Space*; *Administration of a Revolution*; *American Corporations and Peruvian Politics*; *The Public Encounter* (editor); *The Case for Bureaucracy*; *Mission Mystique: Belief Systems in Public Agencies*.

SAGE research**methods**

The essential online tool for researchers from the world's leading methods publisher

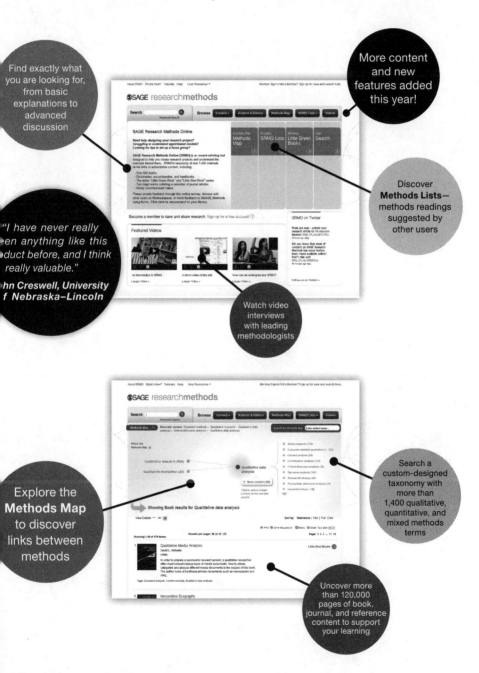

Find exactly what you are looking for, from basic explanations to advanced discussion

More content and new features added this year!

Discover **Methods Lists**—methods readings suggested by other users

"I have never really seen anything like this product before, and I think really valuable."

hn Creswell, University f Nebraska–Lincoln

Watch video interviews with leading methodologists

Explore the **Methods Map** to discover links between methods

Search a custom-designed taxonomy with more than 1,400 qualitative, quantitative, and mixed methods terms

Uncover more than 120,000 pages of book, journal, and reference content to support your learning

nd out more at
ww.sageresearchmethods.com